KU-131-851

The Sensational
ALEX HARVEY

JOHN NEIL MUNRO

Polygon

First published in 2002 by Firefly Publishing
This second edition published in 2008 by Polygon,
an imprint of Birlinn Ltd

West Newington House
10 Newington Road
Edinburgh
EH9 1QS

www.birlinn.co.uk
9 8 7 6 5 4 3 2 1

Copyright © John Neil Munro, 2002, 2008

Every effort has been made to trace the copyright
holders   d
        b

All right   y
be reprod   or
by any me   ng,
recording   n

The right   e
author of   ce
with the   .

ABERDEENSHIRE LIBRARY AND

INFORMATION SERVICES

2647441	
HJ	731656
B HAR	£9.99
AD	ANF

ISBN 978 1 84697 088 7

British Library Cataloguing-in-Publication Data
A catalogue record for this book is available
on request from the British Library.

Printed and bound by CPI Cox & Wyman, Reading

CONTENTS

PHOTOGRAPHS

Alex as a child, with his grandfather, father, brother Les, July 1946
Alex aged three, Dunoon, August 1938
Alex on banjo, brother Les and Charlie Carsware, c. 1955
Alex and the Soul Band (*Milk Marketing Board*)
Alex and Les onstage during the Soul Band era
Alex with Tommy Steele
Alex and Trudy at their wedding
Les Harvey at home
Alex with son Tyro
Alex with snake charmer
Trudy Harvey with Bill Fehilly
Alex, Tyro, Trudy and Alex Jnr
Alex revisits the Gorbals
The Sensational Alex Harvey Band (*Fin Costello/ Redferns*)
The Sensational Alex Harvey Band (*Gems/Redferns*)
Alex on stage, 1980 (*Ray Conn collection*)
Ian Dury and Alex
Trudy, Tom Robinson and Alex
Alex, 1980 (*Ray Conn collection*)
Alex rehearsing (*Ray Conn collection*)

(*All photographs unless otherwise stated are from Trudy Harvey's collection*)

INTRODUCTION

In December 1975, Glasgow's disaffected youth had more than their fair share of reasons for feeling disillusioned with life. The weather was awful, Scotland's national football team was underachieving again and the economy was in a complete shambles. Unemployment was soaring and house prices were rocketing. Harold Wilson's Labour Government was under fire from both the Left and the Right, and the Cod War was raging in Iceland. To add to the sense of foreboding, Margaret Thatcher had just arrived on the political scene and the *Black and White Minstrel Show* was the main draw on television. It hardly seemed to be the season of good cheer.

But in the week before Christmas, the city's youngsters found some salvation from their troubles at the Glasgow Apollo theatre, a ramshackle old concert venue on Renfield Street in the city centre. For three consecutive nights, the hall seemed to shake to its foundations as it hosted a series of festive parties to welcome home the city's favourite son. Those lucky enough to have been there swear to this day that those were some of the greatest concerts ever staged at the legendary Apollo.

As the house lights dimmed and 3,600 voices let loose a primeval roar, an army of longhaired, denim and leather-clad kids rose to their feet. While the band coiled up the tension with a dark pulsing beat, a small, middle-aged man decked out in a maroon smoking jacket, a hooped T-shirt, blue denim jeans and a pair of cowboy boots stalked to the centre of the stage. After a seemingly interminable wait, the spotlight shone on the wee man and with a sweet smile he started to speak to the crowd: 'Good evening, boys and girls, my name is Alexander and it really is a gas to be here. I would like to take this opportunity to introduce you to my band, The Sensational Alex Harvey Band.' The audience – fired up on a combination of booze and hash – suddenly forgot any pretence to decorum. For the next two hours it was going to be party time – their Faith Healer was back in town.

*

In the winter of 1975, Alex Harvey was at the peak of his powers. Music critics used to say that Alex served the longest apprenticeship in rock 'n' roll history. It dragged on through almost two decades, during which the working-class boy from Thistle Street in the Gorbals must have despaired of ever making the tantalising leap from the dancehalls of Scotland to the national record charts. Alex once had the modest childhood ambition of becoming a post-office clerk until one of his uncles did the world of music a favour and bought him a guitar. Gradually his love of music came to become the most important thing in his young life and he saw it as a way of escaping from the rat-infested tenements of the Gorbals.

Many people will only know of Alex through his Sensational Alex Harvey Band (SAHB) – in fact they only took up about a fifth of a career that lasted over 26 years. His musical career predated Presley, and as rock 'n' roll matured so did Alex Harvey. Soaking up all the strands of the 1950s music scene, Alex soon earned a legendary reputation in his native Glasgow as a charismatic performer. On a constant round of dance-hall gigs, in a variety of bands of varying abilities he would belt out an electrifying blend of blues, country, skiffle, jazz and rock 'n' roll. In 1957, he even won a Scottish newspaper talent contest to find the new Tommy Steele!

Along the way he sometimes drifted out of the music business, disillusioned by being ripped off by just about every money-grabbing manipulator around. He also suffered more than enough in the way of personal heartache and tragedy. In the 1970s, Alex lost his younger brother and his best friend – both dying in the most awful of circumstances.

Over the decades, Alex noted every passing musical trend – from Gene Autrey through Bob Dylan and The Beatles to Slade and the Sex Pistols. Alex learnt from them all but never became too closely associated with any one style – he always had enough class and originality to stand apart from the crowd.

And by the early 1970s, at long last, he had made it – and he was loving every minute of it. He had found the perfect band, four talented West of Scotland musicians who would power him to the top. They were guys who could indulge his tastes in blistering hard rock, jazz, blues, country and even vaudeville. His new band wouldn't miss a beat – even when Alex spiced up the set with cover versions of everything from Jacques Brel to Alice Cooper via The Osmonds and Del Shannon. For record company executives, the SAHB's eclectic approach was a nightmare to market, but for everyone else it was just great fun.

For five glorious years, The Sensational Alex Harvey Band tore up the rock 'n' roll rulebook. They chalked up hit singles together with critically acclaimed albums, and built what seemed like a large and ultra-loyal record-buying fan base. But it was up on stage where Alex was really most at home. A gentle guy away from the limelight, in concert he was transformed – mesmerising his audience with a bizarre series of personae and a groundbreaking stage set. It's too easily forgotten that during the mid 1970s the SAHB regularly beat groups like Pink Floyd and Genesis when fans voted for their favourite live act.

When Harvey was on stage performing, anything could happen.

Imagine the lead singer of a band dressed as Tarzan, swinging on a rope into the audience to haul an unsuspecting female back up on stage – just for a dance. Think of a rock star – naked apart from a plastic bag to cover his head – swimming through a lake before clambering up on stage just in time to start the first song for thousands of fans. Imagine a performer who would have the nerve to dress as Adolf Hitler and then lecture a huge crowd of German fans about the dangers of Fascism – or who would want to go onstage blacked up as Al Jolson at a concert in America's Deep South. Visualise a rock band arriving on stage at a massive festival in Belgium – all sitting aboard a 3.75-ton Bren Gun carrier which they had commandeered from the set of a Richard Attenborough film. Can you think of a modern-day musician who would re-enact the crucifixion live on stage wearing a crown made out of real barbed wire which would leave his forehead soaked in blood?

Alex did all these things and a lot, lot more.

In the old days he used to share the bill with Jimmy Logan or suffer the ultimate indignity of getting booed off stage by Uriah Heep fans. But by the mid 1970s, he was being feted by superstars like The Who and Elton John. The three 1975 Christmas shows at the Apollo, followed quickly by more sell-out concerts in London were proof positive of the band's appeal. When Alex, appearing on *The Old Grey Whistle Test* around that time, told the host Bob Harris that he thought his band were the 'best in the world' it didn't sound like an idle boast. It seemed like everyone loved Alex.

But somewhere along the line, it all went horribly wrong. Plagued by ill-health, drinking heavily and left isolated by the break-up of the band that was so crucial to him, Alex went into a tailspin of poor record sales and dispiriting comeback tours, playing to half-empty halls. The SAHB which had been one of the biggest British live acts during the 1970s split up owing hundreds of thousands of pounds. Disillusioned by debt and stripped of his fan base, he was lost in the whirlwind of the punk rock revolution. Even his 'ain folk' seemed to turn on him and just five years after the 1975 shows he was back at the Glasgow Apollo – but this time only for the one night and even then only a couple of hundred took the time to see him. Embarrassed bosses even let fans in free to bolster the crowd numbers.

Two years later Alex Harvey was dead.

Rock stars live a bizarre life – whisked around the world in private jets to glamorous, sunny locations. Some musicians even manage'glamorous' deaths, all wrapped up in whispered tales of drugs and debauchery. Alex Harvey died in distinctly unglamorous surroundings on a cold grey morning in Belgium. As he waited for a ferry in the seaport of Zeebrugge he was struck down by a heart attack. He was rushed to hospital but while in a coma he suffered a second and fatal attack.

To his family and close friends, Alex Harvey's death was a devastating blow. Those who knew him and loved him were well aware that they had lost an irreplaceable and dear friend. But news of his death also touched many others – not only in Scotland but also throughout the world – who had never met Alex but who felt that they knew him. Through his records and his concerts he gave his all with total conviction, and he had become their friend too. To them he was a unique individual whose talent touched their lives and who has never really been replaced.

Alex didn't fit the image of the standard 1970s rock star. He wasn't a bronzed Adonis with bare chest and long flowing hair. He was a scrawny wee guy with a shock of untidy black hair and scary teeth who sported a three-day stubble long before George Michael's vain attempt to make facial hair fashionable. He had a smile that was as menacing as it was welcoming. Though he had a limited education, Alex was an intensely intelligent man – a lateral thinker who could, and often did, talk for hours on the many subjects which fascinated him.

Alex didn't own a swanky sports car – in fact he didn't drive at all – because he didn't have a driving licence. He never owned a mansion in the sun, instead he settled for suburbia in East Finchley. There he spent time with his family and read from his vast collection of Marvel Comics, sci-fi magazines and *Boy's Own* story books or played with his huge collection of Edwardian and Victorian toy soldiers. (He was also genuinely convinced that in a previous life he fought in the frontline at the Battle of Waterloo!) The mechanics of war fascinated him just as much as the gory reality of battle repulsed him.

In every sense, Alex was a real one-off, a true original. He paved the way for a long line of Scottish singers and musicians – people like Maggie Bell, Lulu, Frankie Miller and Jim Kerr who were all inspired and fascinated by Harvey and his music. Further afield, musicians like David Bowie, Tom Robinson, Ian Dury and even John Lydon have acknowledged a debt to Harvey. A less well known admirer is the Australian Nick Cave, who has covered seven SAHB songs in both The Birthday Party and solo sets. As Cave succinctly told *The Scotsman* in January 2003: 'Alex Harvey was where it was at, man. And the band were extraordinary ... And his lyrics, which are just the most twisted thing ... the places he went, nobody went ...'

In suburban Crawley, The Cure's Robert Smith, sans eye-shadow and liner, grew up listening to Alex. Smith told *The Guardian* how Harvey was 'the physical manifestation of what I thought I could be. I was 14 when I first went to see him and then I followed him around to all the shows. He never really got anywhere, even though he had something so magical when he performed – he had the persona of a victim, and you just sided with him against all that was going wrong. I would have died to have Alex Harvey as an uncle.'

And Harvey's influence doesn't just stop at rock stars. On a recent radio interview, Sarah 'Fergie' Ferguson, aka the Duchess of York, selected SAHB's 'Boston Tea Party' as one of her all-time favourite oldies. Truth is indeed sometimes stranger than fiction.

And now, 26 years after his death, it seems strange that no one has taken the time to document what was an incredible life. (Martin Kielty, who wrote the official SAHB biography, estimates that there have been eight different attempts to chronicle Harvey's life in book form. All of them came to nothing, for one reason or another.) Indeed there seems to be a danger that people are beginning to forget the man who was undoubtedly Scotland's greatest rock 'n' roll star. Sure, when they hear his name

mentioned, people of a certain age will give you a knowing smile and recall vague recollections of a certain concert or TV show all these years ago when The Sensational
Alex Harvey Band blew them away. But for the younger
generation, Alex just doesn't seem all that relevant any
more.

If anything, this book is meant to redress the balance
and to try and help ensure that Alex's memory will live
on forever.

*

First off, I have a few sensational revelations of my own
to make and also some cautionary notes. I never met
Alex Harvey. I never even saw him play live. If truth be
told I wasn't that big a fan of his music when I was young
– I was too busy being duped by dodgy progressive rock
bands. But gradually I grew interested not just in his
music but also in the man himself. It seemed unusual
to me that no one had written his life story when other
'stars' who weren't fit to tune his guitar had reams written about them. So, I decided to try and rectify things.

Writing a biography about someone whose career
spanned almost 30 years is no easy task. It's made even
more difficult because Alex passed away 26 years ago.
Given the nature of the rock 'n' roll lifestyle and the fact
that so much time has elapsed, total recall is nigh on
impossible – many of the people I interviewed honestly
couldn't remember facts and dates. Alex Harvey crammed
an awful lot into his 46 years and this book isn't meant
to be a definitive recollection of every concert he ever performed or of each record he released. This biography isn't
aimed solely at the obsessive fan who will want to know
which song The Sensational Alex Harvey Band played for
their second encore at a concert in the Bracknell Sports

Centre in 1976. I'm sure such a book will be released some day and I look forward to reading it.

Alex was a very talkative individual, and the many interviews he gave during his career are a good starting point for any writer. Another cautionary note, however, is that Alex could spot a gullible reporter from a good distance. So, for a laugh, he would often exaggerate or even make up nonsensical answers. On tours of America, he wasn't averse to telling reporters that his biggest musical influence wasn't Elvis or Ray Charles but his 'Aunt Betsy' – a three-fingered blues guitarist who lost her fingers after she was tortured by the Gestapo when she worked for the French Resistance! Another favourite was his story about once working as an apprentice lion tamer at a circus! He also gleefully put a story about that he had been thrown out of the Black Watch for brutality to recruits.

Reporters sometimes were treated to Alex's favourite fantasy yarn about when he worked as a cabin boy in the Merchant Navy and was threatened by a gay tattooed stoker who gave him the choice of his dick – which he held in one hand – or a beating with a shovel. When the wide-eyed reporter would ask what choice he made, Alex would just growl 'D'you see any shovel marks on ma face?' Amazingly some of those stories actually made it into print and added to the Harvey myth. Sorting out the truth from the fantasy is a challenge in itself.

When I set out to write this book I didn't realise how difficult it would be to get some people to speak openly about Alex. Initially I was a bit confused as to why certain of Alex's friends or old bandmates didn't return my calls, or even have the courtesy to reply to my letters. Gradually I began to realise that although some of these people had their own agenda and were working on similar projects to my own, the majority of them were just suspicious about my motives. It's hard to exaggerate just how well-loved and respected Alex was by those who knew him. I lost track of the number of people who said that he ended up being like a brother or a father to them. Not surprisingly they were concerned that I might want to trash his reputation in print. Unfortunately several key players in Alex's life couldn't be persuaded to talk and I respect their right to do so. Just for the record, those who wouldn't talk were Zal Cleminson, Maggie Bell and Richard O'Brien. Letters to other key players went unanswered.

All of which makes me especially grateful to the following for taking the time to answer my questions: Trudy Harvey, Alex Harvey Junior, Hugh McKenna, Tom Robinson, Derek Nicol, Eddie Tobin, John Miller, Matthew Cang, Barbara Birdfeather, Ray Conn, Janet Macoska, George Butler, George McGowan, Gordon Sellar, Manni Ferri, Jimmy Wray MP, Derek Wadsworth, Laurie Scott Baker, George Gallagher, Tommy Eyre, David Gibson, John Waterson, Marianne Price, Loudon Temple, Bob Fish, Daniel Bennett, Tam White, Steve Toal, Roy Neave and Tony Hadland. Special thanks to the leading Alex Harvey fan Dougie McMahon for allowing me to view his great collection of memorabilia and for taping some of the rare early records for me.

Thanks for assistance and encouragement go to Dave and Mick at SAF Books, Russell Leadbetter, Calum Angus Macdonald, Donald John Munro, James McNair, Martin Kielty, Terry Houston, Ronnie Simpson, Neil and Shannon, Hugh Murray, Gillian Taylor, Wade McDaniel, Donnie Macleod, Simon Eyre, Nick Low, Ronnie Anderson, Alf Sludden, Aaron Childress, John Reed, the *Daily Record* Library Staff, Glasgow and the Central Music Library staff, Edinburgh. Thanks for getting this latest edition printed go to Roger Hutchinson, Stan, Kate Pool, Peter Curran, Neville and Alison at Polygon.

Finally, thanks to my mother for never fulfilling a threat to throw away all my old *NME*s.

1

HE WAS JUST A CHILD ...

'The folk heroes were gangsters. I'm not
knocking them, they were the friendliest
people I have ever met, some of the greatest
people I've ever met in my life. The same kind
of conditions that breed a kind of dark terror
and fear also breed a form of humanity – like
if you leave your door open, people next door
just walk in and out.'[1]
Alex Harvey

Way back in the fourteenth century, long before even
Alex Harvey had been born, a tiny village to the south of
the River Clyde in Glasgow was the site of a hospital for
lepers. The desperately ill people were taken across the
river to be cared for at the hospital, which was dedicated to St Ninian. Over the centuries, as the population
increased, the leper colony disappeared but the area
known as the Gorbals never really lost its reputation
for being a place best avoided by the upwardly mobile
in society.

By the 1930s, the Gorbals had earned an unrivalled and unwanted worldwide reputation for all the worst excesses of urban, working-class life. Name a social problem and the Gorbals had it in spades. Dismal housing, filthy sanitation, high levels of tuberculosis and other deadly diseases, overcrowding, unemployment and distinctly unfriendly gangs armed with razors – the ghetto just south of Glasgow's city centre had the lot. All in all, it wasn't the healthiest of places for the young Alex Harvey to grow up in.

Crammed into the rows of four-storey Gorbals tenements were around 90,000 folk – many of them poor immigrants from the Highlands of Scotland, Ireland and from the Jewish areas of Eastern Europe. Yet, despite the deprivation, the Gorbals had a great community spirit – the old cliché about people leaving their doors open at night actually rang true back then. Jimmy Wray, who grew up in the area and went on to become a Glasgow MP, recalls that there was very little in the way of bitterness: 'Maybe it's because we were all poor, but the people were humble and generous. We had nothing, but we were all friends together.'

And whatever problems the locals faced, they also knew how to drown their sorrows. Never mind the rat-infested homes, outside toilets and the all-pervasive poverty, 130 pubs still managed to do a roaring trade in the Gorbals of the 1930s.

*

Alex Harvey was a true son of the Gorbals. It's true that technically he spent part of his Glasgow years in the neighbouring and slightly more up-market district of Kinning Park, but he was born on 5 February 1935 at a time when his family lived briefly on Govan Road in the

14

Gorbals. And for 17 years, the Harvey family lived at 301 Thistle Street, slap-bang in the centre of all the inner-city decay.

When he became famous, Alex seemed to personify the Gorbals. The enduring image of Harvey is of the hard-drinking, tough-talking, working-class hero with the uncompromisingly honest Glasgow accent. The perception was of a man who was no stranger to violence and an individual determined to succeed against all the odds. Anyone who knew him well recognised that the image was somewhat exaggerated, partly by Alex himself. But there's no denying that Alex Harvey had a tough upbringing. In a radio interview, he once told how he, his young brother Les and their parents all lived in one room and had to share a communal toilet with 100 other people.

In September 1975, at the height of his commercial success, Alex took *Melody Maker* journalist Allan Jones back to what was left of the Gorbals of his youth. Fuelled by strong drink, Alex went on a hazy nostalgic trip around the area. He pointed out the church where he used to sing 'My Cup Runneth Over' on a Sunday. Then he and Jones wandered to the street corners where the kids used to keep themselves entertained by dropping bricks onto the heads of rats or cutting off the heads of police dogs with bayonets and sticking them to the walls – allegedly!

Later on in the interview, he told Jones how he remembered the wartime blitz by German bomber planes of the nearby town of Clydebank and how people were burned alive in their tenements. Seeing the futility of war and the squalor that surrounded him obviously made an impression on the young Harvey and he seemed to have a deep resentment towards the ruling upper class. After the war, when they came looking for Alex to do his stint of National Service they found him less than willing. In the interview with Allan Jones, he recalled:

I wasnae gonna fight for the fuckin' English. I'd been brought up in a single-end in a tenement. Me and my old man and my mother and my brother ... And these people come along and say, 'Fight for your country'. In this place where I lived there were rats crawling through the walls. Fight for what? ... I couldn't have cared less if the fuckin' Germans had come and taken the Gorbals ... They were welcome to it ... This is a place where 100 kids had to share the same shithouse ... That was our country – rats and tenements.[2]

(Any readers south of the Border should bear in mind that Harvey was no hater of the English, whatever this drunken quote might imply. Indeed he married an English girl and the Harvey family lived happily in East Finchley, London, for almost 20 years.)

Alex's parents, Leslie senior and Greta, looked after their two boys well; working hard to ensure they got as good an education as possible and they always had healthy food on the table. The boys' father was a clever man with humanist ideals. He was well-read, especially in Scottish history, and was a brilliant storyteller who held strong left-of-centre political views. Like many working-class men of the time, he realised that the quickest way out of the urban squalor for his children was to get a decent education. He encouraged his kids to go to the cinema and dream of Hollywood, to read about history but also to learn about the reality of war. Leslie Harvey senior had been a conscientious objector, as was his father before him. (Young Alex proudly carried on that tradition and on 27 January 1954, Alexander Harvey of 30 Durham Street signed on as Case Number 9,264 on the city's register of conscientious objectors.)

Despite holding these strong pacifist views, young Alex soon developed a contradictory obsession with the military, building up a massive collection of lead soldiers and adventure books on the British Empire. A childhood fascination with wars stuck with him throughout his adult life. In particular he was drawn to the Battle of Waterloo of 1815 and eventually became convinced that in a previous life he had been a Highland soldier caught up in the horrors of that battle. Alex often spoke of how he could easily conjure up a mental picture of himself in the middle of the fray – with the smell of gun smoke, sweat and leather and the grotesque din of war all around him. Late on in his life, he even visited an American psychiatrist who was an expert on reincarnation to try and set his mind at rest.

By all accounts, young Alex was a bright and conscientious student at the local Camden Street Primary School before he moved on to Strathbungo Senior Secondary. He was also a keen member of the local Boys' Brigade division.

A visit to Glasgow's Mitchell Library failed to throw much light on Alex's schooldays – the only remaining record for Strathbungo school shows that he was pupil number 1,869 and that he enrolled on 1 September 1947. His medical inspection is mysteriously listed as 2C. The only other fact cited is that he left school on 30 June 1950, because of his 'age'.

Given that he left school so early in life, it's pretty certain that Alex had no formal qualifications. Like countless other bright working-class kids of his age he was cheated by the education system under which he toiled. In many ways, Alex was the classic example of the under-educated Scot – someone who had great natural intelligence that was forever struggling to get out. The received wisdom of the time was that kids like Alex should leave school, sign on the dole or work at the docks, keep their mouth shut and start a family. Alex was a bit too clever to fall into that trap.

In the long run, that intelligence found an outlet through his music but early on in his life, things didn't look that straightforward. For a few years he struggled to find a steady job – drifting from one occupation to another. By his own reckoning, he started out on 36 different careers. Though he did tell a BBC interviewer that he was a carpenter by trade, he also apparently had spells working as an office clerk, a fruit porter, a brickie's labourer in Doncaster, a plumber's assistant, a cooper, a tombstone maker and a lumberjack. He definitely worked on a coal boat running from Shields to London and in a whisky bottling plant. Most bizarre of all – considering he lived in the centre of urban Glasgow – he often told reporters that he had once earned a living as a lion tamer!

The love and affection shown by Mr and Mrs Harvey to their two sons was reciprocated by the boys. In an interview in 1974, Alex recalled how he used to travel with his father to the Highlands where they would try to sell lengths of suit material to families in areas where decent tailors were thin on the ground:

My old man used to drive a car for these tinkers and salesmen that sold material and things in the Highlands of Scotland and I went with him a couple of times during the school holidays. The first time was when I was about ten and I was very impressed by this guy that was a sort of leader, you know he acted his part. Whenever he was selling, before he went up to the house he used to pick me up and say 'This is the best stuff money can buy – why should I sell it to these people? I am giving them a bargain', and he walked up to the door like that. I used to love him, he was magnificent – the real thing. He overcharged but his goods were not shoddy and I do believe that he brought magic to their doors. I believe that.[3]

Besides his business trips up north, Alex's father had a variety of jobs. He worked in the dairy industry when he was young, before becoming a van driver for many Glasgow-based companies. In his latter years, he worked as a night watchman at the Apollo Theatre (where his son would enjoy his greatest triumphs) and as a stage-door-man across the street at the Pavilion Theatre. Though he wasn't driven to be successful, he always worked hard to ensure that the boys were looked after. His wife Greta worked as a seamstress and played a vital role in bringing up the kids. Alex Harvey junior told me:

As far as I'm concerned my grandmother was the root and the heart of all that happened. She was the stabilising influence and like 'Papa' she was also a fantastic storyteller. She was the kind of woman that people used to bring sick children to in the days before there was a National Health Service. She could take kids out of convulsions, that kind of stuff, even though she had no formal training.[4]

One lesson passed on quickly from father to son was that they should both steer well clear of the gang violence that had long plagued Glasgow. Alex was small and wiry but he knew how to look after himself and early on in his teenage years he seemed to be drawn towards the glamour of the local gangsters, with their big Studebacker cars, glamorous girlfriends and flash suits. An impressionable Alex used to think that the way to a young girl's heart was by acting the hard man and he soon earned a reputation as a bit of a hoodlum with a penchant for rearranging the insides of phone kiosks. In his own words, he didn't have either the bravery or the superior intelligence needed to avoid getting involved in the gang culture.

In the Gorbals, demarcation lines between rival gangs

were strictly respected. When the lines were crossed, the resulting violence was invariably brutal. In interviews, Alex often alluded to being on the fringes of the gangland scene and of having a criminal record. He told *NME* that he had seen two people shot dead in front of him and had found the experiences horrible and heartbreaking. Some members of Harvey's family were fans of Rangers FC, who traditionally draw their fan base from Glasgow's Protestant community – but Alex had little time for the religious bigotry that was often the root cause of gang violence. Indeed, later in his career, fans of Rangers and their city rivals Celtic were encouraged to put their knives into specially provided dustbins when they arrived for Harvey gigs in Glasgow.

Alex was just a young street punk, but unlike many of his contemporaries he secretly preferred his violent fantasies to be played out on the cinema screen or on the pages of a comic book. In later discussions with journalists, he made his views on violence plain and admitted that many of the youngsters he grew up with in the Gorbals ended up in jail after mixing with the gang culture. But as he grew older and wiser, Alex came to realise that there was more to life than violence and he came to use his fame to counter the effects of the gang culture:

I never believed in it [violence]. There's just no fun in breaking someone's nose. I sincerely believe that I neutralise any image of violence I may portray on stage with my humour, which descends from that unique Glasgow wit. The Gorbals was violent, I suppose, but you could always leave your door open – there were very few burglaries because no one had anything to steal.[5]

Alex's widow Trudy, who knew him better than anyone, confirms:

Alex wasn't a wild man at all. I can remember watching him at a small club gig once and someone behind me said, 'Oh, I wouldn't like to get on the wrong side of him!' That was the impression Alex gave off but to me it was just unbelievable. He was actually an incredibly peaceful person – when he wasn't working he preferred to read. He used to get through a book a day. And he was incredibly friendly and welcoming to people when they came to our house. I think I saw him once kick a bus door but only because he was angry with the driver. And that really is the sum total of my experience of him being violent.[6]

So despite the hard-man image and his menacing, aggressive stage persona, Alex was a gentleman away from the limelight. He understood violence but rarely felt the need to use it. Only when his sweet powers of persuasion failed did he opt for the last resort. The SAHB keyboard player Hugh McKenna told me how he had once seen Alex take care of a drunk at the Speakeasy Club in London as the band unwound after a show in 1972. The unfortunate individual was by all accounts being provocative, by deliberately bumping into Alex and at one point kicking out at the singer. He was asking for trouble and he got it – Alex nutted him twice after failing to make the man see reason. According to Hugh, this type of incident was extremely rare.

A story told by Eddie Tobin, who was part of The Sensational Alex Harvey Band's management team, would seem to confirm that the 'Glasgow Kiss' was Alex's favoured mode of attack. When push came to head butt, Alex knew how to look after himself – even if he was a pacifist:

He stuck the head on a member of the press once when he bumped into him. For a pacifist he could be a very angry man. He was really intense, when he talked to you sometimes you thought 'This guy is going to hit me!' and when he laughed it was really, really menacing. When he laughed it was as frightening as when he was angry!

2

... WHEN HIS INNOCENCE WAS LOST

'In those days, to walk down the street in a
pair of jeans was an amazing thing. I nearly
stopped the world.'[1]
Alex Harvey

Many of his relatives were keen amateur musicians and
Alex was soon taking trumpet lessons, though – in his
own words – he only ever learnt 'to play in B-flat!' He
was irresistibly drawn to the weird names and wonderful
music of jazz musicians like Jelly Roll Morton. In 1954,
one of Alex's uncles, Jimmy Wallace, who had a liking
for jazz records and those of virtuoso guitarists Django
Reinhardt and Eddie Lang in particular decided to give
his young nephew a nudge in the right direction. Notic-
ing Alex's strong attraction towards music, he gave him
his old pre-war Gibson guitar and even taught him a few
rudimentary chord sequences.

Armed with his new toy, Alex started busking, and per-
fected the art on weekend trips to picturesque villages like
Drymen or Luss, near Loch Lomond. On those summer
evenings, he and his pals would sit around the campfire

singing Gene Autrey and Hank Williams' songs. Sometimes the gang would even get a gig keeping the locals entertained in the village pub and a grateful manager would allow them all to bunk down free in a room for the night.

Back in the city, Alex – who by now had also learnt the basics of banjo and trumpet playing – was starting to get noticed. With his long hair in a headband, he was difficult to ignore. He made his pro debut playing trumpet at a family wedding and really loved the trad jazz and Dixieland scene which was so popular at the time. Revival bands like the Clyde Valley Stompers were cashing in on the resurgence in popularity of 1920s jazz.

Along with saxophonist Bill Patrick, Alex often rehearsed at Bill Paterson Studios in Glasgow. Paterson ran a touring roadshow, and soon Harvey and Patrick were playing at those gigs alongside stand-up comics and tapdancers. Bizarrely the same musicians often played in two different bands at the gigs. Prior to the interval they were the 'respectable' trad Clyde Valley Jazz Band. Later on in the night they reappeared in less formal clothing to play country-tinged rock 'n' roll as the Kansas City Skiffle Group, hammering out Woody Guthrie songs.

Alex Harvey was around the music scene long before rock 'n' roll really took off. But once he started to hear the electric blues and early rock 'n' roll records which were being imported from the United States, he realised that you were either a believer or an outcast. He quickly became a zealous convert to the cause:

I was the first to get a Muddy Waters record. It was on the old Vogue Jazz Collector red label. At first I didn't know whether I was going to buy it because it was so different from what we were used to already – which was acoustic guitars – so I got it. And then within a few years … 'Heartbreak Hotel', 'Long Tall Sally'.[2]

By 1956, rock 'n' roll was even starting to make inroads into the sleepy West of Scotland mainstream society. In September of that year, one of Glasgow's biggest ballrooms, The Locarno on Sauchiehall Street, experimented by inserting a weekly half-hour long session of rock 'n' roll music. The brainchild of resident bandleader Benny Daniels, the experiment was advertised under the slogan 'just to keep the youngsters happy!' The bored teenagers loved it and later that same month they almost went apoplectic when the Bill Haley movie *Rock Around the Clock* was released in Scotland. Police in dozens of stations across the Central Belt were put on alert after earlier screenings in London triggered riots.

For Alex, the new rock revolution couldn't come quick enough. He was a regular customer at the Locarno dance nights and also at the fabled Barrowlands Ballroom in the East End. Alex liked the dancing and the weekend boozing, but his real obsession was with the wild raw electric sounds that were increasingly coming to dominate the 1956 hit parades. One such song was 'Giddy Up a Ding-Dong' on the Mercury label by Freddie Bell, which an impressed Alex filed away in his memory bank for future use. (Bell's group The Bellboys were the first rock 'n' roll group to play Glasgow, and it's a fair bet that the young Harvey was a member of the audience that night.)

Dressing like a Teddy Boy, Alex had a reputation for wearing the tightest drainpipe trousers on the Glasgow scene. He was earning a living playing trumpet for a local jazz band called the Kinning Park Ramblers and increasingly getting a tremendous reception when he himself took centre stage. Late in 1956, police had to be called to clear the aisles of the St Andrew's Hall in Glasgow after Alex played an impromptu gig during the interval of a trad jazz gig.

Much as he loved the music of Louis Armstrong and Jelly Roll Morton, Alex wanted to branch out into rock 'n' roll full-time. His chance came bizarrely in 1957 through the Scottish tabloid newspaper *The Sunday Mail*. Eager to show their youth credentials they organised a country-wide competition to find Scotland's answer to Tommy Steele – the former bellboy who had signed to Decca Records and was reputedly earning an impressive £400 a week. Steele had once been hailed as the UK's answer to Elvis Presley.

The Sunday Mail ran regional heats throughout Scotland, including one held in Kirkcaldy Mission to the Deaf and Dumb, where the winners would each receive £5. After auditioning 600 hopefuls, Alex, armed with a guitar bought for £3, emerged as the winner. The competition was organised by David Gibson, then a 24-year-old journalist at the newspaper. Now retired and living in Tighnabruich in the Highlands, he recalled:

Tommy Steele was tremendously popular at the time and he had just had a huge hit record with Guy Mitchell's original 'Singing the Blues'. So we thought it would be a great idea to find Scotland's own Tommy Steele. We set up these auditions all over the place, and almost everyone we heard tried to do 'Singing the Blues'. I heard so many bad imitations of that song … I never wanted to hear it again in my life!

The last audition was held in Glasgow and Bill Paterson, who helped arrange it, asked Alex to take part. He stood out head and shoulders above the rest. He just had so much charisma and personality. He had a good act, very punchy and aggressive – and he didn't play 'Singing the Blues' until we asked him to! Incidentally the guy who came second – Joe Moretti – was a much, much better guitar player than Alex but he lacked the strong personality. The competition did Joe some good too, and as I remember he gave up whatever job he had and went to London where he became a leading session musician.[3]

On 28 April 1957, *Sunday Mail* readers were given the long awaited news that the winner of the competition was Alex. At the time, he was 22 years old and worked as a cooper at the docks. The article concluded:

He is a first rate rock 'n' roll singer (but he's not limited to rock 'n' roll) and his vitality is unlimited. Brought up in Kinning Park, he left school early to get to work and bring in some money. When he was 21 he married his girlfriend – a cinema usherette. The only house they could get was a single-end on Crown Street, a cramped little apartment with walls, which showed signs of dampness. Some time ago, Alex bought a smashed-up guitar for £3. He worked on it with loving care and transformed it into a bright gleaming instrument. With that £3 guitar he sang his way to the top of our contest against guitars which cost anything up to £100. So to Alex Harvey, a youngster from the dark back streets of Glasgow, goes this chance to be a star.[4]

To help him escape those very same dark back streets, Alex was presented with £25, a film test and an auditioning contract with a record company. To publicise his win, Alex was pictured leaping off a chair into the air, guitar in hand and with his long hair blowing in the breeze. He later complained that the shot had taken ages to get right.

Harvey was presented with the award at the end of a jazz concert run by the newspaper at the St Andrew's Hall in Glasgow. Doing the honours was Kitty Kallen – an American who was one of the most popular female big band singers of the era and who had a number one hit a few years previously with 'Little Things Mean a Lot'.

David Gibson remarks:

Kitty Kallen was appearing at the Glasgow Empire theatre at the time, and the idea was for her to come along and just present the prize. But when Alex came on he did some rock 'n' roll numbers and the place went crazy. There were people dancing in the aisles, which was almost unheard of at the time and something which was strictly forbidden due to the fire regulations. The ushers in the hall had a real job trying to get everyone under control.

Kitty Kallen got up on stage but under the terms of her contract at The Empire she wasn't allowed to perform anywhere else. She got so excited that she ended up doing a duet with Alex while her manager was standing in the wings having kittens because she was breaking her contract! It was an incredible night.

Bill Haley and the Comets were an international success at the time and here we were in Glasgow with one of our own giving us the same kind of roof-raising music. Hundreds of people in the audience were on their feet trying to dance in whatever spaces they could find. Nothing like Alex had been seen before and I didn't see that type of audience reaction again until Alex played the Apollo nearly 20 years later.

That show in 1957 really marked a sea change in the Glasgow music scene. At that time, there wasn't a lot for young folk to do – the pubs shut at some ludicrously early hour like 6 p.m. and there were only a half a dozen jazz clubs which were all teetotal. When Alex and rock 'n' roll arrived, traditional jazz began to take a back seat – it was the very beginning of what became the 'disco scene' and from there it grew and grew into what we have today.[5]

The show may have marked a turning point. Alex became a minor celebrity, roped into events like photo signing sessions in stores that sold 'trendy' suits – in Dundee! But it's difficult to see any real comparison between Alex and Tommy Steele. While Harvey was cultivating his image of being a wild stage performer with a real knowledge of his musical roots, Steele was fast settling into a niche as the loveable face of rock 'n' roll – the type of singer a mother would approve of.

Irrespective of their differences, there was obviously some respect between the pair. They were pictured together soon after the competition, and when Steele returned to play at the Empire Theatre the following year, the two met up in the backstage dressing room after the show. David Gibson went along with Alex and recalls how the two singers shared a liking for a wee refreshment:

We all sat in the dressing room after the show till about 1 a.m. They got on like a house on fire, just strumming their guitars, having a drink and a laugh. I went home around 1 a.m. but when I met Alex a couple of days later he told me that he and Tommy had gone down to Govan docks after I left. Tommy used to be a cabin boy on a merchant ship that just happened to be in Govan that night.

They were both pretty merry by then and apparently they got through a hole in the perimeter fence, got onto the vessel and woke up the crew. They had a party which just got louder and louder. Now at that time the docks area was very busy but notorious for thefts. So the security men were alerted by all the racket and came and chased Tommy and Alex off the ship. They managed to get through the hole in the fence and were last seen running down the streets of Govan with their guitars in hand![6]

Looking back on the competition, Alex Harvey junior told me that his dad took a lot of good things from the Tommy Steele contest:

My dad found positive aspects in just about everything he did. He thought the competition was 'a ball'. It was there, he done it and he won it – and he met Tommy Steele. I'm not sure if it was necessarily the best label for him at the time – no disrespect to Tommy Steele – but it's not the best compliment in the world. My dad was the type of person who thought 'What's the point of analysing it all?' That was the only opportunity available to him at the time.[7]

Emboldened by his success in the newspaper competition, Alex soaked up the new sounds of Bill Haley and Elvis Presley while also joining in the tail end of the skiffle boom and the new blues scene, covering songs by Big Bill Broonzy, Muddy Waters and Jimmy Rogers. But the success had its down side, according to his close friend and bandmate Jimmy Grimes; after Alex won the competition he was appearing in four different places in one night and people were even pretending to be him. It was an omen of hectic times to come.

3

BIG SOUL BAND

'Rock 'n' roll is like an atomic bomb – those
involved in the business are soldiers, but
they won't hurt anyone. If I was attacked by
500 million Chinese I'd rather have a 1000-
watt amplifier and a guitar than a gun – they
might like it and it might just stop them.'[1]
Alex Harvey

Alex Harvey could have been forgiven for thinking that
in 1958 he was on the brink of nationwide fame and
chart success. Irrespective of whether the Tommy Steele
competition was a blessing or a hindrance, it had given
him much needed publicity and made his name known
throughout Scotland. With the rock music revolution in
full swing and with his given talent and enthusiasm,
Alex must have thought fame and fortune was just
around the corner. In fact he would spend the next 15
years in a succession of failed attempts to make the
big time. Incredibly he went through the whole decade
of the 1960s almost unknown while his contemporaries
and rivals – many of whom paled in comparison to Alex
– notched up hit singles and albums. It must have been
a soul-destroying time for him.

*

Back in 1958 the first obstacle Alex faced was the indifference of the Scottish music establishment. If rockers like Alex were beginning to make a modest impact in Glasgow, the walls of the music establishment were still far from tumbling down. Most promoters were still wary of change and opted for the safe option of big bands playing slushy ballads and trad jazz instead of the raw and dangerous new sounds of rock 'n' roll.

For Alex Harvey, the key to the rock revolution that was about to take off was the electric guitar. Kids who had previously felt hemmed in by the safe society of postwar Britain now had the option of buying a cheap guitar and amp on hire purchase, and learning a few chords. Forming a band was a sure-fire way of attracting the girls and offending their parents.

Like the punk rockers 20 years later, Alex and his pals were learning the thrills of challenging the old order. He later recalled:

It became possible for a young person that didn't know anything about music to get hold of a guitar and turn it up loud, whether he could play it or tune it didn't matter, but he could make everyone know that he was about and make his presence felt ... and there really has not been anything like that since ... I suppose until they invent an atomic sax or something there's not going to be anything ...[2]

Alex used to draw comparisons between the guitar and the machine-gun. His musical instrument was the safe – if noisy – way for him to work off excess energy and pent-up emotion.

Now in his early twenties, Alex had more than enough experience and working-class Glasgow charm to lead his own band. He was level-headed and knew what it would take to achieve his ambition of success. First off, he formed the Kansas City Counts, a pop outfit who often shared the bill with another West of Scotland band – the Ricky Barnes All-Stars. Legend has it that 'Counts' soon got fed up with that name – especially as their detractors were preferring to omit the letter O from the third word! In any case, Alex was gradually becoming more confident with his role as frontman and the band's name evolved into the Alex Harvey Band.

Largely forgotten now, the Kansas City Counts did have the distinction of being one of, if not the first ever touring Scottish rock bands, and had the dubious honour of triggering Scotland's first ever rock 'n' roll riot after a gig at Paisley Town Hall. Peter Curran was one of the two sax players in the band and remembers that they mostly played the McKinnon circuit – named after one of the leading promoters of the time, Duncan McKinnon. Peter, who now lives in Kirkliston, first met Harvey in 1956 when Alex went seeking advice from a mutual friend on how to play the cornet. Alex at the time was working in the Glasgow fruit market, and Peter remembers visiting the Harvey household on Crown Street which had a clock that, rather spookily, only started ticking prior to their being a death in the family.

In 1957, Alex invited Peter, who had been playing in dance bands on the same bill as Harvey, to join the fledgling Counts as second sax player behind Bill Patrick.

I spent an unforgettable few months with them, touring – and starving – in an old Austin hired car, which somehow held all of us, travelling, eating and sleeping. The other key band on the circuit around then was the Ricky Barnes band. They were a fine band and a Bill Haley clone, with smart jackets and choreographed movements, but they were a dead-end in rock, whereas Alex was the beginnings and also the future of true rock 'n' roll.

Life with the Counts was great fun, but it was never going to make the boys rich. The guitarists had to share Alex's 15-watt Selmer amp and had to tie broken guitar strings together because of the lack of replacement strings. Shifty management didn't help – once leaving the boys stranded outside a public lavatory in Carlisle for a week, where they took turns to sleep in the back of their car and lived off Oxo cubes, tins of beans and vegetables liberated from a nearby farm. Busking in the pubs would sometimes get them a half-bottle of whisky and a bed for the night.

Peter Curran recalls:

Apart from the McKinnon circuit, which was well-managed and paid up on the button, we got involved in a very strange set of charitable concerts under the banner of the Spastics charity (I think they got a donation from the concerts, but weren't involved in the management side). These were stage-based variety bills. The main arguments on money arose from these concerts.

Curran says that even in those early days, Harvey was just a little bit different from the rest of the band.

I remember Alex's fascination with the occult and its theatrical manifestations. We used to stop after midnight outside graveyards in the Borders, and Alex would climb on the shoulders of Big Dougie, our double bass player, then pull on a huge long greatcoat, creating a sinister giant. They would then wander onto the road, and hail passing motorists, to their consternation and terror, causing near pile-ups. Alex also used to insist that we walked backwards into the graveyard, as a sort of test of nerve. Nobody could do it but him!

George White, our drummer, was older than the rest of us, but a real extrovert. He had a drum kit illuminated from the inside by coloured light bulbs running off mains power, and did spectacular drum solos with the lights. However, the bulbs were always exploding with the force of his drumming! Our first truly theatrical performance (which prefigured a lot of Alex's later brilliant characterisations) was in a hall at Galashiels. We had to put on a wide range of items on the bill, to attract the stolid Border folk as well as the young rock enthusiasts. I played a duet with the tenor sax player Bill Patrick on 'Buddy, Can You Spare a Dime?' and Alex had a number of little theatrical skits, including one where, naked to the waist with a rope tied round him, he was pulled off the stage, then reappeared, still on the rope on the other side. He also wanted to kill a chicken on stage in a voodoo skit, but was dissuaded by Bill and me, fearing the Border farmers would lynch us. Believe me, Alex was way ahead of Alice Cooper!

If any of the punters at these early shows had been asked which of the performers would eventually go on to sell over 15 million albums, perform for over 50 years and be awarded an MBE for services to entertainment they would probably have plumped for Alex. In fact another young kid on the bill, Ayrshire guitarist Sydney Devine, would eclipse Harvey in terms of sales and longevity. Scotland's very own rhinestone cowboy had been a contestant in the *Sunday Mail* quest to find the Scots Tommy Steele, and he and Alex became good friends. In his biography, Sydney recalls how they played together soon after in a tour organised by the newspaper, sharing a taxi with the rest of the musicians.

Alex was up for anything in a skirt, and he put the taxi's back seat to good use ... we would watch what was going on and wait our turn.

Devine later joined the Counts on the McKinnon circuit, aged just 17 and billed as 'The Tartan Rocker', decked out in full Highland dress and singing songs like 'Hound Dog'. The two young lotharios were soon scouting for girls again

– after a gig at the Meeting Rooms in Inverness they bedded a pair of local twins!

A few months later the Counts, without Sydney, were being billed as Alex Harvey and the New Saints before finally becoming The Alex Harvey Soul Band or Big Soul Band in 1958. This outfit was to last until the mid 1960s though, for whatever reason, Alex occasionally appeared with musician friends under a number of different names such as The Alex Harvey Showband or Mad Harvey and his Insane Six.

The new Soul Band was performing long before the advent of the type of music of the same name that would eventually be popularised by artists like Wilson Pickett and Marvin Gaye. In fact the use of the word soul in the Glasgow band's name came about when they read an article in the US magazine *Crescendo* which made mention of the 'soul jazz' sound of pianist Horace Silver. The Big Soul Band had numerous influences but perhaps the strongest was Ray Charles, the blind American pianist whose catchy tunes like 'I Got a Woman' and 'What'd I Say' made a lasting impression on Alex.

Alex wanted the new band to be the best around and to put the rest of the Scottish music scene in the shade. When people went to see the Soul Band he wanted them to remember the experience. Jimmy Wray (who had declined an early offer to manage the band) helped instead by buying them their first uniforms – natty yellow and maroon outfits. Later, they graduated to even more gaudy gold or silver crushed velvet suits with bright red shirts, gold bow ties and white stack-heeled boots. It was difficult for audiences to ignore them.

A Soul Band gig was as much a treat for the ears as it was a pain for the eyes. Basically they were a showband playing covers – but to make them stand out from the competition, Alex added two saxophones, congas, timbale and maracas. Punters could expect to hear any new recordings by Ray Charles, Elvis or Bo Diddley with an exotic flavour of calypso or Art Blakey's distinctive African drum sound thrown in for good measure. Women in the audience weren't safe from becoming part of the act. Alex had one routine where he would dress up in a leopard-skin outfit and leave the stage to run through the crowd Tarzan-style and pick up a girl before carrying her over his shoulder back up on stage!

It made for an exciting and – for the still repressed West of Scotland at least – an exotic night out. The Soul Band were soon spreading the rock 'n' roll gospel outside Glasgow and Edinburgh to the North of England and throughout Scotland, even turning up in outposts like Wick, Stornoway in the Outer Hebrides and Orkneys. But their main strongholds were to be working-class areas in cities like Glasgow, Liverpool and Hamburg. In some places the band felt like missionaries bringing the new electric sound to the non-believers. Alex recalled that sometimes when he would ask the manager where they could plug in, they were asked 'plug in what'?

The original band featured three local musicians – Charlie Carsware on bass, drummer Willie White and singer Bobby Rankine. As the band evolved, Alex chopped and changed the musicians – paying them on a weekly basis and selecting them from a pool of talented players on the Glasgow scene. Musicians came and went and even played for 'rival' combos run by the likes of Ricky Barnes and Bobby Patrick.

One man who made the switch was drummer George McGowan who first came across Alex Harvey late in 1958:

I was playing with Ricky Barnes All-Stars at the time and they were the biggest band around with Alex's band number two. I had met Alex on the circuit a few times and when Ricky decided to change his band, I was out of work. Fortunately for me, Alex's drummer at the time had to leave and I got the job. As I recall, the band became The Soul Band around 1960 and with the congas and timbale we had a totally different sound from all the others. Although we did copies of songs, we did them in our own style.[3]

Bobby's Patrick's brother Bill played sax in one of the early line-ups, and other regulars were Jimmy Grimes on bass, Robert Nimmo on rhythm guitar, George 'Hoagy' Carmichael on sax, and a conga player called Big Wally Stewart.

The one certainty in all this fluidity was that Alex would be the focal point – the real leader of the band. With his immaculate outfits and long hair he immediately looked the part. He also had a natural talent – both as a musician and an organiser. He had a forceful, rasping vocal delivery and knew how to ape his own singing heroes, Big Bill Broonzy, Hank Williams, Little Richard and Elvis Presley. He also drove the crowds wild by hammering away at his guitar. Alex might not have been in the same league as future axe heroes like Pete Townshend or Jimi Hendrix when it came to musical ability, but he could match them when it came to manhandling the instrument, mangling the strings as he thrashed out songs.

He also had a real empathy with his audience. They loved his highly individual sense of humour and he seemed to know intuitively what to say to the crowd and when to say it. Soon the band were big enough to play support to their idols John Lee Hooker, Eddie Cochran and Gene Vincent when they came to the UK to play.

Despite having a growing popularity beyond Glasgow, Alex didn't forget his roots. Jimmy Wray recalls how the

Soul Band would play charity gigs for Gorbals pensioners, helping to raise cash which Wray said put a smile on the old folks' faces and paid for their bus tours and Christmas parties. Once, in 1959, Alex and the band played an open-air concert at the League of the Cross Hall on Errol Street in aid of a benevolent fund for Jimmy Murphy. The unfortunate Mr Murphy was a pensioner with no relatives who was found lying in his home on Caledonia Street with a rat chewing away at his foot.

Elsewhere there were gigs to be played at the new jazz or art clubs which were starting to open up in Scotland – but the bread-and-butter concerts were in town halls, miners' welfare clubs and village halls around the country. Bass player Jimmy Grimes, a former merchant seaman from Parkhead, Glasgow, recalled those frenetic early days in the book *Blue Suede Brogans*:

We did a lot of work at this time ... In one 24-hour period we did six jobs. La Cave [a music club in Midland Street, Glasgow], then down to Alexandria, back to Glasgow, then on to an all-nighter at a club in Leith Walk with Andy Fairweather. Then La Cave twice again on the Sunday. Even wi' aw the pills – purple hearts that women could get on prescription for slimming – you still fell asleep.

Grimes was to become a lifelong pal of Alex Harvey. Known as the General, he had first seen Alex in action around 1955 playing 'Sweet Georgia Brown' on the trumpet at a church hall in Springburn, Glasgow. When the General returned from his trips to sea, he would bring back calypso records, which the pair feasted over. They both worked together on a coal boat which ran from the north of England to London before Alex eventually persuaded the General to turn his back on life at sea and join the Soul Band with the immortal words 'how would you like to get into debt?' Jimmy obviously fancied the idea and within months he was the proud owner of the first Fender Jazz bass guitar in the country.

Grimes recalls how that bass drew admiring glances when The Beatles met the Soul Band in Alloa around 1960. The embryonic Fab Four and a singer called Johnny Gentle once apparently backed the Soul Band at a concert in Grangemouth Town Hall. In the book, Grimes remembers:

They were called the Silver Beatles and they wore black gear. Also, they used four guitars ... they didn't have a bass and were interested in mine .... we didn't actually play with them ... they didn't make much impression on me either.[4]

Other gigs saw the Soul Band support teenage idols like Marty Wilde, Billy Fury and Johnny Gentle – young guns managed by London impresario Larry Parnes. By 1961, Parnes was considered to be the most powerful man in British rock 'n' roll and was running 'value for money' concert tours around the UK.

But by then Alex was starting to feel restricted by the Scottish 'beat' scene. In comparison to London it was less sophisticated and had fewer venues willing to entertain rock 'n' rollers. The few clubs that would take the risk were saddled with bizarre licensing regulations. Getting to the gig was also a problem and after a couple of years the band were soon fed up with being cooped up in a beat-up old Bedford Doormobile van or shivering half-asleep at a greasy-spoon roadside café. Space was even more limited in the back of the van when the group invested in a vibraphone, which they carted around in a coffin-sized case. When they carried it out of the van, passers-by took their hats off, imagining that they were witnessing a funeral. The money was poor too, drummer George McGowan recalls that depending on bookings, he would earn only £12 a week in Scotland.

Getting paid was the biggest problem of all. Alex was convinced early on his career that there were too many 'managers, agents, shysters, sharks and hangers-on' in the business. The Glasgow singer Maggie Bell – who was just starting out on her own illustrious career in the early 1960s – agreed. She later told a reporter:

We all grew up together, there was a time when we were prostituting ourselves musically for 30 bob a night. I tell you there was one place in Glasgow where you got paid with a glass of champagne and a chicken leg.[5]

Jimmy Grimes had similar painful memories of the early days on the road:

Back then Alex and I would look at the promoter, size up the cut of his jib and often as not Alex would say, 'You lift this, I'll lift that and if we get paid we'll put them back.' As we moved on in the business, the promoters' methods changed but the net result was the same – screw the workers. You'd get a cheque issued by the Bank of Outer Mongolia and by the time it bounced back by slow camel the guy had disappeared. I think he [Alex] actually got accustomed to being ripped-off in those days. I reckon two out of three cheques used to bounce – and there were nights when we would have to carry the piano out of the hall if we wanted to show a profit.[6]

In addition to the rip-offs, bands also had to contend with their concerts degenerating into violence. In particular, Glasgow gigs were plagued by knife fights between rival gangs in the crowd. At one gig where his brother Leslie was on the bill, a bouncer was stabbed to death. An added, though much more pleasant, consideration for Alex was that he now had the responsibilities of being a parent. He and his wife Mary now had a young son to look after, Alex junior who was born in 1959. The need to bring in more income led Alex to look outside Scotland for work.

4

HAMBURG AND HOME AGAIN

'We went to Germany in 1963 and one of the
first things I thought about was my uncle
had been bombing Germany twenty years
previous. And I made a better impression
with an electric guitar. I made a lot more
friends than they did.'[1]

Alex Harvey

By the early 1960s, jaded British rockers were being offered an unusual escape route from the conservative UK
music scene. Salvation lay across the North Sea in the
German port of Hamburg. There, a couple of adventurous entrepreneurs had an ambition to transform the
city's seedy red-light St Pauli district and cash in on the
growing popularity of rock 'n' roll among German kids.
But they faced two problems – their own German bands
weren't very good and the real thing, American stars like
Elvis, were just too pricey.

The solution was to hire British rockers who both looked
the part and also made a passable impersonation of the

Americans. Club owner Bruno Koschmider travelled to London's legendary 2 i's coffee bar where he met an old band mate of Alex, organist Ian Hines – the brother of actor Fraser Hines who went on to star in the BBC's *Dr Who*. It was Ian who helped recruit the first wave of bands to invade Germany – including The Beatles. The British bands were soon pulling in large crowds at clubs like the Top Ten or the Kaiserkeller.

In his excellent book detailing the history of the Hamburg beat boom, Alan Clayson paints a convincing picture of why so many British musicians were per-suaded to go to Germany. Among the musicians lured there were 1970s rock icons like Deep Purple's lead guitarist Richie Blackmore, Paul Raven (aka Gary Glitter) and Black Sabbath's singer Ozzy Osbourne. They dis-covered that, compared to Hamburg, British cities like Glasgow were still desperately dull with archaic licens-ing restrictions and conservative promoters. Finding a chip shop open after dark in Glasgow was difficult enough – so finding a hip and happening night club was near impossible. The newly opened La Cave club, off Jamaica Street, and the Maryland Club, which spe-cialised in jazz and R&B were still the exception. In the UK, rock music was still seen as intrinsically worthless and only good as a stepping-stone to a career in light entertainment.

In Germany, the musicians were paid more respect. Also there was no soul-destroying touring to contend with – there was plenty of work in the Hamburg clubs to keep them happy. And the amps and instruments were set up and ready to go. They could also earn a steady wage of £20–30 a week plus an abundance of women, cheap strong beer and amphetamines like Preludin to fight off the tiredness. There were also good times to be had when the group was off duty, gathering in places like 'Mutti's' to drink the bar dry. It certainly beat playing at a miners' welfare club on a dreich February night. Drummer George McGowan – who had left the Soul Band in 1961 – rejoined in 1963 for a stint in Germany:

Hamburg was pretty wild really. We played shifts, we would do a morning show and then try and sleep, then we would do an afternoon slot and then finally we would do a night shift. The club would only shut for one hour in 24 so they could clean the place, then the whole thing started again. And of course the Preludin was on the go.

(Interestingly, George McGowan is still very active on the Glasgow music scene and plays regular jazz gigs in the city's pubs and clubs along with Bobby Wishart – another graduate from the Soul Band. (Wishart went on to lecture in music at Strathclyde University and to lead the Scottish Youth Jazz Orchestra.)

Prior to making the move to Germany, Alex Harvey had hitchhiked to London to audition at the famous 2 i's coffee bar in Soho's Old Compton Street. His ambition at the time was to win a spot on British pop pioneer Jack Good's TV series *Oh Boy*. Instead, he was soon signing up to join other Scots like Ricky Barnes and Bobby Patrick to play in the clubs of the Reeperbahn. Barnes had already won the plum role of resident sax player at the Top Ten Club. In 1962, the Soul Band began a stint at the Star Club in Hamburg. The decision to move to Germany before the band had even played as a unit in London was a gamble. London was the undoubted capital of the European music scene even back then. It looked even more risky when they were given the bullet after two weeks when one of the band – bassist Jimmy Grimes – allegedly did an impromptu strip on stage. But no matter, within hours they had signed up to play at the rival Top Ten Club.

Alex's reputation went before him. Alan Clayson recalls how he was a 'feared man' but was also respected for his leadership qualities and knowledge of music – which stretched to owning rare early Tamla Motown discs and Chicago blues records that were difficult to find at the time, even in the USA.

Writing in the history of Scots pop, *All That Ever Mattered*, Ricky Barnes recounts:

He (Alex) was way ahead of the competition both as an experienced player and his feel for the blues. None of the Liverpool groups had it – and I mean none of them – they were more like showbands. Alex built an atmosphere. It was a driving, swinging thing and you could see the excitement on the faces of the crowd.[2]

Alex himself enjoyed the new 'beat boom' He thought that establishing the 'beat' background gave him the opportunity to sing just about anything – he could even swear and sing obscene songs! Still, he sometimes felt a bit confused by the beat explosion. He later said:

It puzzled us, we found difficulty understanding when people called us a beat group. But looking back, I can see exactly what they meant. It was a recognised thing, wasn't it? Two guitars, bass and drums. Before that it was either solo singers being backed by someone or a band. The Beatles were a phenomenon, though.

The beat boom was great for us because we spent a lot of time in Hamburg in '63, '64, '65 – the first album was cut there, that was amazing for us straight out of Glasgow. We hadn't even been to London and there we were in Hamburg. It was 24 hours a day, and inside the first month I heard Ray Charles, Bo Diddley, Fats Domino, The Ink Spots, Jerry Lee Lewis and Little Richard.

A lot of the groups that went there couldn't stand it, the singers used to get what we called 'Hamburg Throat' through such long hours. And a kind of thing developed where the drummers cut right down on everything that was superfluous, because that beat had to be there and the two or three singers primarily would come in because one singer on his own could not handle it. I found that if you could supply that beat you could virtually get away with anything.[3]

Hamburg, according to Alex, had given birth to the beat movement in much the same way as Chicago had spawned the blues and New Orleans gave rise to jazz.

The Hamburg nights also allowed for a bit of experimentation instead of the run-of-the-mill top ten songs and Alex – not for the last time in his career – started to introduce some more eclectic numbers, including The Isley Brothers 'Shout'. Alex had first heard the record playing on a jukebox in a Wick café that was owned by his future manager Bill Fehilly. The song soon became the signature tune for the Soul Band.

Despite enjoying the round-the-clock Hamburg craziness the band also worked hard enough on stage to win their first recording contract. Polydor Records were desperate to cash in on the popularity of The Beatles and one of the company's A&R men, Liverpudlian Paul Murphy was first to spot the Soul Band. He received a 3 a.m. phone call from the manager of the Top Ten Club on October 13 1963, imploring him to get out of bed and come to listen to 'the most fantastic sound since sliced bread'. Murphy later wrote on the Soul Band's debut album sleeve notes that 'all hell broke loose' when the group took to the stage and after only eight minutes of listening to the Scottish group he had decided to sign them up.

So, in October 1963, Alex entered Polydor's Hamburg studios at the rear of the Top Ten Club to record the album *Alex Harvey and his Soul Band*. Paradoxically, the record company insisted that some of the Soul Band step aside from the sessions. Instead, members of another Liverpool group King Size Taylor and the Dominoes backed Alex. The album took only 12 hours to tape from plug-in to final mix. For whatever reason, the record lay around for five months until in March 1964 it was released in the UK, just a month after the Big Soul Band had made their long overdue London debut at the 100 Club on Oxford Street.

Music historians have since dubbed this disc as Scotland's first rock 'n' roll album, though if truth be told the Scottish influence is negligible. Alex adopts a very dodgy fake American accent on most of the tracks. The pressure was obviously on him to try and persuade – even dupe – the listener into believing they were hearing the real American product. Later on in his career Alex seemed to rebel against this and would sing proudly in broad Scots tones. But back in 1963, it was difficult to be so daring.

The accent is most notable on the version of Leiber and Stoller's 'Framed' which opens the 13-track album. Slower and slinkier than later versions by the SAHB, it still manages to get things rolling effectively. From then on in it's a frenetic if somewhat rudimentary run through some rock 'n' roll standards with the slow acoustic blues number 'The Blind Man' tagged on to close the set. Considering they hardly knew Alex, the back-up band does a good job in getting the toes tapping. The saxophone player in particular drives the whole album, even leading them into experimental territory on 'Bo Diddley is a Gunslinger'.

But overall, the record itself is a curious affair, dragged down by the bizarre canned applause added on to achieve a 'live' effect. Apparently the Top Ten Club didn't have a licence to record concerts. Still, the inclusion of 'Framed' was an appetiser of greater things to come and the record still has a weighty reputation among critics. In 2003 *The*

Scotsman placed it at number 61 in a poll of the top 100 Scottish rock albums of all time. Nowadays a copy of the original album in good condition can fetch over £100 at record fairs. But back in 1963 the album flopped, as did the two singles lifted from it – the high-energy version of Willie Dixon's 'I Just Wanna Make Love To You' and a jaunty cover of Muddy Waters' 'Got My Mojo Working'. Alex was discovering that working in Hamburg had some drawbacks – by late 1963 the 'scene' had moved away from the German city back to places like Liverpool and London.

According to the writer Brian Hogg, Alex and the Soul Band also cut a number of one-off singles in the Top Ten studio – including covers of Elvis's 'Jailhouse Rock'. For some unknown reason, they were recorded under bizarre pseudonyms such as Bruce Wellington and his Rubber Band! Sadly only one of each disc was cut and although they ended up on the club's jukebox they have long since been lost to the general public.

The manager of The Soul Band at the time was a New Zealander called David Firmstone. According to Alex's second wife Trudy Harvey, the manager was quite unlike the band members:

David spoke with a very posh accent, he was a lovely guy, but to be honest he was fairly ineffectual as a manager. He loved the guys in the band and the music they played. He absolutely adored Alex – I think Alex was everything that David wanted to be but could never be. Really, David was too much of a nice guy to be a manager. He also had a job as a night manager at the London Elizabeth Hotel in Paddington. He had a room there which had faulty heating and gave off fumes – and one night he just died in his sleep.[4]

Just as rare as the *Soul Band* record – and equally valuable – is *The Blues* album, which was recorded in June 1964 in Hamburg, and featured Alex's 16-year-old brother Les on acoustic guitar, providing the sole back-up. At the time, Les was playing with The Kinning Park Ramblers which were managed by his dad. The album was released a year later to a decidedly lukewarm response. With sparse, lacklustre covers of songs like 'Waltzing Matilda' and 'Strange Fruit' it sounded completely at odds with the music scene that was emerging throughout Europe.

Again, the album was the brainchild of Paul Murphy of Polydor who believed that Alex had a natural talent when it came to belting out his interpretation of blues standards. Murphy felt that Alex had never been given the chance to show this talent to the world. The idea to cut such an album dated back to February 1964 when Alex made his London debut at the 100 Club on Oxford Street. The gig took place on the day before his first single, a version of Muddy Waters' 'I Just Wanna Make Love To You' – also covered by The Rolling Stones – was released. But the plans for the recording had to be postponed because of Alex's busy schedule. In the summer, a chance cancellation of some gigs allowed Alex two days off, and on 8 June, manager David Firmstone flew with the Harvey brothers from London to Hamburg to do the album.

At the Polydor studios, after a quick photo session the Harvey brothers started recording at midnight. The PR puff to go with the album said that hearing the music blew away everyone in the studio – one unfortunate studio lackey apparently was overcome with emotion by the version of 'TB Blues' and fainted on the spot! The first day's session ended at 2.30 a.m. and after a long sleep the whole group gathered again to complete the project later that day – in the presence of Polydor's head honcho Horst Schmolzi. The record company boss had initially been reticent to back a project which featured just two guitarists, but was apparently soon won over by what he heard – calling Alex an incredible talent. In the early hours of 10 June the album was complete, with 15 songs in the can after only nine hours of recording! Two of the songs, including 'Good God Almighty' were apparently written by Harvey on the spot.

When *The Blues* was released in November 1965, it carried sleeve notes that lied about how old Alex was. Nervous Polydor bosses claimed he was actually four years younger than his actual age. It also came with a warning that it was definitely not for the unimaginative listener. Forty-three years on, that advice still rings true. The jury's still out on whether a white man from the Gorbals really can sing the blues. It certainly is an uncompromising album – songs about tuberculosis and the St James Infirmary were never going to make for easy listening.

But the real problem is Alex's vocals, which really dominate the album. Even his most loyal of fans would have to admit that his voice was not the strongest and here it undoubtedly proves to be the weakest link. He just tries too hard and finishes almost every song wailing like a drunken banshee. Still, Alex knew all about poverty and he could certainly handle songs like Jimmie Cox's 'Nobody Knows You When You're Down And Out' – later recorded by Derek and the Dominoes – with feeling. Maybe it's best to file the album under the category of worthy but misguided efforts. Perhaps he just needed to get it out of his system, and tellingly his later more successful work was never to be so authentically bluesy.

With both Alex's first two albums being collectors' items, it's been difficult for Harvey fans to gauge what their hero sounded like back in the early 1960s. A couple of years ago the Bear Family Label managed to rectify matters by releasing the previously unheard third album from that period. It was cut at Landsdowne Road studios in London during August 1964 but was never commercially released at the time.

Listening to the album more than 40 years on is a strange experience. Sure, it reflects Alex's wide-ranging tastes but you can only guess what the pilled-up Hamburg youths made of oddities like 'The Liverpool Scene' – a bizarre tale of musicians travelling to Merseyside in a hearse. It opens with the dreadful line 'We came fae Scotland, we musta been full, we heard about the scene down in Liverpool' and doesn't get much better. Other weird tracks are a calypso version of 'The Canoe Song' and the tearjerker 'The Little Boy That Santa Claus Forgot'.

Most of the rest is made up of songs that are definitely best heard in a boozy sweaty night club. Songs that must have been magic live seem to lose their impact on CD. Still, Alex shows his potential as a hit writer with songs like 'What's Wrong With Me Baby?' and there's no doubting the band's energy on the driving R&B of covers of Chuck Berry's 'Reelin' and Rockin'' and 'Shout' by The Isley Brothers.

'Shout' opened the Soul Band's set and was a major favourite for the audiences. On one trip back home to Glasgow, an unknown singer called Lulu was amongst the audience of a Soul Band gig. In a recent radio interview she told how she had broken a 10.30 p.m. curfew to stay out and watch the band:

I begged my mum to let me go and see him, Alex Harvey was dressed in tight black leather and looked totally emaciated. It was exciting – like the whole of Glasgow was aware of his talent and there was a tremendous atmosphere. He had been away in Germany for so long.

In 1964, Lulu herself recorded 'Shout' with her backing band The Luvvers, and the song became a worldwide hit for her.

The Soul Band did hundreds of gigs during this era, though sadly most of them are by now long forgotten. Their rock 'n' roll mission did however definitely take them to the Scottish Borders on Friday, 25 September 1964 to play at Peebles Drill Hall. They topped the bill at the 'Great Festival of Rhythm and Blues' and the few hundred devotees that turned up got in for five shillings before 9.30 p.m. and for six bob thereafter. Also on the bill that night were The Diamonds, a Hawick-based combo who were at the forefront of a mini-R&B boom in the region and who shared the stage with Alex on a number of occasions. They had a much admired 18-year-old lead guitarist called Bob Fish who was a remarkable talent when he strapped on his Stratocaster and belted out the blues and Chuck Berry standards.

Back in the early 1960s, The Diamonds supported future superstars like The Bee Gees, Little Eva, The Who and The Animals when they did gigs north of the Border. They also hung out with Robert Plant and John Bonham in their pre-Led Zeppelin outfit Band of Joy. It's a little known bit of rock trivia that the future Zeppelin men stayed in Galashiels for over a month and used it as a base for touring around the Scottish borders. In fact Bonham, who was down on his luck at the time, actually accepted an offer to join The Diamonds before having to return home to Birmingham due to a family illness.

The Diamonds' lead singer Loudon Temple, who went on to become one of Scotland's best known journalists, recalls with a shudder and a smile one of the nights they backed up the hard-drinking Soul Band:

The posters were for this guy called Alec Harvie [sic] and said that the Soul Band were just back from 'their great tour in Germany and the Home Counties'. We were second on the bill and when the local lads from Selkirk, called The Avengers, were on stage, Alex and the other Soul Band guys produced some duty-free booze that they'd brought back from the Continent.

As far as I can recall, liberal measures of Scotch and vodka were being poured into teacups and passed around to be swallowed neat. We had a shit-hot harmonica player in the band called Wattie Robson. Now, Wattie and I were both just 16 and shouldn't have been anywhere near a pint of shandy, never mind neat spirits. The last thing I recall is seeing Wattie cartwheeling across the floor of the dressing room, making *wheeee* sounds as he went. He collided with the table where the teacups were standing, sending sugar scattering everywhere.

Then, he collapsed in a heap and no matter how much we tried, we couldn't revive him. We went on to play a stormer of a set despite his absence and the fact that we had to drop the instrumental, 'Country Line Special' which was the hot last number and his chance to show off big time. Alex and the other lads in the Soul Band stood in the wings and took in the whole set, whooping and applauding and shouting words of encouragement to us, even though they told us we'd be a hard act to follow.

Our bass player, Sid Cairns, wrote a few lines in the band's scrapbook after that night. Referring to Alex Harvey and his Big Soul Band, he noted: 'Fab R&B. Great lads. Lots of encouragement.'

That just about sums it up. The Soul Band were really fantastic – more earthy and real than all the other big name acts we supported. Alex was quieter than the rest, he just sat in the corner chuckling when all the drunken mayhem was going on. He wasn't a particularly good guitarist or singer but he had incredible charisma and real star quality.[5]

The Diamonds' guitarist Bob Fish actually recalls Harvey playing with The Kinning Park Ramblers in Hawick in the late 1950s. Bob is still wowing audiences today with his rockabilly trio Johnny and the Roccos – their last CD was recorded live at Munich's Rattlesnake Saloon in the year 2001. He remembers that Alex was a dominating presence on and off the stage even back in the days of The Soul Band:

Alex had a very risqué, raunchy act and the group were totally unique in the songs that they played and the way they delivered them. Alex was quite a sinister guy up on stage – a very imposing personality. He came across very mean and menacing – a small, scrawny dark guy like Richard the Third. He used to play this cheap old Burns Trisonic guitar which was like a cricket bat and he got an amazing sound from it. But we all thought he should have had a foxy Gibson as he was a very good blues guitar player.

Off stage he was a nice guy, and very approachable – until anything went wrong. Any fights or bother in the audience, and Alex was straight in there to sort it out. Maybe that's why he used to play such a cheap guitar – to whack punters who were causing trouble! Les played bass for them and he took a great interest in a new Gretsch guitar I had. He tried it out and, man, he was a phenomenal player. He could knock spots off Alex when it came to guitar playing.

Anyway, Alex came backstage and saw Les playing the Gretsch and he just yelled at him, 'You – put that down! You're just a bass player.' I don't think he was too happy about being shown up by his kid brother![6]

After making their long overdue move to London, the Soul Band were beginning to make a name for themselves in the south of England. One regular gig was at Eel Pie Island every Wednesday where audiences of over 1,000 were not uncommon. A contract for a show at the Marquee on 14 January 1965 reveals that the Soul Band and Alex only got a quarter of the total salary of £26 6s 10d. So for all their hard work, money was in short supply and the band often went hungry and lived in cramped accommodation. By 1965, Alex was fast becoming disillusioned with both Hamburg and London, and with the music scene in general. The Soul Band – with Jimmy Grimes and Les Harvey to the fore – continued to gig in

London and the south-east of England, once touring with Sonny Boy Williamson. But compared to young upstart bands like the Yardbirds, Bluesbreakers and The Rolling Stones, the Soul Band were stuck in first gear.

5

THE GIANT MOTH EXPERIMENT

'Someone says to me, what's all this angry
stuff, man? ... But, OK, we're gonna be
anarchists, communists or whatever ... But
somebody has still got to wash the dishes!'[1]
Alex Harvey

By 1965 the Soul Band was dying on its feet. After almost a
decade in the business, Alex Harvey and the Top 20 were
as far apart as ever. He was sick of being ripped-off and
frustrated by the lack of success. In a later interview he
lamented the mistakes he had made in the years prior
to making his big breakthrough. Like many young musicians he had erred by trusting in people who did not have
his best interests at heart and by signing up to contracts
that he should have given the widest of berths to:

I got myself tied up with the wrong people and the wrong companies. One company put a record out of mine that sold 1,200
copies in ten days, which was phenomenal in those days, but
they did not make any more. I did TV, radio, theatre and club
work, gigs and one-night stands, tours and trips abroad, the
lot.

At one time I was paying ten per cent of all my earnings to an agent, ten per cent to a manager, £20 a week to a road manager, HP on equipment, and on top of that having to fork out for the bands' wages, petrol, insurance and all sorts of other expenses. I used to cart around a suitcase stuffed with £4,000 worth of pieces of paper signed by promoters who had beat it when it came time to pay up.

There was even a time when I found out I was apparently appearing in four places hundreds of miles apart on one evening. When the band was booked into some village hall on the strength of a good record and some good broadcasts, who in the village would know what we looked like? Would the real Alex Harvey please play up.[2]

While it's undoubtedly true that Alex was on the wrong end of a few dodgy deals, it shouldn't be forgotten that he was no innocent himself. If people were impersonating him to make a few quid then he was more than willing to do the same himself. He never tired of telling how in the very early days, the Soul Band did a tour of the remote Outer Hebrides pretending to be Johnny and the Hurricanes, a band who were high in the charts at the time with a song called 'Red River Rock'. Apparently the Soul Band were told to use fake American accents or better still, just to keep their mouths shut. All in all it was an eventful tour which reached a climax when the sax player took a tumble into Stornoway harbour on the Isle of Lewis.

*

With the Hamburg scene fading, Alex and the band headed back to London for a series of gigs in and around the capital. In July 1965, Alex tried his luck with another single 'Ain't That Just Too Bad' – his final effort on Polydor, but it also flopped.

Undeterred, in September, he switched to the Fontana label and released a barnstorming cover version of 'Agent

00 Soul', with a standard tale of a no-good hard-drinking woman, 'Go Away Baby' on the B-side. 'Agent 00 Soul' had been a debut Top 30 US hit for Edwin Starr on the Detroit Ric-Tic record label. Backed by a brass section and female vocalists, Alex does a more than passable imitation of the Secret Service man who had no need for Continental suits or high-collared shirts (the single was later released on the 1968 compilation album called *British Blue-eyed Soul*). The Harvey take on the song featured a young Steve Winwood on piano and was produced by the Old Harrovian Chris Blackwell who would later form Island Records. Yet despite their best efforts and a promotional push which featured Alex posing as James Bond by an Aston Martin, the record bombed. The following year, another single 'Work Song' also failed in the charts. A deeply disillusioned Alex headed home to his 'ain folk' in Glasgow.

In 1966 he played in the house band on the revolving stage at the Dennistoun Palais in Glasgow. This time round, his fellow band members included his brother Les and saxophonist Bill Patrick, both of whom had moved onto playing in the Blues Council – a much admired group which disbanded after two of the band died in a car accident while returning from a gig in Edinburgh.

The Dennistoun Palais band also featured Dougie Paul on bass, Miff Paterson on drums and two other vocalists beside Alex – George Gallacher and Isabel Bond. Gallacher was already a name to reckon with on the Scottish music scene. In 1961, aged just 19, he had formed The Poets, a band that shone brightly during the early part of the 1960s before fading. The Poets only released a half-dozen singles but they stood out from the competition due to the quality of their songs and the fact that they wrote their own material. Their talents were soon being noticed far beyond Glasgow and when Rolling Stones' manager Andrew Loog Oldham came across the band in 1964 he rapidly signed them up to Decca Records.

Sadly, The Poets only managed one hit single, the moody 'Now We're Thru' which skirted the edge of the national charts. A move to the Immediate label late in 1965 also didn't work out as Oldham – perhaps understandably – preferred to concentrate on The Stones, whose career was by now taking off in spectacular fashion. The Poets soon fell apart and by 1966, vocalist George Gallacher's career was in limbo. The offer to team up with Alex Harvey – who was also at a career crossroads – was one Gallacher was eager to accept. He recalls how he barely knew of Alex aside from the obscure Tommy Steele link:

It's a mystery to me how the gig came about – but somehow Alex got in contact with me and invited me in – I think he maybe saw me as the pop element in the band. Alex was brilliant to work with and he allowed me and the others in the band complete and equal say in things. Isabel Bond was a girl from Pollok – which was and still is one of the toughest housing schemes in Glasgow. She had an amazing voice that could knock down walls! She was a friend of Maggie Bell's and Isabel had also played with Alex in Hamburg. She was a real tough girl and could handle herself against the hardest men – but she was also one of the nicest people I ever met. Later, I took her down to London where she cut a single for Major Minor records. I believe she now lives in Canada.[3]

Though Alex on rare occasions played acoustic guitar and George played the harmonica, the Dennistoun Palais group – which was known simply as The Alex Harvey Band – was still somewhat unique in that it had three lead vocalists. Depending on the song, each of the three singers took it in turn to sing lead. They only played on

Fridays and Saturdays, and George Gallacher recalls that each night attracted a different type of audience:

On Fridays the audience was mainly over-25s – so we could indulge in the old standards. But Saturday was a younger, more hostile crowd who were looking for the latest chart sounds. This caused some problems if Alex was in an uncompromising mood on the night. There would be a couple of hundred people in the hall each night and occasionally the gang violence thing would happen. But we came from the same background so we managed fairly well.

Alex had an unfortunate habit of informing us of what chart numbers we would play on Saturdays only an hour before the gig, so we all gathered round this little Dansette record player trying to master the latest sounds. Sometimes we had to master maybe three or four songs with only minutes to go before we got up on stage. Most songs we could generally make some reasonable attempt at but some were disastrous! One song in particular that caused us problems was The Beatles' 'Paperback Writer', which started with multiple harmonies without any instrumental introduction. Every one of us started in a different key and the result was bedlam!

We tried about half a dozen times to get it right but the boos from the crowd made it even more difficult to pitch the harmonies and we gave up. They booed every number that night and were actually encouraged by Alex, who thought that the whole thing was hilarious.

The core of our material was soul and R&B standards and we didn't do any original material. I cannot remember what we were paid but it was a paltry amount and it was shared out equally. Alex never tried to play the part of leader in the band.[4]

The Palais gigs were enjoyable but by now Alex wanted to make a clean break from the showband covers scene. In any case the four-month stint at Dennistoun had to come to an end because the arena was due to be converted into a roller-skating rink.

Soon he was back in London again – drawn by the exciting developments in music, fashion and art which were to make the English capital the focal point for all things creative. The Harvey family had already tried once before to move to London. In 1963, when young Alex junior was just four years old, they attempted to migrate south of the Border. But Mary Harvey was unhappy about making the massive step of leaving her native Glasgow and the plan was abandoned. In truth, the constant touring and inevitable separation was putting pressure on the marriage, and she and Alex gradually drifted apart, eventually divorcing near the end of the decade.

George Gallacher remembers that when he and Alex eventually made the switch to London, things were far from easy for either of them:

Alex and I both went down to London in 1967 independently of each other, but we met regularly in a café in Denmark Street. I was doing session work for United Artists with Elkie Brooks and others. Alex and I were both starving and I remember him never being off the phone in the café calling what I thought was a phantom agent. I kept thinking, you poor fucker, Alex, nobody wants that fantastic talent nowadays, for goodness sake give it up and take a job on the buses![5]

Alex later admitted that those were his darkest days in the music business. No one in the industry seemed willing to take a risk on him. At the time he was living in a basic bedsitter in South Kensington and didn't have much contact with his family back home in Scotland.

London was a magnet for musicians from all over the country, including a group from Kilmarnock in Ayrshire called The Anteeks who had decamped down south in an ultimately vain attempt to catch some of the falling stardust of the Swinging Sixties. Their drummer George Butler chanced upon Harvey one afternoon outside the Giaconda Café in Denmark Street late in 1965:

I was looking for some work and someone said, 'Oh, look, there's Alex Harvey.' Even then he was well-known, for a young man like myself he was frightening, a legend. He was a million light years from where I was musically and he had this reputation of being a fearsome character.

I went up to him and said, 'Hello, d'you know anyone who is looking for a drummer?' He said, 'No, but give me your number.' I was only about 18 and I was pretty scared. He was a ferocious-looking character and he also looked really miserable. He had no money, he was absolutely down on his luck.

I really didn't think anything was going to happen. About three weeks later though I walked into the Ship pub in Wardour Street, which was the place where everybody involved in music hung out. Alex was the first person I saw and he says, 'Where the fuck have you been? I've been looking for you – I know someone looking for a drummer.' I asked him who it was, and then he just growled, 'Me!'[6]

The pair eventually teamed up with another ex-Anteek, Jim Condron on bass and a mysterious chap called Mox who played anything that extracted wind and who, with his long red hair and beard, resembled Jethro Tull's Ian Anderson. They picked the unfortunate name Giant Moth in a forlorn attempt to sound both psychedelic and ecologically aware. Sessions in a Soho studio produced a weird mix of driving R&B and Incredible String Band-style mysticism. They also had a stab at the bizarre 'There's No Lights On The Christmas Tree Mother, They're Burning Big Louie Tonight' which was to eventually appear on the first SAHB album. A deal with Decca Records was secured and two singles, 'Sunday Song' followed by a version of the Incredible String Band's excellent 'Maybe Someday', were released but failed to impact on the charts. The Giant Moth was resolutely refusing to take off.

On 22 July 1967, *Melody Maker* reviewed 'Sunday Song'. Back then a guest reviewer was played the singles and then invited to guess who the artist was before giving their opinion on the song's merits. That week Pink Floyd's Syd Barrett did the honours and his review of Alex's single is well worth documenting here.

Nice sounds – yeah. Wow. Lot of drumming but it avoids being cuttered [sic]. The people in the background seem to be raving a bit more than the people in the front. English? One of the young groups like John's Children? It moved me a little bit. But I don't think it will be a hit. Very snappy.

A couple of weeks later, the same newspaper carried a front page story that Barrett was suffering from nervous exhaustion and added that Pink Floyd were having to cancel a series of lucrative gigs.

The choice of 'Maybe Someday' as a single was an interesting one and an early sign that Harvey would never be shy of delving into his own eclectic record collection when it came to doing cover versions. The original was penned by Mike Heron and had been the opening track on the String Band's remarkable 1966 debut album. Harvey replaced the violin on the original with some Ian Anderson-style flute courtesy of Mox and after a slow intro the song thunders along with some thumping drumbeats. Backed with a Kinks-inspired B-side, a song called 'Curtains For My Baby', the single really should have been a big hit but it sold poorly.

'I suppose we split because we were crap!' laughs Butler with disarming honesty. But the band did stick it out for two years and along the way played numerous gigs including a stint supporting John Lee Hooker. Alex initially intimidated George Butler, who remembers listening to Harvey records on a local jukebox while he was growing up. But the two soon became close mates and remained friends for the next 15 years. Butler recalls:

He almost turned into my uncle. He was an extraordinary man to know and to work with, though he could be very, very stubborn. I remember sometimes when he was in a really bad mood he would run a knife across some of the demos we had made. Alex had a very varied musical taste – he liked to do sleazy blues but also liked a cabaret slant to the show, so you never quite knew where he was coming from.[7]

Living in South Kensington and with one marriage on the rocks and his new love Trudy expecting a child, Alex had to make some tough decisions about the future. He spent lots of his time in London hanging out with hippies, but the working-class man from Glasgow didn't really fit into that middle-class scene. He later told a reporter that 'no bugger would wash the dishes ... I eventually turfed them all out and I got mad, y'know?'[8]

Even if his own career wasn't working out, Alex was at least hanging around with the right people. They were a disparate group of hippies and wannabe musicians including singer-songwriter Lesley Duncan who had started out as a backing singer for Dusty Springfield and later achieved some fame of her own when Elton John covered her 'Love Song' on his *Tumbleweed Connection* album. Vince Taylor, a leather-clad performer known as 'The Black Leather Rebel' who would arrive on stage on a motorbike swinging chains around his head also hung around the Swinging London scene with Alex. Vince recorded a number of classic rock songs including the magnificent 'Brand New Cadillac' covered many years later by The Clash. Another of Harvey's circle of friends was a rocker called Jackie Lynton, an offbeat performer who sang covers of 'The Teddy Bear's Picnic' and 'We'll Gather Lilacs'. He later went on to front the band Savoy Brown.

The focus of much of this activity was a large, palatial apartment on Reddington Road in Hampstead. Trudy

Harvey recalls that when she lived there, David Bowie and Elaine Paige were among the regular visitors:

It wasn't really a commune, but a lot of people did come and go from that flat. It was 1967, a really magical time of hippies and flower power. It was an era of mad parties when everyone took pills and smoked a lot of dope. Very bizarre things tended to happen – I remember going to Hampstead Heath one day because a woman called Yoko Ono – who no one really knew of at that time – was going to show people 'how to catch an imaginary butterfly!' You could do things like that back then, it really was a very strange era. We used to have a meeting in this house every week called 'Contact', where around 30 people would gather from all around – if they wanted to send out good vibes into the universe in case there were people out there – to encourage them to come down to earth!

Alex was very much part of this scene, though he always used to say he felt slightly outside of all that. He used to complain that no one ever invited him into these groups!

6

HAIR

'Distinctly shagadelic music'
Hair Rave-up CD sleeve notes

The need to put food on the table led Alex to seek work in London restaurants and clubs like The Pontiac singing standards like 'I Left My Heart In San Francisco' and 'Begin the Beguine'. Times were so tough that he actually considered quitting the business. Fortuitously, he met ex-Animal Chas Chandler around that time who persuaded Alex to check out his new prodigy, Jimi Hendrix. Harvey told friends that he left the concert feeling reinvigorated and more determined than ever to make a success out of his music career.

One of Alex's lengthier gigs was at the 800 Club in Leicester Square, a high-class night club once frequented by Princess Margaret, where he played in a small band led by tenor sax player Manni Ferri. The Scots-Italian needed a singer-guitarist to round off his group and Harvey fitted the bill – eventually playing six nights a week for almost a year at the club and earning around £30 a week in the process. It was tough work, with the group working from 9 p.m. until the club shut at 3.30 a.m. Ferri was in an indirect way to play a key role in the Harvey story when he persuaded him to try his hand at a song that would eventually become his biggest chart hit:

Alex was recommended to me and I knew that in many ways he was more or less on his arse at the time – he was doing nothing and he needed the regular work. He was keen on doing stuff like Wilson Pickett and his rock 'n' roll stuff. But it wasn't really the type of club for that music – we needed to cover a wider spectrum of music. Middle-aged men came into that club and they liked to hear the oldies. At the time I wanted to do a cover of the Tom Jones hit 'Delilah'. I said to Alex that it would be good for him, but initially he was very reticent to do so. I don't know why, maybe he thought it was a bit naff, but to please me he eventually agreed. Alex was a very capable player and was a quick learner. He could be quite a volatile character but when he was with me he was always a model professional. He went down very well with the audiences – the hostesses loved him.[1]

The round of cabaret gigs soon brought Alex into contact with Derek Wadsworth who was to become musical director for the London stage production of the Gerome Ragni and James Rado musical *Hair*.

Wadsworth had been a musician since the age of 11 when he first started playing in brass bands in the north of England. By the mid 1960s he had a growing reputation as a man who could arrange rock 'n' roll for artists like Dusty Springfield, Georgie Fame, The Small Faces and The Rolling Stones. Derek also played for a while with trumpeter Derek Andrews and drummer Peter Woolf in a band called The Echoes who backed Dusty Springfield. All three musicians would later join the *Hair* band.

Like Alex, Derek was drawn to the easy cash to be made playing in Soho nightclubs where rich businessmen took their floozies for discreet, if expensive, cocktails.

Wadsworth was instantly impressed by Alex's musical abilities. The pair soon discovered that they shared a fondness for Chicago jazz and strong beer. The Englishman recalled:

I was playing in these pick-up bands and you seldom knew the guys you were playing alongside. We used to play stuff like 'Girl from Ipanema' and 'Lady is a Tramp'. I was introduced to Alex and immediately noticed that he was very knowledgeable about music. I liked him a lot, he was very forthright and enthusiastic about everything.

One night he got up and sang Bob Dylan's 'Like a Rolling Stone' – which is quite a long and complicated number to do – and I just thought, shit this guy is good. He wasn't a great guitarist though, he played it like you would play a banjo, strumming it. But he always sang from the heart, he was a very pure and direct artist.

We discovered that we were both born on 5 February and eventually Alex became like a soulmate for me. We got on really well and kept in contact.[2]

In 1967, the Canadian composer Galt MacDermot was looking to put together a band for the London production of *Hair* and after a recommendation from Mickey Waller, who was then the drummer with the Jeff Beck Group, MacDermot contacted Wadsworth. Derek was eventually persuaded to take the gig and when it came to picking the band, he immediately thought of his old pal from the club circuit:

I knew Alex was struggling at the time. To be honest he wasn't good enough to do studio work on a regular basis. He hadn't been discovered and there weren't many outlets for what he wanted to do – he was geared to be a recording artist in his own right. He had had quite a few disappointments and had reached a point where he was asking himself why he should play in sordid pubs for the rest of his life, especially when he had that talent to do much better.[3]

The prospect of a steady income of around £50 a week in a band consisting of two trumpets, two guitars, saxophone, percussion, bass and keyboard was too much to resist, and Alex joined the band. In an indirect way, he had finally made it to the big-time. The controversial play was the talk of London with its nudity and detailed dissection of themes like drugs, war, peace and sexuality. For many, the explicit nature of the material was just too much to handle. The Lord Chamberlain – who at that time had the power to censor stage shows – for one was less than impressed. He blocked the show's opening until finally it got the go-ahead after a Bill was passed scrapping his licensing powers.

Alex – as singer Marianne Price recalls – fitted in straight away as he strummed chords for Galt McDermot songs like 'Good Morning Starshine' and 'Aquarius':

The *Hair* Band (as they were known), used to be on an old truck on the side of the stage. It was decorated with psychedelic paint and at the front by the bonnet was a small armless wooden chair. This was riveted to the side of the bonnet and was known as 'Alex's chair'. No one else would sit on this chair except Alex and if he was off the chair then it would be left empty. The show had a storyline but also an informality (which was groundbreaking for its time). And this meant that when not involved in scenes, cast members could sit where they pleased and do – within reason – whatever they wanted. We were known as The Tribe and in the show we lived on the streets so the stage was our home.

It was the kind of show that people could see many times as, although there was the storyline with ad libs, the spontaneous party finale at the end meant that people didn't get bored. When I was not in a scene, I used to sit just by Alex's feet and chat to him. We would talk, eat or drink or look at a paper or whatever. I remember him sitting in his chair quite quietly, except when he got annoyed with someone or something. It was obviously a very different side to the extrovert solo performer he was to become. He came across as a very deep person indeed.

His eyes had the look even then of someone who had seen too much of life and this was before his own career took off. He was definitely his own man and not one to suffer fools gladly. There most definitely was an aura about Alex that made people respect him.[4]

Looking back now, Derek Wadsworth reflects:

In a way, *Hair* was a bad career move for Alex, it wasn't taking him where he wanted to go and it put his own solo career on the back burner for a while. But he was still writing his own songs though. Also, because *Hair* was such a radical show where the band were encouraged to take part or run about on stage, that helped Alex. At the end of each performance, the band was allowed to play their own songs and they also did gigs together away from the show.[5]

Intriguingly, one of Alex's deputies – who would fill in for him playing guitar on nights when he wanted a break – was a very young Mike Oldfield. Derek Wadsworth recalls that Harvey and Oldfield actually rehearsed together away from the show and were eager to secure a record deal for their new 'band'.

Laurie Scott Baker, original *Hair* bass player, confirms that for a few months in 1970, Harvey and Oldfield played in a gigging band: 'It was Alex's band and Mike was pretty incidental to it, he was just the guitar player. But Alex recognised that Oldfield "had something". He went round telling everybody, 'You really must see this guy.'

No deal materialised for the band, and both men went on to great success in their own right – Oldfield eventually signing for Virgin Records and releasing the multi-million seller *Tubular Bells* and a string of other best-selling albums in the 1970s. A rumour persists that it was Harvey who encouraged Oldfield to pester record companies with his original demos.

Besides being an international phenomenon, *Hair* was a springboard for musicians and actors around the world. Besides Harvey and Oldfield, the London production featured future stars like the Nigerian-born Patti Boulaye who went on to be a stalwart supporter of the Conservative Party. Also involved were the actor Oliver Tobias, singer Marsha Hunt and Sonja Kristina who later fronted 1970s rock band Curved Air.

Another future star who played a lead role was Gary Holton who would go on to front The Heavy Metal Kids, before gaining more success as an actor in the TV drama series *Auf Weidersehen Pet*. Holton and Harvey were kindred spirits and spent many hours together drinking and discussing music and theatre. Away from the UK, Meat Loaf made his name with the American cast and future disco queen Donna Summer starred in the German version. The Dutch show featured the talents of Jan Akkermann and Thijs Van Leer, the engine room of Focus, the much respected prog rockers of the early 1970s.

Another member of the *Hair* band was bassist Laurie Scott Baker, an Australian with an impressive CV, which takes in experimental music, jazz, folk and contemporary classical. Laurie knew vaguely of the Soul Band through adverts in the music press and recalls meeting up with Alex around the time *Hair* started in London:

The band and key members of the cast did one rehearsal with the writers Ragni and Rado along with the composer Galt McDermot – most of the musos knew of him already, as he had a minor hit back in the early 1960s with a song called 'African Waltz'. Then there was a long wait followed by a week rehearsing and then the run started properly.

In early 1968, I was living in a basement flat, full of musicians, in West Kensington where the guitarist Andy Summers (who later played with The Police) had stayed. Andy had gone to the States with the Soft Machine as they had been picked by Jimi Hendrix to open for him on his inaugural US tour. My partner Brigid and I shared this flat with the drummer Colin Allen, who later worked with Lesley Harvey and Stone the Crows.

Colin was going to be the drummer for *Hair* and he did the first rehearsal, but in the meantime he joined the John Mayall band. I got the gig through Colin's recommendation, and this is how I first met Alex. I remember Alex telling me that he had met Hendrix in the pub across the road from this house! Incidentally Alex sang on one of my songs, 'Let Me Tell You This'. Leslie Harvey and Colin Allen also took part on that session.[6]

Laurie says that the *Hair* band days were enjoyable but were always hard work:

At the start of it we rehearsed during the day and did one show per night along with two at the weekends. It was quite a lively time and we were always meeting lots of new people because *Hair* was *the* show in town. Both Alex and I did gigs after the show where we would play till about 3 a.m. I was playing in the Pickwick club with a jazz trio and Alex was playing in a club nearby in Leicester Square. We usually walked down together after the show and that's when I got to know him quite well. But with all the session work on top of this it meant that all we did for the first six months was work and sleep![7]

The musical was soon the hippest show in town and pop-stars, tourists and even Lord Longford flocked to see it. For the first eight months or so Alex worked in the 800 Club after the shows, but eventually he gave that up. Later, following the nightly *Hair* shows – which started at 8 p.m. – he and his mates would often team up in a Greek diner on Tottenham Court Road or go late-night drinking at the Intrepid Fox pub in Soho, where they would share anecdotes and discuss future plans. Sometimes the gang would adjourn to all-night parties where Alex would strum his guitar while the others sang along.

Invariably too much strong drink was consumed, but Derek Wadsworth says Alex was still in control in those early days:

We drank too much but we could hold it well. It was a lot of fun and Alex was never aggressive. Saying that though, he could quieten things down pretty quickly. Alex was the type of guy who you could quite easily imagine on the waterfront with a knife in his hand. He could handle trouble but really he was a humanitarian at heart. I never saw anything but love and kindness from him.[8]

In a feature in *Mojo* magazine, the actor Richard O'Brien told how he and Alex became firm friends when he worked on the show:

Alex was cheeky, special. Very charismatic. A naughty boy who didn't want to grow up. He was full of stories, but no one ever knew if they were true, half-true or what. One night he told me about a time when he was arrested in Sweden on suspicion of being a part of the Baader-Meinhof Gang. He said, 'The police got me stark bollock naked against the wall, and the next minute one of them had his finger up my arse. I told him he looked like a big strong boy!'[9]

The four years spent on the show were very happy times for Alex. The *Hair* job meant steady cash and it also allowed him the opportunity to play countless lucrative sessions. One unreleased acetate has him singing 'Jerusalem' backed by the Brighton Festival Choir and a rhythym section. Apparently Alex sings it beautifully, not tongue-in-cheek at all. The acetate was rescued from a rubbish skip by David Firmstone's nephew, and when Firmstone (Alex's manager at the time) died, many of these rare recordings were thrown away.

One-off club gigs were slightly less profitable. A contract drawn up by bosses at London's Marquee for 3

March 1970 shows that Alex and his unnamed backing band were only due 50 per cent of the guaranteed minimum payment of £50. Alex employed the extra-curricular *Hair* band for several one-off gigs, where he used them as a template for the SAHB days. Laurie Scott Baker recalls that they played a regular gig in Ipswich, where Harvey first wore the trademark striped T-shirt and played Brel's 'Next' for the first time.

Alex now had stability in his private life, and he spent days off relaxing with his new love Trudy and their infant son Tyro, picnicking and visiting museums. Trudy Harvey first met her new husband around 1964 when, as an impressionable teenager, she had seen The Soul Band support blues legend Long John Baldry. The gig was at the London Marquee – which at the time was an alcohol-free club where everyone had to make do with soft drinks. A mutual friend introduced the couple. Trudy recalls how, once she saw him on stage, she immediately knew that Alex would be a star.

I must have been about 17 or 18 when I saw him at the Marquee. I had gone along to see Long John Baldry because I was a big fan of rhythm and blues at the time, but when Alex came on I just thought he was amazing. Jimmy Grimes was playing with him at that time and so was his brother Leslie and they were playing stuff like 'Let The Good Times Roll' and 'I Just Wanna Make Love To You'.

I had gone along with a friend from Glasgow who knew Alex slightly, so after the gig we went around to the little cubbyhole backstage where the band were. The band were quite raw. I was a middle-class girl from Leigh-on-Sea in Essex and – you won't believe this – but I don't think I had even heard the word 'fuck' being used! So when we went backstage I was amazed to hear these guys shouting things like 'Get to fuck!' or 'Fuck off!' I remember thinking, mmm, this is a bit interesting – I don't think my father would approve. Great!!! Alex was 11 years older than me, so initially I just sort of followed him around.[10]

Shrewd, intelligent and attractive, Trudy was to play a major part in Alex's subsequent success – offering inspiration and support away from the lunatic world of rock music. When they met, she was working for the Foreign Office. Trudy refused Alex's marriage proposals until their son Tyro was old enough to attend the wedding! After their marriage in 1971, she studied at teacher training college, but that meant she was seeing precious little of her new husband, so Trudy decided to concentrate on staying at home instead. Friends of the family told me that although she was much younger than her husband, Trudy eventually became almost like a mother figure to him – looking after him and becoming extremely protective of him during the difficult final years of his life. One friend told me: 'She seemed to hold him together as best she could. And he was a handful – unlike anybody I ever met. He could be very insecure and I suppose Trudy was like a rock in his life.'

The *Hair* job also taught Alex a lot about music and about arranging. Most important of all, it taught him how important discipline was if he was ever to be successful. The *Hair* years also saw more vinyl adventures. In 1967, the *Hair* group recorded *Band On The Wagon* for Bell Records, produced by Alan Price, a former member of The Animals who would later find chart success in his own right as a solo artist. Alex is credited with contributing to writing four of the album's 11 songs and he also takes the lead vocal chores on six of the tracks.

Playing every night in the *Hair* band didn't allow too many chances for the musicians to impress an audience outside of the theatre, so when the chance came to record an album themselves they took it with both hands. *Band On The Wagon* is a real mix of styles but the big brass arrangements dominate proceedings. Derek Wadsworth's

'I'm Living', a convincing jazz instrumental 'The Golden Egg' and the classic 'There's No Lights On The Christmas Tree ...' are the outstanding tracks but overall the record was just too diverse and offbeat to make much of an impression on the public.

In 1969, Alex also contributed to the *Hair Rave-Up* album for Pye Records, which was recorded live at the Shaftesbury Theatre and produced by Cyril Stapleton. Recording started at midnight before a specially invited audience and was only completed at 5 a.m. The album featured a version of Bob Dylan's 'All Along the Watchtower' along with the band's take on Lennon and McCartney's 'Birthday'. Harvey takes lead vocal duties on both songs and his assured laidback delivery on the Dylan classic was a marker for his talents. Indeed, his vocals throughout the record showed that Alex was learning that there was more to singing than wailing in a fake American accent – now his delivery could be laconic or energetic and the hint of menace which came to characterise his later vocals was also taking shape. The recording took place just after the band had performed the musical that night so they were probably eager to try something different. As a result, only two songs from the show – 'Hare Krishna' and 'Hair' make it on to the record.

In June 2001, the *Hair Rave-Up* album was re-released on CD by the Castle Music label for Sanctuary Records as part of their Psychedelic Pstones (sic) series. For readers wanting an inkling of the style of the *Rave-Up* recording, then the clue is in the names of some of the tracks – like 'El Pussy Cat' and two of the Harvey-penned songs 'Royal International Love-In' and 'Bond Street Baby'. If the spoof secret agent Austin Powers had ever cut an album then this would have been it. As the sleeve notes for the CD say, this is 'distinctly shagadelic' music. Sadly the CD is also like the Mike Myers movies. You start out thinking this is a brilliant montage of Swinging Sixties London but by the third or fourth track you are glancing at your watch and looking for a way out.

The band performs well enough together – which is hardly surprising given that they knew each other so well. The ensemble initially played a set at the end of each night's show with the aim being to send the audience home happy. Gradually they became more confident, adding cover versions and original songs – most of which were written by Alex. So they were soon performing concerts away from the theatre at venues like the Marquee. But reproducing that magic on vinyl was never going to be easy – especially on extended instrumentals like 'Hare Krishna' – and the record never made the charts.

In October of 1969, Alex released his first solo album in almost four years – *Roman Wall Blues* – on Fontana Records. The 11-track record came replete with a W.H. Auden poem of the same name on the sleeve. It featured some of the *Hair* gang like guitarist Mickey Keene, flute player Ashton Tootle and Derek Wadsworth – plus Les Harvey. Like all of Alex's solo work, the record is a real hit-and-miss affair. Most of the songs hurtle along at breakneck speed on the back of beefy brass arrangements by Wadsworth and Frank Ricotti. The record opens with by far the best track – a swaggeringly confident version of 'Midnight Moses'. Listening to it now, it still sounds great – even before Ted McKenna and Zal Cleminson got their teeth into it.

That song and another *Roman Wall Blues* effort 'Hammer Song' would both resurface on the *Framed* album in 1972. Another curio for Harvey collectors is the title track that was to appear again on his last ever album *Soldier on the Wall*, released posthumously in 1983. The song, with lyrics by Auden, featured Alex playing the part of an ordinary centurion carrying out unpleasant chores in rotten conditions. Also included on the 1969 outing was a brave cover version of The Rolling Stones' 'Jumping Jack Flash' – which manages the not inconsiderable achievement of being both raucous and perfunctory at the same time.

Overall the album is certainly worth checking out. A couple of the lesser-known tracks – the thoughtful, plaintive 'Maxine' and the moody instrumental 'Down at Bart's Place' hint at greater things to come.

Around this time, Alex also worked with a jazz-rock combo called Rock Workshop, which included Derek Wadsworth and guitarist Ray Russell. Two tracks on the Rock Workshops' 1970 self-titled debut album featured Harvey – 'Hole In Her Stocking' which was to resurface on SAHB's *Framed* album and 'Wade Into The Water', a tune by jazz pianist Ramsay Lewis.

The album is a curious mix of experimental styles, with everything from sub-Jimi Hendrix guitar histrionics to weird electronic doodling and thumping brass backing thrown in the mix. The end result is far from convincing and again it's an example of Alex simply marking time and having some fun in the studio. Musos will pay up to £100 nowadays for a mint copy of the record but back in the 1970s the public resolutely refused to show much interest. Harvey quit Rock Workshop soon afterwards though the band did release one more album without him in 1971. Later, the influential critic Charles Shaar Murray was to claim that the band were 'criminally underrated'.

7

FROM TEARS TO TEAR GAS

'They were very rocky, loud and
undisciplined. They needed my experience
and I needed their enthusiasm and balls. It
was a very happy marriage.'[1]
Alex Harvey

Hair may have given Alex some financial stability, but by
early 1972 it was plain that his music career had all but
stalled. He was 37 and surely way too old to make an
impression in an industry where youth was so important.
Younger upstarts like The Rolling Stones, The Beatles and
The Who had whizzed past him and were now international superstars. By contrast, Alex was stuck in a rut.

Thankfully, his sense of humour was still intact. In a
Sounds interview in March 1972 with Ray Telford he told
how he had recently played a solo gig at the Marquee in
London and had been met with a 'very positive kind of
silence'. Alex had become jaded with the routine strumming in the *Hair* show, he even admitted to being bored
with seeing the same naked women on stage every night.

The future of the show itself was also in the balance after the theatre roof literally fell in early one morning. There was talk of sabotage as property developers were at the time eager to redevelop the theatre site.

So Alex quit the *Hair* band and eventually formed a new group with Ian Ellis, who once played in a group called Clouds, on bass and ex-Velvet Opera drummer Dave Dufont. In a taste of things to come they played an eclectic set which included 'Isobel Goudie', Frank Zappa's 'Willie the Pimp', 'Roman Wall Blues', alongside rock standards like 'Honky Tonk Women', 'Shakin' All Over', 'Jailhouse Rock' and a version of Jacques Brel's 'Next'. The trio had potential, but Harvey wasn't happy with what he perceived as their lack of musical tightness. They soon drifted apart and Alex seemed to be back at square one.

Sadly, it was to be a tragedy that was to change the course of Alex's career. On 3 May 1972, his younger brother Les died after being electrocuted as his band Stone The Crows prepared to play a concert at the Swansea Top Rank Theatre. As he moved forward to announce the opening number, Les touched a badly connected live microphone and was thrown into the air. He landed with his guitar in contact with the microphone stand and other band members received minor shocks as they tried to pull him clear. Frantic attempts were then made to resuscitate him. Ironically the gig was a coming-out ball for Swansea University medical students and had been moved to the Top Rank because the local university hall was not big enough to meet the ticket demand. Les was rushed to hospital but was pronounced dead later that evening. He was 26 years old.

What made his death even more poignant was that the band's lead singer Maggie Bell was Les's partner. The couple had been teenage sweethearts and Bell was effectively part of the Harvey family. She actually stayed with them for a while at Durham Street, Glasgow, in a home that had 'This is the house of music' chalked on the wall. On the night of the tragedy, Maggie Bell collapsed and was kept in hospital overnight under heavy sedation. Almost 30 years on, she told *Mojo* magazine:

I remember Leslie saying, 'There's something wrong here – but we want this to be a good gig so bear with us.' He put his hand on the mic, and he was gone, it was just as quick as that.[2]

In the *NME* of 16 February 1974, she told readers:

It's a funny thing to explain but I died when Les died and I experienced a rebirth. I was born again and I knew that I really had to go on singing. If I'd quit, Les would have known and I know that he would not have wanted that.

Les was an accomplished musician who had been taught guitar at a very early age by Alex. A quiet and delicate child, Les had an allergy to milk and used to be fed carrot juice instead. In 1957, aged only 11, Les was part of the Kinning Park Ramblers skiffle band. Alex taught him how to play the guitar and showed him various songs, including the old blues standard 'Blind Man' which would appear on the first Stone The Crows album. During the mid 1960s, Les had played in the highly rated Blues Council band who were tipped for stardom but split after the tragic death of vocalist Fraser Calder and bassist James Giffen. Both were killed in a road accident in March 1965 as the band returned from a gig in Edinburgh. A few years later, Les was offered the guitar slot with The Animals, but turned down the opportunity after taking advice from Alex.

In 1969, Les had been a co-founder of Stone The

Crows. Under the guidance of Led Zeppelin manager Peter Grant, the band was on the verge of great things. Les briefly played lead guitar in the backing band for Aretha Franklin when the queen of soul performed some gigs in Europe – her own regular guitarist, Cornell Dupree, had taken ill. Stone The Crows had supported Joe Cocker on a US tour and the ebullient Maggie Bell was being touted as the new Janis Joplin. Quiet and contemplative, Les was a perfect foil for Maggie's more raunchy style. Les was frailer than Alex, but he shared his brother's interest in music and history. A big fan of Bob Dylan, Les was a guitarist with immense potential. *Sounds* reckoned that he was the best guitarist to emerge on the British music scene since Eric Clapton and George Harrison, the author concluding, 'had he lived there is no telling ... what degree of brilliance he would have attained.'

Stone The Crows initially looked to the mercurial former Fleetwood Mac guitarist Peter Green as a replacement, but he backed out at the last minute. Steve Howe of Yes helped out at the Great Western Festival in Lincoln before Stone The Crows finally replaced Les with another young Scottish guitarist, Jimmy McCulloch. But the spirit of the band died with Les and they split up soon after, unable to convert their popularity as a live act into record sales.

Peter Grant paid for some of the Harvey relatives to travel to Swansea for the cremation. Maggie Bell was still inconsolable and could not face the ordeal. Over time it became clear just how crippling a blow the tragedy was to Alex. Many of his friends felt that he never really recovered emotionally. George Butler, who dined with Les and Maggie the night before the tragedy says, 'Les's death affected Alex hugely ... I think he never ever got over it. Leslie was a sweet guy.'

Trudy Harvey recounts:

The verdict was death by misadventure. There was a strong feeling in the family that the blame should be laid somewhere. The death left Alex feeling very disillusioned with the music business, but I think it also made him more determined to succeed by himself. As a child, Les apparently was very quiet and dour, he didn't talk much. It seems that after Alex taught him the guitar, the guitar almost became like his voice. Even as an adult, Les was not a terribly talkative person. I remember thinking he would turn out to be a wise old man. But he was only 26 when he died. Les and Maggie stayed with us in a flat in Highgate. At the time he was such a good guitarist that he was playing with Aretha Franklin. Then he and Maggie went off to the States to do their first American tour. Alex and I were in the Highgate flat on the night Les died. Alex took the phone call – he was absolutely devastated.[3]

In the letters page of *Sounds* on 9 September 1972, Leslie Harvey senior sent a message that drew a poetic veil over the whole sad episode:

Just a humble intimation to any fan of the late Leslie Harvey of Stone The Crows. Leslie's ashes will be scattered on Morar Sands, Inverness-shire on Sat Sept 9th at 3 p.m. No mourning garb or useless tears. Assembly! by the Sound of Sleat where saint did pass and Prince arose. On Morar Sands in sweet repose.

The Harveys rented a house in the Highlands during September and around 50 friends and family attended the event at Morar. Alex Harvey junior – who still has 8mm-film footage of the ceremony – recalls the effect that the tragedy had on everyone who knew Leslie well:

It was devastating for the whole family and for my old man in particular. But he held a lot of it in. See in the 1970s, counselling – talking to someone about bereavement – just wasn't considered right. I reckon we all needed someone to talk to including me, because Leslie wasn't really my uncle, he was more like a brother to me. I was brought up with Leslie – he was a gem.[4]

Eddie Tobin – one of Glasgow's leading music agents who eventually ended up on the SAHB management team – remembers that after the tragedy he took Alex to Wales. Tobin says that the heartbroken singer had an unusual initial reaction when he first saw the face of his dead brother, who appeared to have a grin on his features:

I had taken him to Swansea, to see Leslie's body. When Alex came out he told me 'He [Leslie] is smiling, he's very, very happy, he's happy because he is playing with Jimi Hendrix. He's playing now with the other great guys who are dead.' Alex was happy because he thought Les was happy now. That was the view that he took. I think in many ways he may actually have believed that.[5]

For Alex Harvey, the only answer to the pain he was feeling inside was to immerse himself totally in his work. But he told friends that he still needed a band – preferably Scottish – who would back him in every sense of the word in his battle to succeed in the tough music business. An old friend, the promoter Bill Fehilly, knew Alex had the potential to be a huge star if he could only find the right backing band. Eddie Tobin told Fehilly of a 'progressive' Glasgow band called Tear Gas whom he had managed and that had great potential. Alex soon headed north to check them out.

According to interviews in *Melody Maker* and *Sunday Mail* he first saw the band play in Arran during the Glasgow Fair holiday. In other interviews he said he first saw them in the Burns Howff pub in Glasgow, apparently sauntering into the bar and introducing himself to the band. Alex was impressed, telling friends that the band sounded like a grenade going off. He thought Zal's playing was 'brain-bending'.

That may have been the first time he had paid any attention to the band but they knew of him from way back. In fact, Tear Gas had supported him at the Marquee during Harvey's ill-fated attempts at getting the right sound back in the early 1970s. Zal Cleminson says they were less than impressed with their future boss and also slightly intimidated by him. On that occasion they never spoke to him, though standing in the audience they were won over by his charisma and latent talent. Zal was confused that Alex no longer seemed to sing in the James Brown style of the Soul Band days – and he wasn't impressed by his guitar playing:

Alex was bad, you know, he was trying to put across several songs that we've done with him since then, but it just wasn't working. Nothing was happening in his band. The sound was all wrong and having Alex playing an instrument was all wrong too.[6]

When they first got together to jam, the band members were initially nervous, but once they rehearsed the Harvey song 'Midnight Moses' they knew they were onto a good thing. They quickly agreed to ditch the progressive rock sounds, which had held them back and concentrated instead on beefing up Alex's simple rock riffs and ideas. In a radio interview, Alex recalled:

They were a bit introverted on stage at first and extroverted off stage. I had to change that about ... they had incredible talent and I thought they were probably the greatest band in the world.

Alex was correct that Tear Gas needed him as much as he needed them. The band were progressive and aggressive on stage – legend has it that they employed one roadie solely to ensure that the amplifier stacks stayed upright when Zal launched himself at them. The band lacked leadership but had still managed to release two good albums. The bizarrely titled *Piggy Go Getter* in 1970 featured Zal Cleminson and Paisley-born bassist Chris Glen along with drummer Willie Munro, pianist Eddie Campbell and singer David Batchelor. The following year saw the release of a second record *Tear Gas*. Over time, three of the group – Munro, Campbell and Batchelor – were replaced by two cousins, Ted and Hugh McKenna.

But, whatever the line-up, album sales were poor and spirit in the camp was low. Sales for the first record were around 5,000 with the second album shifting just marginally more at 7,000. The band members were living six to a room in overcrowded London digs. According to guitarist Zal Cleminson: 'Tear Gas was a progressive band. We all grew beards and turned our backs on the audience. When we met Alex he bought us all a drink and I said, "Right, you can be our singer."'[7]

Ted McKenna was originally from Coatbridge and had been playing drums since he was a teenager. His father was very supportive and made him his first pair of drumsticks. In a recent BBC interview with Tom Morton, Ted told how, aged just 16, he was doing three or four gigs a week with schoolmates – including his cousin Hugh on piano – in a band called Rare Breed: 'Nobody had any particular aspirations to be pop stars, it was just a case of playing something you loved and you learnt your trade. That's very, very important.'

Rare Breed eventually mutated into a professional band called Bubbles before Ted briefly did the drumming chores for Dream Police – an outfit that gradually evolved into the Average White Band, Scotland's only true soul superstars.

Ted – who was an admirer of jazzy drummers like Billy Cobham – joined Tear Gas in time for their second album. He was brutally honest when he told *Mojo* that Harvey's intervention came at just the right time. Tear Gas was on the brink of calling it a day:

Tear Gas wasn't in great shape. We'd been roughing it in London, paying off gear. Financially things were falling to bits. Alex had a lot of experience, and way of doing things that demanded attention and respect. We thought, what have we got to lose?[8]

Another recruit was Ted's piano-playing cousin Hugh McKenna. Born in 1949, Hugh was also originally from Coatbridge and had started teaching himself the piano at the early age of eight. Hugh believes he was fortunate to hail from a family who were immersed in music and the variety scene in particular. His dad had rejected a career down the mines in favour of playing piano accordion and his mum was also a talented soprano singer. Hugh's father worked for over 35 years on the variety circuit alongside legends like Jimmy Logan and Jack Milroy – and his son soon felt there was something inevitable about him taking to the stage.

Hugh left school when he was 18 armed with an A-level in music and worked for a year in the civil service, where he was – in his own words – a 'really bad wages clerk', before concentrating full-time on a music career. By that time he was already a fairly experienced musician having started fooling around in bands years earlier.

My first experience of pop music was with my cousin Ted – playing mostly Beatles stuff, but also records by The Rolling Stones, The Who, The Hollies and The Kinks. Ted had a Dansette-type record player whereas we just had a 78 player. There were three kids in my family but Ted was an only child. His parents weren't any richer or poorer than mine but because Ted was an only child, they could afford a record player. Another cousin had given my brother Johnny a snare drum and Ted started playing around with it. Ted's house had a piano and we just started messing about doing things like The Stones song 'Little Red Rooster' and I found that I had a feel for blues right away. I just kind of assumed that I was going to be on stage. I always had that belief since childhood. I just bought into the whole idea that my family are musicians and I seem to be quite good at it too.[9]

By the age of 16 or 17, Hugh and his cousin were both in Rare Breed, playing venues like The Place in Edinburgh where they supported groups like The Stoics and Rory Gallagher's first band Taste. Rare Breed were in Hugh's own words 'a fairly good pop band made up of local guys'. They decided to change their name to Bubbles after a concert in Paisley one night when a local wag defaced a poster featuring the group's name – stroking out the word Rare and substituting it with the word Pan!

In total, Rare Breed and Bubbles lasted for about three and a half years. But soon after Ted left the group, Hugh also quit and then worked for a while with a couple of bands – Merlin and then Nickelson (who also featured Davey Nicholson, who would later join the much praised outfit Blue).

Hugh McKenna:

By that time, Ted had left Dream Police and joined Tear Gas. I knew of Zal and Davie Batchelor through their work with a group called The Bo Weevils. So I started going to a few gigs with them in their van – but I had no real ambition to join them. Nickelson were getting almost £100 a gig at that time, they were one of the top bands in Scotland and I was doing all the singing.

I thought Tear Gas were a good raunchy, heavy rock band – they always had a lot of power, with a very tight rhythm section and a powerful guitar player. But they had gone as far as they could in Scotland – I think in 1971 the guys were earning about £10 a week. My main motivation in joining Tear Gas was because Ted played with them and he was the best drummer in Scotland by a mile. Ted had turned me on to a lot of music – people like Miles Davis, Oscar Peterson and Nina Simone. He was much more adventurous in his tastes and he used to talk in such an enthusiastic way about what people were doing.

Alex must have seen us at the Marquee because we supported him there. I wasn't that impressed by him on that occasion, though there was something about him that was definitely very charismatic. I remember him coming on stage while we were having our soundcheck and him walking up to the mic to tune his guitar. Later I heard a report that he thought the piano and guitar sound of our band were nice. So if he wasn't actually out in the audience then he must have heard the band from the dressing room.

The second time he saw us would have been at the Burns Howff when he came in to meet and rehearse with us. I remember him walking in with a guitar strapped around his shoulder. He went up to the bar, bought himself a pint, and came over and sat down. The first thing we rehearsed was 'Midnight Moses' – I was aware that he was in the position of leader right away.[10]

Soon after that, following an early gig at the Burns Howff, Alex and the band adjourned to the Lido Café across the road and Bill Fehilly offered the Tear Gas boys a retainer of £25 a week – roughly £15 more than they were making at the time.

Tear Gas manager Eddie Tobin says:

Tear Gas were the biggest rock band in Scotland at that time – one of the heaviest and loudest rock bands around. They had released two albums but the truth is that they had reached their peak, they had gone as far as they could go. They were looking for alternative avenues to bring them success. At that time a friend of mine – Derek Nicol – had moved to London and we talked about this singer he had – he said, 'What about Alex for Tear Gas?'

I went to London to see Alex – I think I saw him play at the Music Room. Alex at that time had a three piece band – but the truth is the band were not very good, they were just good musicians but that was all they had going for them, they had no emotion. Alex was performing a hotchpotch of songs that he liked – including some Jacques Brel.

When I listened to him I thought he was very, very intense and angry. He came across as an angry, threatening, menacing singer – so much so that he intentionally angered some guys in the crowd. I remember that one of them offered him a drink, which he threw away. I talked to him afterwards and he had the intensity of an angry Glaswegian, I don't know if the world knows what that is – Glaswegians are all angry, to be honest, especially the working-class ones. Him and Frankie Miller were the two archetypal angry Glaswegians of my lifetime. They were very close friends. They conveyed the anger of the shipyards.[11]

Tear Gas were initially not enamoured with their new boss barking out orders and heated arguments soon flared up. Alex had learned from working with American showbiz types in *Hair* that discipline was crucial. So if band members were just a matter of minutes late for rehearsal they got told off in no uncertain terms. With his daunting reputation and tough-guy image, Alex invariably won the arguments, confiding to friends: 'They always do what I say because they know I can beat all of them at once anytime.'[12] Hugh McKenna remembers: 'Alex would work people really, really hard – past the point where everyone else wanted to throw in the towel for the day. We would end up working into the early hours of the morning.'[13]

Eddie Tobin had a close-up view of how things were developing and comments:

It's unfair to say there was tension initially, that's the wrong word. There was a degree of caution because Alex was older than any member of the band, so he was immediately a father figure. He had been in London and done the circuit, had played in places like the Krays' club. He'd really been around and the band had a lot of respect for him. But there was a lot of caution too because he didn't understand who or what the band were and – in a way – he was finding his feet.

When the band heard it was Alex, it wasn't like they said 'Wow, that's sensational!' Alex was a historical figure in Glasgow even then. He was respected for what he had done because he had once had a great band. But he was certainly not 'current' – he was seen as a part of history, he had been away, had played in *Hair* and now nobody knew where he was.

But Alex loved the violence of the band, the aggression and the anger. They were absolutely perfect for him as a vehicle for the messages he wanted to convey.[14]

Ted McKenna recalls how the fact that Alex's age – he was almost 38 and about 15 years older than them – was a factor early on:

I never forget when he came to the house when we finally went down south and we were moving into a flat in Hornsey, he came to the house and my dad was there and it was almost like my dad was handing me over to this other old guy. My dad would have been well into his sixties at this point. I got the feeling that he was basically saying, 'OK, you better look after my boy or I'll be down to see you.' Yeah, he was like a father figure, no doubt about it at all.[15]

In an interview with *NME*, Zal reflected on the early difficulties:

Alex has very simple ideas musically and we used to have constant battles, us trying to express four or five ideas in one song and him trying to clear away the debris, because he doesn't think the audience should have to grasp more than one at a time. And now I think he's right. We're confused enough up here sometimes without confusing them down there.[16]

An added complication was that Tear Gas had a small but vocal following that were initially hostile towards Alex. At an early gig supporting Stone The Crows at Clouds Disco above Glasgow's Apollo Theatre the crowd almost booed Alex off stage. The younger fans had no idea who he was and the older ones didn't like his theatrical arrogance. Indeed a combination of Alex's hard-man image and the group's uncompromising attitude meant that there was often an air of pent-up violence at early gigs. Undeterred, Alex swore back at the hecklers. To him, a hostile reaction was better than none at all.

8

SO SENSATIONAL

'Rock 'n' roll is entertainment – it's got to be
entertainment. If people pay money to see a
group, they're going to be entertained. If it
was only for the music they'd put a big
screen in front of the band.'[1]
Alex Harvey

Alex knew he had the perfect band and now he wanted
people to know about them. Ever eager to provoke reaction, he modestly agreed to call them The Sensational
Alex Harvey Band. The name had been suggested by
Derek Nicol and harked back to soul bands like The Fabulous Younghearts. The name may initially have been
seen as a joke by some but it certainly courted attention and set the group apart from others starting out. By
choosing the prefix Sensational, Alex also seemed intent
on issuing a challenge to the newly formed band – now
they had to go out and prove to the doubting public that
they really were worthy of the title.

The SAHB was a perfect platform for Alex and allowed
him to experiment with his musical fantasies. The band

– used to playing in the hard-rock style of their heroes Deep Purple and Led Zeppelin – now had to learn songs by Jacques Brel and Frank Zappa. Everyone agreed that it was going to be fun. Hugh McKenna:

Our first reaction was 'Who is Jacques Brel?' I'd never heard of him, and to this day I still haven't heard that much of him aside from the odd David Bowie or Scott Walker cover. But the whole of the band were open-minded about these type of excursions – we thought of everything in musical terms.[2]

His experience with the Soul Band taught Alex that musical dexterity wasn't enough. In the early 1970s, there were simply too many rock bands on the road, all vying for the public's attention and hard-earned cash. The SAHB also needed to compete with overblown pomp-rock theatrics from groups like Genesis and glam kings like David Bowie. These musicians were soon selling truckloads of records on the back of fantastic stage shows, spectacular lighting and brilliant costumes. A SAHB show had to become a theatrical event – something the audience would never forget. Alex said:

Being flash is the story of rock 'n' roll ... even Ravi Shankar, he's flash. As soon as you stand up on stage it's show business.[3]

In the same interview, to explain his attitude, he recalled an early gig in Glasgow:

I played the Metropole with Jimmy Logan ... [he] played something on a little accordion with the house lights down. The crowd were crying and going crazy for that simple melody. He communicated with those people, that means it was entertainment.

Limited budgets meant the SAHB gigs were never going to rival the Pink Floyd in visual spectaculars. Instead they had to improvise with basic props and sets which served to reinforce the stories and characters that Alex created. Usually Alex's trademark stage outfit was centred on a tatty black-and-white hooped T-shirt, but as the show developed over the years he became more adventurous. For a song like 'The Man in the Jar', Alex stood under a blue street lamp dressed as a private eye in a grubby raincoat bought from Oxfam for 25 pence. For 'Vambo Marble Eye', Alex harked back to the Gorbals gangs he ran with as a teenager. Dressed as the eponymous street hero he would climb on top of the speakers and use a tin of spray paint to daub an imitation 'brick' wall with the slogan 'Vambo Rool!' Later on in the show, during the song 'Framed', Alex would punch his way through the wall.

Other stage props included a blackboard, teacher's cane, pirate outfit and judicious use of scantily clad females. Alex saw the theatrics as a method of selling the music – like wrapping the act in an attractive bright ribbon. Doing things on the cheap actually suited him. If he was singing a song about a character escaping then why not use a ladder that was lying backstage to express the meaning? He also believed that a simple thing like using kilted Highland pipers on stage helped spread international goodwill and also moved the audience.

It was cheap and very cheerful, what Harvey himself used to call a matt – rather than a gloss or glitter – finish. In a 1975 interview he explained:

You might think that the David Bowie theatrical thing is new – it isn't. The difference is that Bowie and the others like him are glittery and involved, and we like to be street theatre, where it's cheap, where you can use instant props and use anything you can find and improvise on it, rather than having a big organised thing.'[4]

The show had to be fun for the audience. They had to be entertained. There were already scores of bands playing mainstream hard rock. So Alex required that the band learn to play jazz, blues, cabaret, country & western, punk rock and heavy metal. That way every base was covered – Harvey wanted the widest possible audience from the teenyboppers to the 'serious' music fan. And though he may have played the role of mad scientist, he was in fact the perfect front man. No one could milk a crowd like him. Sometimes he got the fans so mesmerised that he took the opportunity to lecture them on drugs, violence or the environment; 'I get them in the palm of my hand and then I do my bit for the world,' he once told David Gibson of the *Glasgow Evening Times*. On other occasions he would don a smoking jacket and a pair of horn-rimmed glasses and chew the petals of a rose!

When it came to writing songs, he used every tool at his disposal. For a working-class man with a limited education, Alex was pretty well-read, and he could quote freely from classics like Fenimore Cooper's *Last of the Mohicans*. He also took a keen interest in science fiction, and admired how that genre broke conventions and pushed the boundaries of exploration. His love of history – everything from cowboys and Indians to the Battle of Waterloo – was a rich source of ideas. His affection for movies like *King Kong* and his admiration of actors like Marlon Brando was another avenue of inspiration. Then there was his own personal experience of Gorbals gang violence, which many see as the basis for the Vambo songs. In short, everything he had ever seen or done in life was a source for his songwriting.

Underscoring everything Alex did was his genuine affection for the fans that spent their hard-earned cash on his records and concerts. Like many performers, he often took time to tell his audience that he loved them. But unlike the false sincerity of some of his contemporaries, Alex genuinely meant it. He belonged to his fans and they belonged to him. If they spent their money on the SAHB, then they were owed some aural and visual stimulation. Bouncers at concert venues who were notorious for dishing out brutal beatings to over-enthusiastic fans were told in no uncertain terms by Harvey that such behaviour was not acceptable at a SAHB gig.

Hugh McKenna:

He definitely had a policy – that the band were happy to adhere to – about the fans, particularly those who had travelled a long way to see us. Some fans would often travel a couple of hundred miles to one of our gigs. It was a bit like giving them the 'star fan' treatment – these were people who actively supported us and who were telling all their mates about us as well.

Even from a cynical point of view it was just good politics. I do believe that in a way Alex would never forget where he came from – maybe it's a thing that people from Scotland have, that you might get found out or something. My impression of him as a person was that he was quite sophisticated in many ways but after all was said and done we are all working-class guys from central Scotland. So if some kids are travelling hundreds of miles to see our gig then the least we can do is show our appreciation.[5]

Alex summed up his views on his young fans in a US promotional interview in 1974:

I don't know what I mean to those kids. I don't know whether I'm supposed to be their uncle or brother or whatever. I only know that I don't lie to them and maybe they can tell that, because they're not as silly as lots of people think they are. They're a whole lot smarter – a whole lot more intelligent. I worry that they might think I'm some kind of leader. They don't need any leaders. It's up to them – they can be their own leader.

In the early days at least, Alex also had an almost

evangelical belief in the power of rock music to be a force for positive good in society. Speaking to radio DJ Tony Hadland in 1974, he commented:

I believe in rock 'n' roll ... that it's possible to have a universal understanding and communication through a form of music and they don't have to know what the words are or understand what the song is about ... the message is there ... When you think of 'Hound Dog' ... what the fuck does that mean? ... or 'Long Tall Sally'.

We went to Germany in 1963 and one of the first things I thought about was that my uncle had been over bombing Germany 20 years previous ... and I made a better impression with an electric guitar, I made a lot more friends than they did. It's very positive, it's got a lot of power and aggression.[6]

And if the audience ever tired of Alex, well, there was always another natural-born star to entertain them – guitarist Zal Cleminson. As a teenager growing up in Glasgow, Zal had initially toyed with the idea of becoming a post office clerk but thankfully at the age of 16 he bought a cheap acoustic guitar and started working on his Chuck Berry and Stax Records riffs. On the radio series *Vambo Rools OK* he remembered how – as a young man – he had seen the Soul Band play at a club called Picasso on Buchanan Street in Glasgow. Zal was immediately impressed by their slick, brassy sound. He thought the group made an unbelievable noise and was won over by their discipline and professionalism.

Between 1965 and 1968, Zal had served his time with a pop band known as the Bo Weevils, a Glasgow group who were probably best known for having the gall to wear pink suits and white shoes on stage. Zal and Alex both shared a liking for the music of Frank Zappa and an understanding that audiences were there to be entertained. Standing still and churning out riffs wasn't enough. Zal used to say that he would fall asleep on stage if he had to play in the style of Status Quo for more than three minutes.

After the formation of the SAHB, encouraged by Alex and Bill Fehilly, Zal took on a whole new persona on stage. Fans were soon mesmerised by his weird harlequin catsuits and his ghostly white face and black diamond colouring around his eyes. Stalking the stage or leaning forward on the monitor leering into the audience, Zal was a uniquely talented and intense performer. *NME* got it right when they called him a one-man freak show. His look was part-Marcel Marceau and part-The Joker from *Batman*. Another of his trademarks was to pull exaggerated faces as he wrenched out riffs from his Cherry Red Gibson SG or Fender Stratocaster guitars. It could be an unsettling sight for those not in on the joke.

He once explained that his philosophy was not to upstage Alex but to always look like he was just about to, adding:

Guitarists always pull faces when they play from the sheer effort of playing. The faces I pull have always been pretty funny but ... It's just the classic guitar players' thing. Someone suggested I should accentuate it and as it happens it really works, both in terms of a comic thing and a heavy thing. I have been told that at the same time it can be daft and comic and yet quite macabre. It's a bit of acting and I enjoy it. But in the same way it must also be part of me. Alex is the front man and my role is that of the shadow, his colourful sidekick. It's like we'd rather go on and create something that completely overwhelms people. I've seen people open-mouthed at some of our gigs, you know, completely agog so that when the number finishes they won't even clap. I'd rather that to the more vociferous reaction we're attracting now.[7]

In conversations with friends, Alex would talk fondly of the individuals in his new band. He saw Zal as an amazing guitarist who also happened to be a perfect comical sidekick on stage for him – the two feeding off each other. Chris – who had originally worked for two years as a quantity surveyor before graduating to music – was always described as the anchor of the band – the punk one and the pretty one. Alex used to tell reporters that he had plans to manage Chris and launch him in a new musical career as a teenybopper idol called Glenn Benson – a David Cassidy-style balladeer who would dress in ocelot suits and be the ultimate narcissist. Hugh was considered to be the brainiest and most talented musician of the group while Ted was praised for his intuitive understanding of the group and their music.

By 1972, with the pieces now in place and brimming with confidence, The Sensational Alex Harvey Band launched their assault on the record-buying public. Alex was at long last on the verge of the big time. Thanks to his new manager Bill Fehilly's contacts, the SAHB soon had a deal with Vertigo Records. For the next four years they worked flat out in a bid to reach the top. They toured almost constantly and released seven albums. The agenda was straightforward – commercial success as quickly as possible.

9

EVERYTHING IS COMING UP ROSES!

'I didn't come into the business to become rich but when this present band started it was conceived as a definite business proposition.'[1]
Alex Harvey

The decision to tie his future to Bill Fehilly was a wise one. Apart from Jimmy Grimes, Fehilly was probably Alex Harvey's oldest and dearest friend. A self-made millionaire, he had started as a housepainter in Coatbridge, Lanarkshire, before moving with his brother Dave to the northern town of Wick in Thurso. There they opened a café and dabbled in the fishmarket business. Bill maintained a base in the northern outpost and used to jokingly tell business associates in London who were seeking money from him that they would only get paid if they turned up in person in Wick – a mere 700 miles to the north!

Bill Fehilly had an uncanny and happy knack of making money in whatever venture he turned his hand to and he soon moved onto promoting artists like Big Bill

Broonzy. Even when he bought a couple of horses and started racing them they kept on winning despite the odds. He eventually built up a lucrative business empire, which included a string of bingo halls, racehorses, Mountain Management and Mountain Records. But to Alex he was much more than a businessman whom he could trust. He was one of the few people who held sway over Alex – he was his mentor.

Derek Wadsworth recalls:

Fehilly was a larger than life character. He was a millionaire who made his money from a chain of bingo halls. Alex told me that he used to do flyposting for Bill way back in the early days. Bill had said to Alex, 'I'm going to make you into a star' – and he did. He hyped Alex into a star, it was Bill's money that paid for it all. He put a guy called Derek Nicol in direct control of the band with instructions to make them stars.[2]

Derek Nicol was another Scot who had made his name in the frenetic music business of the 1960s. Straight out of school he ran the Stardust Club in his hometown of Rosyth in Fife and managed the quaintly named local band Mike Satan and the Hellcats – who featured a youthful Manny Charlton on lead guitar. Charlton went on to play in The Shadettes, which ultimately became successful as the hard-rock quartet Nazareth. During the 1960s, Nicol moved to Dundee and then on to Glasgow where he promoted a host of major touring bands when they headed north of the Border – including The Kinks, Deep Purple, The Who, The Troggs, Fleetwood Mac and Otis Redding. Around the turn of the decade, he headed for London and set up Mountain Management, concentrating on managing the SAHB and fellow Scots rockers Nazareth. In the following years he helped set up the Mountain group's recording and publishing arms.

Nicol told me how he and Fehilly set up Mountain:

At one time in the mid Sixties, Bill and I were promoting head to head in Stirling. I was running the Albert Hall on Friday night and he was running the Plaza Ballroom across the road. I was doing all the business on the Friday and he decided to get out of music and convert the Plaza to bingo. And he never looked back.

Around the end of 1969 Nazareth approached me, asking me to manage them. They presented me with this demo tape and about three weeks later I got this call out of the blue from Bill Fehilly – who was in Glasgow at the time. He said he wanted to have some fun again and get back into the music business. He had discovered a singer from Birmingham called Mike Alexander who did original Tom Jones-style songs and who eventually went on to become Shirley Bassey's MD and also did lots of TV work.

Mike was a bit middle of the road – so I said to Bill, 'What's happening now is this' – and I played him this reel-to-reel Nazareth demo tape. Bill said, 'Right, it sounds great – we'll do them both!' Next day, I'm on a plane to Birmingham to see Mike Alexander playing piano at the Embassy Club. Bill wanted me to move to Birmingham and set up a management company, but I said to do this seriously we have to move to London.

A week later I was in London on my own with a suitcase with this brief from Bill to set up a company. I was living in a Bayswater hotel and on the lookout for property. I found a three-bedroom apartment in Knightsbridge – and set up office there. It was my suggestion to call it Mountain Management. The choice of name maybe had something to do with Bill, who weighed about 20 stone! Our first signings were Nazareth and Mike Alexander. Armed with demo tapes I started going round the record companies.

Neither Bill nor I knew much about the London music business, apart from the agents. It was a case of let's meet everybody and anybody in the business and wine and dine them. We got turned down by just about every record label for the demo tape, so we just decided to do it ourselves, find a studio and make a record. It was as naïve as that.[3]

Both Fehilly and Nicol remembered Alex from his Soul Band days and decided to try and track him down in

London. They eventually found him strumming a rhythm guitar in a pick-up band at The Green Banana Club off Charing Cross Road. After a brief chat they decided to sign Alex up to Mountain and soon had him playing one-man shows in pubs and clubs like the Marquee and the Speakeasy. At these gigs, he was using a form of wah-wah foot pedal called the Tootle Bug Drone, which had been designed by Ashton Tootle who played in the *Hair* band. After the failed experiment with Ian Ellis and Dave Dufont backing him, Mountain agreed to Alex's request to bring Tear Gas down from Glasgow to London and The Sensational Alex Harvey Band was born.

Derek Nicol:

I knew of Tear Gas – they had been support to Deep Purple on Scottish tours I promoted. We decided that their old singer David Batchelor would be the SAHB sound engineer and road manager. We put all of Tear Gas, their wives, kids, dogs and cats into a house in London. It was almost like a commune.

I came up with the name 'Sensational' – it's one of those words that make the media go, 'So they're sensational? Sez who?' We got a logo designed for £15 and the group did all the showcase gigs like the Speakeasy and Marquee. We invited all the record companies and press along – by this time Mountain was getting a reputation, we knew a lot more people.

The way it worked was that the band was signed to Mountain. We made the records and licensed them to the Vertigo record company. We were actually delivering the product to them. We did two albums a year in those days.[4]

Alex was keen to encompass the business side of things to maximise the chances of success.

Years ago I just wanted to be in a dance band, but now you've got to come to terms with the businessmen and you've got to make a reasonable amount of money just to be able to keep a band on the road. The band is a business venture with businessmen running the top part of the show. It's just a question of

reaching a good balance between the two. But our management are also behind us musically. They're into the music and
that gives us a lot of confidence.[5]

Hugh McKenna agrees that Alex was keen to make a success of it and adds that he knew what the business could
do to musicians. Tellingly though, he doubts whether
– away from the brash quotes – Alex had much ability
in doing business with businessmen. As for the band,
Hugh adds: 'We were all just like daft musicians – we
didn't really have any interest in the business.'

Harvey rounded on his critics, who questioned whether a 37-year-old veteran who was 15 years older than his
fellow band members – let alone his fans – could make
any impact in the pop world. Nervous management lack-
eys actually wanted Alex to lie about his age, but they got
short shrift when any such suggestion was made. As an
enthusiastic Harvey told reporters:

I see myself as being really fortunate because I'm not hung up
on my own generation. I'm lucky because I can still understand
what young guys see in singers like Gary Glitter. It's just a
question of awareness. I have a son of 14 and I'm on his level.
I can relate to him and he can relate to me. He knows about
dope and sex because I've told him and we can laugh about the
same things together. I'm not hung up on the '50s, '60s or '70s
– I'm hung up on the '80s.[6]

Much of 1972 was spent gigging in London's rock clubs
and around the UK at places like the Caledonian Hotel, Inverness, and the Bellshill YMCA in Lanarkshire. The first
few weeks of December were especially gruelling, with the
group playing 15 concerts around Scotland and England.
The band was relying on word-of-mouth to build a small
loyal following. They got some additional bizarre publicity
on a promotional photo shoot in Glasgow during October

1972, when a man attracted by the free booze wandered into one of the photos. The picture was shown in the local *Evening Times* and immediately set off a massive police manhunt. A Mrs Harvey (no relation) had called the paper and the local police to say that she recognised the man as her long lost son!

Gigging at small venues was hard graft and was never going to bring the cash flowing in. Like many aspiring Scottish rock stars, Harvey and Tear Gas couldn't be choosy where they played and when. Good venues were thin on the ground, even in their native city of Glasgow. The Burns Howff in West Regent Street was one of only a couple of venues in the city centre that would allow in kids with long hair and wearing denim to hear live music. The venue had been opened in 1968 by local businessman John Waterson who has no qualms about now admitting that he paid performers a modest ten-pound note per show – irrespective of how many were in the group!

Waterson recalls:

I remember paying Billy Connolly and The Humblebums £2 a night – and I overpaid them! But at the Burns Howff, no matter how many were in the band, the wages were £10 a night. But part of the deal was that the groups got to rehearse in the Howff during the morning – instead of paying for studios. Also, I allowed them to play their own music, which was good because we never had problems with paying copyright.

The Howff started out with Top 20-type of bands, but that died a death. When we started with bands like Tear Gas, initially there were ten people there. The next week there would be 50 in the crowd and the following week it was packed. And it became an easy place for London agents to visit. They would phone me up and if I said there was a promising band playing they would just jump on a plane and fly up to Glasgow.[7]

The shrewd Waterson had recognised the potentially huge market of progressive music fans that wanted to see their heroes play live. The Howff became a Mecca for aspiring bands like Beggar's Opera, Tear Gas, Nazareth, and a useful outfit who lived up to their name of Power. The latter band – which featured Maggie Bell, Jimmy Dewar and Les Harvey – became like the resident house band at the Howff, playing four or five nights a week. They eventually evolved into the formidable Stone The Crows. Waterson knew that Alex Harvey and Tear Gas would make a powerful unit:

Tear Gas were pretty level-headed boys, they were switched on enough to know what a great front man Alex was. I don't think Tear Gas were the best band around but they were the most available at the time. Alex was shrewder than most people give him credit for, he was quite intellectual in his own way and knew he had this great ability. I've never seen a performer who put so much work into his rehearsal. If anything he worked harder in the rehearsal than he did during the actual concert.

The SAHB's intensive assault on the UK concert circuit soon began to pay dividends. And it wasn't just the fans who were taking notice. Bands who shared the bill with the new group were finding out how difficult it was to follow them. Gordon Sellar, who would play with Alex much later in his career, recalls how the band he once played bass in – Beggar's Opera – topped the bill above the SAHB at an Edinburgh University concert in 1972. Beggar's Opera were no slouches themselves, the Glasgow group recorded a number of critically acclaimed albums during the early 1970s and were a fair draw on the concert circuit. But, according to Gordon, when it came to the SAHB, there was no comparison:

It must have been one of the first gigs they ever did and we were absolutely knocked out by them – they were fantastic. We're thinking, Christ almighty, we are top of the bill here – what is going on? They were blowing the place apart. I remember they played the song 'Runaway' and thinking what a bizarre song to play. Alex just had an incredible stage presence. You weren't quite sure what he was going to do next. That manifested itself a lot later on.

As the SAHB shows developed, new spots were added, including the Highland pipers and a regular talent competition which would see Chris Glen – resplendent in his codpiece – doing ace Elvis impersonations. For his talent showcase, Zal tap-danced on a metal tray while reciting Hamlet. Hugh played the accordion! Besides being good fun, it was different to the run of the mill rock 'n' roll fare – and that was important to Alex. His reckoning was that anything was valid if it was going to sell. If some kid laughed at the talent show it might just also win him over to the music on offer. Hugh McKenna says the talent spots just grew out of an idea someone had suggested as the band sat around having a cigarette and a beer: 'Alex was very good at picking up on a chance remark – he would zone in on it and develop it.'

And in charge of all this organised chaos was Alex, who summed his own role up succinctly:

I see it like a movie and I'm the director, every night on stage we're making a movie and we're playing the soundtrack ... There's no such thing as an audience not being our crowd ... we're aiming at everybody ... we trigger each other off ...[8]

People close to the group saw that although Alex liked to hang out with the lads and play the rock 'n' roll game, he was always the boss. Besides being a director, Alex also saw himself as an actor on stage rather than just a straight singer. But he always clarified matters by saying that even though he was an actor playing a role he implicitly believed in what he was doing. For him the act was his take on life, it was his truth.

Confusingly, 1972 also saw the release of *The Joker Is Wild* album. It emerged out of some early London studio sessions Alex played with various musicians, including his brother Les and guitarist Mickey Keene in the late 1960s. Unfortunately, the record company bosses somehow envisioned Alex as a new Tom Jones or Engelbert Humperdink. At the time, Alex thought very little of the record and dismissively called it 'a heap of mush'. It was only released in Germany and subsequently made no impression on the record-buying public. But three years later, when Alex had at last become a success, it was re-released under the misleading title *This Is The Sensational Alex Harvey Band*. This led to some litigation, which Alex won.

The album, on the Metronome 2001 label, featured a couple of tracks penned by Alex including 'Penicillin Blues'. It also contained some interesting cover versions: Frank Zappa's 'Willie the Pimp'; a version of 'Hare Krishna' from the *Hair* show and a cover of 'He Ain't Heavy, He's My Brother', the Bob Russell and Bobby Scott song which became a massive worldwide hit for The Hollies.

The SAHB were eager to capture the energy they were generating on stage and to do it quickly. So, the recording of their first proper album *Framed* took only six days, with the band members taking care of production duties. The resultant nine-track album, released on Vertigo Records, was a strange mix. The title track and 'Midnight Moses' – written about an old schoolfriend of Alex's who only got up around the end of the day – were the standouts. Both songs dated back to the Soul Band days. 'There's No Lights ...' was first tried out by Giant

Moth and its inclusion here was a sign from Alex to rock fans that his band were not going to be straight boogie merchants.

The album's final track, 'St Anthony', told the story of a hermit who was tormented by a woman as a test of faith. The lyrics were based very loosely on the painting 'Temptation of St Anthony' by the 15th-century artist Hieronymus Bosch. Overall, *Framed* was an eclectic mix of songs and the album cover also featured a superb photograph by Jim Wilson showing the band sharing some cheap booze with winos in a slum area of Glasgow. Behind them daubed on a wall was the city's motto 'Let Glasgow Flourish!'

In a similar way to the debut albums by bands as diverse as Led Zeppelin and The Damned, there's a certain exuberance and energy about *Framed* that makes it near impossible to dislike the record. Many of the songs had been kicking around in Alex's head for nearly a decade and the sheer delight he must have felt finally to get them down on vinyl with a band which could do the songs justice is reflected in the feel of the album. The rushed nature of the recording is evident in the fact that none of the SAHB guys get a writing credit on any of the songs – in particular Alex's fruitful writing partnership with Hugh McKenna was yet to surface.

Even if the production is a bit lame, with some vocals too far down the mix, the band still sounds live and dangerous. There's also an undoubted happy vibe to the record – finally after all the years of disappointment things were falling into place. For Alex, it was a relief to get the songs out of his system and now he could move on to experiment with the other ideas he had. When he sings in 'Midnight Moses' that everything he touches is coming up roses you get the feeling that he really means it.

Sadly, the record-buying public weren't quite ready for it all and, despite some encouraging potential-noting reviews, the album failed to make the chart. 'There's No Lights ...' also couldn't make an impression when it was released in an ambitious bid to win the coveted Christmas number one spot. Even Alex himself seemed to admit that the album was a letdown:

The last album was a disappointment to me, at least that's the way I see it now. I know there was a lot of depth and feeling put into the songs but it didn't show because it wasn't produced properly ... but I just wanted to get the songs we had down on record. Just the fact that they were on record was enough – it was a relief to get them down. The next album will be much better presented in every way – it has to be.

We need a hit single. Something that everybody hears and likes right away, something that the BBC won't hesitate to play and that's the next hurdle – we've really got to get into that position.[9]

Interestingly, Zal Cleminson now holds a different view from his old gaffer. In the recent radio series *Vambo Rools OK?* he said the album was one of the best things they had ever done.

The song 'Framed' was now being used as an encore on the live shows alongside pumped-up versions of Martha Reeves and the Vandellas' 'Dancing in the Street' and Sly Stone's 'Dance to the Music'. The gruelling touring schedule continued, and Alex obviously wanted to take the music to as wide a public as possible. In May 1973, *Sounds* reported a gig at Stenhouse Young Offenders Institute in Edinburgh. The concert took place in front of 175 inmates in the Institute's assembly hall. Faced by an audience of youngsters – many of whom probably hailed from Gorbals-type housing schemes – Alex knew he had to put on a top performance. He later told

Sounds that he had never been more nervous in his career. Initially the kids were hostile and during one lengthy break between songs a heckler shouted that he would probably be released from jail before the set was finished!

Eventually Alex won them over and even felt confident enough to lecture the crowd on how they had the power to succeed in life but 'you've just got to be cool about it.' When he invited an inmate called Big Dino up onstage to sing Slade's 'Cum on Feel the Noize' the place went into raptures. Noting their unusual surroundings, the SAHB threw all they had into 'Framed' and 'Runaway'. For Alex, the night was a real treat:

I really fancy the communication thing and I wanted to play places where they don't usually get anybody ... I grew up with a lot of kids like that, they're no worse than anyone else ... and if things do not go right you can find yourself in a place like that ... They gave us incredible vibes, I felt like bursting into tears.

Bizarrely, Alex concluded by saying that next he wanted to play to an audience of apes, chimps and gorillas – just to prove they react to a basic musical beat!

*

Derek Nicol estimates that Bill Fehilly ploughed in the modern-day equivalent of a couple of a million pounds in trying to make Mountain a success – with very little coming back in return during the early days:

There was just small droppings of income coming in initially. And gradually once the deals were done more money would come into the pot. But the outgoings to start with, to run the band, were colossal. The company was all Bill's funding – but I ran it. Bill would come down every now and again. It was two years down the line before we had the first hit records – Nazareth's 'Broken Down Angel' and their album *Razzamanazz*. A lot of the company money was ploughed into Nazareth – they had toured most of Europe and around America, all of which cost money, before they had any hits.

Before the hits started, the debts had built up and Bill was ready to give it up. He was in it for the buzz, we all were, but it was hard work – 24 hours a day. We lived and breathed the music business. I could feel that it was about to happen on the road, and that we just needed another three months. SAHB hadn't broken yet but the audiences were very positive. The communication between Alex and audiences was just magical.[10]

10

NEXT

'I don't want to spend the rest of my life
with people throwing things at me on the
stage. But I can understand it.'[1]
Alex Harvey

The SAHB were maturing into an assured live band and
when the chance came to support Slade on a three-week
tour of Great Britain in the summer of 1973 it looked
like a great opportunity. At the time, the Wolverhampton band was just about at the pinnacle of their career
with four number ones already under their belt. They
wanted a support act who would put a bit of life into the
expectant crowd and would warm the fans up nicely for
the main attraction. With the SAHB they got exactly that
– and a little bit more! Some groups had already balked
at the opportunity to support Slade, but Harvey thought
he had nothing to lose so he accepted the challenge.

The tour meant playing to guaranteed full houses, but
it also meant that 99 per cent of the crowd were in no

mood to sit and watch the SAHB. The upshot was nights of vitriolic abuse from the majority of the audience – often the band played as coins and bottles rained down on them. In response Alex stood his ground, at times he even shouted abuse back at the crowd or squirted them with a water pistol. He understood that even young rock music fans were conservative by nature when it came to the way a concert should be staged. They believed that rock 'n' roll had a strict set of rules that were to be adhered to. SAHB tore up that rulebook and were bound to get abuse in return.

Alex later said it felt like the crowds were acting like football fans that get upset when the opposition played well. He thought the hostile reaction would help to toughen up his band, and he boasted that no other group would have had the guts to take up the challenge:

The stick they gave us, we gave it back to them. I mean I love the kids, anybody who goes to the extent of getting a top hat and writing Slade on it, they are my brothers. We thought it was a good idea – we had nothing to lose. We knew there would be no quarter given or asked, we knew we could not fold up early ... no changes to the set, no compromise. But it's not hard-core premeditated viciousness ... maybe they think that we are a bunch of upstarts, coming on and doing that.[2]

In another interview he said:

After that I don't think there's anything we could not take on. On some of the gigs we got crucified and it was the kind of reaction we could feed off. It was positive, which was better than having nothing at all happen. At one place Mel the promoter – who's a nervous kind of guy – was getting worried because we were not going down well towards the end of the set and I was up there squirting a water pistol at the front row – getting them real mad. The reaction that sort of thing got from the crowd was electric and it was perfect for us because it was real emotion. Slade are an amazingly effective act. Noddy Holder could be one of the most powerful trade union leaders in the country if he felt like it.³

Amid all the flying bottles and insults, Alex nearly always managed to maintain his sense of humour. He would invariably end the set by telling the unruly audience: 'After our show, boys and girls, we're bringing on four young boys from Wolverhampton and I hope you give them a good reception!'

In return, Slade took to Alex and the SAHB and the English band still remember him fondly. The two groups were from similar working-class backgrounds and hit it off well. In fact, way back when the Wolverhampton lads were known as The In-betweens they had shared the bill with the McKenna cousins' first band Rare Breed at concerts in Arran. Slade's lead singer, Noddy Holder, told a BBC radio documentary how much he admired the SAHB's attitude:

They took the audience on ... they played superb stuff but it was very very off the wall ... they were doing a very theatrical act – the songs weren't just heads down no-nonsense boogie ... He'd bring a metal chair on stage and smash it to bits and people would wonder 'why is he doing this?' ... if they were watching the show and listening to the lyrics they would have understood.⁴

SAHB felt even more justified about going on tour with Slade when they started doing headline gigs themselves shortly afterwards. Many of the kids who had booed them before were now turning up to see them play live.

Alex wasn't the only star to get rough treatment from Slade fans. Thin Lizzy were also given a tough time when they had the ill-fortune to support the Wolverhampton band. If anything, the abuse Lizzy received was even worse – their lead singer Phil Lynott had a barrage of racist abuse hurled at him while he tried to entertain the unruly fans.

The SAHB got another rough ride – with abuse and bottles hurled at them – when they supported the heavy metal band Uriah Heep at the Alexandra Palace during the London Music Festival on 5 August 1973. Heep were topping a bill that also included the Heavy Metal Kids, Gary Moore and Manfred Mann's Earthband. It was billed as the biggest indoor rock festival ever staged, with tickets priced at £2 and fans having the choice of five bars and three restaurants. But a group of German headbangers in the crowd apparently took particular exception to the introduction of an old Jack Teagarden type-number in the SAHB's set and the missiles soon rained down on stage.

Alex just smiled as mayhem broke out all around him. Again he realised that such an extreme reaction was better than no response at all. Derek Nicol recalled how the Palace stage was littered with beer cups and bottles and the group had to leave the stage to a chorus of abuse. Derek mischievously suggested to Alex that an encore was called for. Alex responded by saying 'fuckin' right' and turned on his heel, bravely leading the band back on. Promoter Ricky Farr remonstrated with the crowd, saying the only other band that he had seen receive such a reception at the start of their career was Led Zeppelin, arguing that they hadn't done too badly since. Slowly the audience was won over and a wave of applause swept through the crowd.

One of the audience that night was Steve Toal who was at the time a 17-year-old SAHB fan from Scarborough in Yorkshire. Steve made the 240-mile trip to see his idols and to this day he is convinced that the SAHB's choice of opening song that night was like a red rag to a bull:

Alex was on just before Uriah Heep, but there had been major delays all day, with all the bands coming on late. So that by the time Alex was due on, the crowd were very impatient for the Heep to start and whoever was on next would have struggled to quell the unrest.

Not many people in the audience had heard of Alex and, probably because of the stage costumes, the crowd assumed they were some kind of glam-rock outfit and they started booing straight away. The atmosphere was not then helped, when the band opened up with a version of The Osmonds' hit 'Crazy Horses', this just reaffirmed the crowd's initial thoughts.

Looking back, I am sure this was a deliberate ploy on Alex's part to get some kind of reaction; he succeeded rather more than I expect he anticipated! The plastic beer containers then started flying and people all around us started to hurl as much abuse as possible and they set up a chant for the Heep to come on.

I remember Alex struggling to win over the crowd – though he seemed to be enjoying the whole thing. But this proved impossible and in the end they were forced to cut their set short in view of the danger they were in.

This was the first time I had seen the band and, although I initially wondered why they chose to start with 'Crazy Horses', on the way home I appreciated the irony of the choice. Looking back (possibly cynically with growing old) I think Alex encouraged the controversy for publicity reasons as certainly this one gig raised his profile in the press. I think he needed the 'edge'. Whenever you saw Alex live, you just did not know what was going to happen next and this is what is missing from music nowadays.[5]

Alex knew that things were falling into place when the band stole the show at the 1973 Reading Festival. The group interrupted rehearsals for the second album to appear at the show. Even though they were way down the bill, which was headed by Genesis, the SAHB gave what was unquestionably the best performance of the day. According to *NME*, 30,000 fans gave the SAHB an ecstatic reception as the sun set on the horizon, raising their arms aloft in response to Alex. The review in *Sounds* said:

Alex Harvey was as lethal as ever, whipping the crowd up into a state of frenzy. Zal Cleminson looked menacing, like he'd just escaped from a freak show, his face grimacing, as if he was suffering some unbelievable torture as he squeezed the notes out.

Hugh McKenna has fond memories of the triumph at Reading:

We always got a good reception at these big festivals and that was an amazing gig. Something magical happened there. We opened up with 'Faith Healer', which we had only written the week before, it hadn't even been recorded yet. And Alex put his arms up in the V-sign, saying 'Let me put my hands on you.' I remember the sun was just going down and Zal whispered across to me, 'Start it, start it!' I remember thinking this is going to be no ordinary gig – there was something in the air. It was absolutely amazing – we blew everybody off the stage. That gig was really, really special – it moved the band up an echelon. The band started to arrive that day.[6]

Music magazine *Disc* also praised the group's performance at another open-air event, the Buxton Festival in July, saying they were the only genuine triumph of the entire day's proceedings. Alex kept the crowd entertained as he stalked around the stage in a pair of three-inch crepe brothel-creepers.

Never one to hide his light under a bushel when a reporter was around, Alex had no qualms about telling the general public about just how good the band were. Without even a trace of conceit, he told a Belgian radio station:

I should imagine that there are very few bands in the world at present who are as good as mine ... that might sound egoistical [sic] but it's not. It's just a cool evaluation 'cos I see a lot of bands. I think we can be sensational, we've got lots of tricks, a complete new act lined up – different ways of presenting it ...

The band can do a lot of amazing things that we haven't even touched on yet.[7]

The Belgian radio interview was one of a series carried out by English DJ Tony Hadland. Between 1972 and 1974 he spoke to a wide variety of artists from Cliff Richard to Led Zeppelin and Roxy Music. The resultant interviews were broadcast on the Belgian equivalent of the BBC. When he spoke to Alex after a show at Reading Town Hall, he immediately noticed a difference between him and the other, younger stars he had met:

The thing that struck me particularly about Alex was his gravitas. This was not a young man having a bit of fun before settling down to a conventional life. His music was his life and he was fully engaged with it. He came across as very self-confident but with solid foundations for that confidence. There was little sign of the superficiality that one finds with many rock stars.[8]

Work on the second album – which was originally going to be called *I Was A Teenage Idol* – had begun early in August 1973 – with release due in November. Promotional work included recording two concerts for BBC's *Sounds of the Seventies* along with sets on Scottish and German TV. In early October 1973 the group did a series of one-off gigs in the UK, topping the bill at unglamorous venues like Doncaster College of Education, Gravesend Civic Club and the slightly more promising-sounding Penthouse Club in Scarborough. Steve Toal – who had been at the Alexandra Palace debacle – was delighted to see his heroes play in his hometown club on 12 October:

The main thing I remember was that Alex treated this gig as if he was playing to 3,000, rather than the 300 who were there. He put on a full show even though the stage was no bigger than a pub back room. Alex used the huge torchlight to light up the club so no one could hide! No one dared go for a slash![9]

Later that month, the band also travelled abroad, opening for Status Quo on a short German tour and playing nine major cities starting with Helsinki.

But the concert circuit grind was beginning to take its toll, and following the European jaunt, Hugh McKenna was admitted to hospital suffering from nervous exhaustion. John Martin, who played with Marsha Hunt's band, filled in while the keyboard man recovered. The band was discovering that Alex could be a tough taskmaster who pushed them hard to get the desired results.

In September, the album – now to be known as *Next* – was given an early airing at a concert at the London Marquee. *NME* reported that the band got a near hysterical reaction from a mass of crazed youth, most of whom seemed to be exiled Scots. Next month, *NME*'s Roy Carr gave an enthusiastic review to the new single – a ballistic cover version of 'Giddy Up A Ding-Dong' – the old Freddie Bell rabble-rouser which had been a hit back in 1956. Carr concluded that the cover version was 'nothing less than sensational!'

On 8 November, a day before the album was released, the band started their first headline UK tour with Beckett in support on the 32 dates. It was an incredibly demanding tour – a really concerted effort to break the band to the mass market. An extra show, at the Hippodrome on 10 November, was recorded for the BBC's *In Concert* series. Some 25 years later, in 1998, five of the tracks recorded that night were released on the New Millennium Communication label as part of *The Gospel According to Harvey* double CD. The band sounds to be on top form, with Zal in particular at his most menacing

Alex as a child (far right), with his grandfather,
father and brother Les, July 1946

Alex, aged three, Dunoon,
August 1938

Alex on banjo (left), brother Les (front) and Charlie Carsware, c. 1955

Alex and the Soul Band drinking milk (left to right): Bill Patrick, Bobby Nimmo, 'General' Jimmy Grimes, Alex, Bobby Rankine and George McGowan

Alex and Les onstage during the Soul Band era

Alex with Tommy Steele

Alex and Trudy at their wedding

Les Harvey plays electric guitar at home

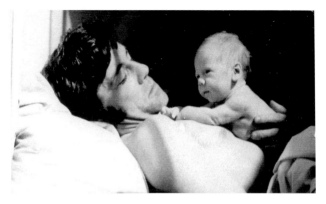

Alex with son Tyro

Alex with snake charmer

Trudy Harvey with Alex's long-time friend and band manager Bill Fehilly

Alex, Tyro, Trudy and Alex Jnr take a family outing during the *Hair* era

Alex revisits the site of his childhood home in the Gorbals, now demolished

The Sensational Alex Harvey Band (left to right): Chris Glen, Alex Harvey and
Zal Cleminson

The Sensational Alex
Harvey Band:
Chris Glen (left), Ted
McKenna (top), Alex
(middle), Hugh McKenna
(bottom) and Zal Cleminson
(right)

Alex on stage, 1980

Ian Dury and Alex

Trudy, Tom Robinson and Alex

Alex, 1980

Alex rehearses with the Electric Cowboys at the Rainbow Studios, 1981, shortly before his death

on 'Midnight Moses'. (The 1998 CD also features five songs recorded live in front of a somewhat restrained audience at the Paris Theatre in December of 1972 and the SAHB's performance at the Reading Festival in August 1977.)

Alex knew that the new album had to be more commercial, so he had drafted in producer Phil Wainman – who had done so much to help The Sweet storm the UK charts. Alex thought that Wainman 'grasped' what the SAHB were all about. He was probably correct in his estimation – while some may gripe at the bass and drum sound, it's undeniable that Wainman brought a new sense of discipline to the SAHB studio.

On 24 November, *Sounds'* influential critic Pete Erskine was almost ecstatic in his praise of the new album, describing it as:

One of the best, most wicked, most intensely aggressive albums I've heard all year. Thank Christ somebody is doing something a little unusual … with depth, tremendous style and the balls of a rampant rhino – if the SAHB aren't colossal next year, I'll eat my Y-fronts.

NME thought it was a solid album and praised the 'gorgeous' guitar and drums. Certainly it still sounds pretty fresh today. The title track with its tales of depravity and imaginative use of a string quartet is a stand out. Lyrics about brothels and sexually-transmitted diseases would infuriate the parents of many young SAHB fans, but Alex's singing never sounded better and he dominates the song with complete confidence. He used to introduce the number on stage by telling the audience that it was 'a tango – the type your mother and me used to do together'! Recording a song by the relatively obscure Flemish songwriter Jacques Brel was a badge of honour for Alex. It totally summed up his desire to approach rock 'n' roll from a new direction and move away from the narrow confines of straight riff-based rock. He was also proud of the fact that he had been the first rock performer to notice Brel's talents. In the interview on Belgium radio in 1974, Alex was reminded that both Scott Walker and David Bowie had also used Brel songs. Alex defiantly replied, 'Yeah, Bowie does "Amsterdam" – but I was the first. I was before Bowie or any of them. I've done Brel songs for eight years now.'[10]

The totally debauched Mardi Gras sound of 'Gang Bang' certainly dates back to an era before political correctness. God only knows how the lyrics influenced less cerebral male listeners. But in the sleeve notes of the post-SAHB compilation *Big Hits and Close Shaves*, Alex set the record straight, telling listeners not to believe a word of the lyrics, which he said were no more than rubbish, adding, 'There's no glory in rape, you must protect your little sisters.'

The one other outstanding track was 'Faith Healer'. With its pulsing intro and killer riff, the song has a dark quality as Alex half-speaks and half-sings the lyrics. As an added treat, the album also contained 'Vambo Marble Eye' which introduced us to the legend of Vambo and featured some nice wah-wah and solo guitar work from Zal. Alex's widow Trudy believes that the character Vambo was derived from the childish talk of their young son Tyro. Variously described as a cross between Santa Claus and Captain Marvel, Vambo is no vandal. Instead, Alex saw him as a streetwise punk who knew that the streets belonged to people like him and as such they had to be looked after. In his spare time, Vambo came to the rescue of those in peril. The character was based on Alex's adolescent years on the mean streets of Glasgow.

The *Next* sessions were the first time that Alex and Hugh McKenna worked together as a songwriting team. It was to be the start of a productive if sometimes difficult partnership – both guys were prone to drinking too heavily and Hugh freely admits to having psychological problems during and after the SAHB years. Hugh – who was eventually to get credits on 59 Harvey songs – says the partnership began when Alex heard him messing about at the piano, on a piece that would eventually surface as part of the song 'Anthem' on *The Impossible Dream*. Alex immediately latched on to the haunting theme, saying it would sound even better played on bagpipes. It was an example of his lateral thinking when it came to music and was the type of idea that would never have occurred to Hugh, who recalls:

The first actual whole song we wrote together was 'Swampsnake'. Alex just read out the lyric to me and we just developed it from there. He always had the entire lyric – the only song that he did that was entirely written by another member of the band was 'Sirocco' – which I wrote on guitar. He did try to change that song too – but eventually he decided that it worked perfectly as it was. That was something about Alex, he would take something that was good to start off with but always try and make it better.

After 'Swampsnake' we wrote 'Faith Healer'. He would read me the lyric and ask what it suggested to me and I would play whatever. I enjoyed writing with him and the freedom it offered. Alex once said to my father, when he met him first at a reception, that 'Hugh is exactly what I've been looking for'. I think it was because I had this very unusual musical background. I had an A-level in music and I also had experience in different kinds of music – I could play little classical things at rehearsal but I had served my rock and pop apprenticeship.[11]

Surprisingly, *Next* failed to sell well and only became a hit album two years later when – at the height of SAHB popularity – sales were given fresh impetus and it entered the album charts in August 1975, reaching number 37. It's an album that still garners respect from those in the know. When *The Scotsman* decided to rank the greatest 100 rock 'n' roll records to come out of Scotland they placed *Next* at number 16 (Primal Scream's *Screamadelia* taking the top slot).

The band closed a successful 1973 with their first appearance in the BBC's *Old Grey Whistle Test* studio on 18 December. At the time, it was the only outlet on British TV for a 'serious' rock band that wanted to reach a wider audience. The band played 'Next' and 'Faith Healer', before having a quick chat with the show's compere, 'Whispering' Bob Harris. The year had been a qualified success and the influential *Sounds* predicted that things could only get better for Alex – whom they playfully labelled the 'biggest anarchist in British rock music'.

11

LIVING THE IMPOSSIBLE DREAM

*'I should imagine that there are very few
bands in the world at present who are as
good as mine.'*[1]
Alex Harvey

In the days before mass media and MTV, the weekly British music papers were vitally important for bands trying to make the big time. Circulation figures for papers like *Melody Maker* and *Sounds* were impressive, and praise from the right music journalist could almost guarantee high record sales and sold-out concerts. Music critics like Nick Kent and Charles Shaar Murray of *NME* almost became celebrities in their own right as they made or destroyed the careers of hopeful acts. The SAHB were fortunate because they invariably got a good press from writers who were eager to praise any act that broke with the boring stereotypes of the time. Charles Shaar Murray in particular became a dedicated fan of the band and devoted fulsome praise to them at every available opportunity throughout the 1970s. (Murray was a good friend of the Harveys, and Trudy attended his wedding in May 1976.)

Murray was present at the band's showcase St Valentine's Rock Ball 1974 at London's Empire Leicester Square – which rather confusingly was held on 11 February. The concert was an event in itself, with DJs Tommy Vance and Jerry Floyd compering at the grand old ballroom, and celebrities Lulu, Marsha Hunt and Maggie Bell were among the audience. Fans were invited to come along in eveningwear or fancy dress – with £50 going to the best costume. Tickets for the spectacular – which went on until midnight – were only £1.

With The Troggs in support, the SAHB were on top form. By now, crowds were getting used to the idea of a show which fused rock and cabaret, and also to the idea of Alex sauntering on stage and saying, 'Good evening, ladies and gentlemen, my name is Alex,' before introducing the band who would then launch into 'Faith Healer'. After a couple of years of conflict and confrontation with audiences, the band was now getting respect.

Harvey had spent the winter months working on jazzing up the stage act, with the emphasis now to be on new songs, visuals and costumes. During the show, Alex punched his way through the imitation brick wall during 'Framed' before munching on the material. The crowd were taken aback by the use of a string quartet, especially as it was largely inaudible, but the most vocal reaction of the night came when Alex's attractive wife Trudy appeared on stage dressed as a St Trinians schoolgirl in suspenders and pigtails during the song 'Gang Bang'. Ushered on stage by Bill Fehilly, Trudy sat on her husband's knee while he tore off her stockings! At one stage, Alex brought out a young lad with a Bowie-style hair cut and Zal make-up on stage. The star told the crowd that the boy – introduced as Mark Oliver – had hitched 240 miles to see the concert. It was the type of devotion that Alex Harvey really admired.

Another influential critic was the laconic Radio 1 DJ John Peel, who wrote a weekly singles review column for *Sounds* during the mid 1970s. Never a total convert to the SAHB cause, Peel nevertheless gave the new single 'Faith Healer' a positive review when it was released later in February. Peel thought the song was crammed with devious sound effects and concluded that it would be nice to see such weirdness in the charts.

The full-scale assault on the record-buying public continued with a massive 23-date headline UK tour starting at Leeds Town Hall on 9 May and climaxing almost a month later with a show topping the bill at the London Rainbow. Prices for most of the UK gigs ranged from 80 pence to £1 and support was provided by Strider, a short-lived English hard-rock outfit who released two albums in the mid 1970s. At one of the gigs, the SAHB had to improvise when sound problems at the Liverpool Stadium meant an encore looked impossible. With the capacity crowd already in ferment and demanding more, Alex treated them to an exquisite acoustic blues set to round off the night. Two days later – on 13 May – Alex made the arduous trip back to the Swansea Top Rank. Not surprisingly, he was overcome with grief at visiting the hall where his brother Les had died two years previously. Underneath the aggressive, menacing exterior, Alex was a sensitive individual and revisiting the hall was a traumatic experience.

The Rainbow concert was the first chance for the band to top the bill at the prestigious venue. Initially they were nervous and the audience seemed reticent to join in the chorus of songs like 'Can't Get Enough'. Alex seemed

more edgy than anyone and over-indulged his trademark lectures to the fans in-between songs. The flat atmosphere eventually picked up and the band finally won
two deserved encores. *NME* said it had been – in places –
the most exciting concert of the year, adding that 'SAHB
are the most perfect fusion of theatrics and rock that this
country possesses'. After a couple of gigs at Southend
and Norwich the band moved onto Scandinavia, France
and Germany.

Prior to all that, the SAHB had entered the studios in
mid March to start work on their third album, which was
given the working title, *Can't Get Enough*. The original
plan was for Phil Wainman to carry on with the production work but when he couldn't fit it into his schedule the
group opted for Shel Talmy, the American producer who
had done sterling work with The Kinks and The Who. In
the event the audacious move turned out to be a disappointment and amazingly the decision was made to bin
all of the first recordings and the band called on ex-Tear
Gas singer Dave Batchelor to take over. Batchelor was
well respected by the group and had already being doing the stage sound chores for them. In the event the
gamble paid off and Batchelor captured the dynamics
of the group perfectly. But the long delay caused by the
re-recording meant that some impetus was lost to the
SAHB bandwagon.

All in all, the SAHB were proving to be a welcome break
from the norm in the stale music scene which was domi-
nated by out-of-touch tax exiles who treated their audiences with disdain, seldom bothering to tour or release
new records. Alex suggested that conservative record
companies were also partly to blame for the malaise:

One of the reasons for the stagnancy is that if you are going to make a hit record, the record company says you have got to do something that's up-tempo and it's got to move and it's got to have a chorus and it's got to consist of these words and it's got to have 'baby' in it – so that for a start restricts and flattens ... I'm only saying that because we are not in the charts![2]

The critics were invited along to the Leeds City Hall gig and were united in their praise. In *Sounds*, Simon Orrel said the band had an immense talent and had matured since their visit to Yorkshire in 1973 where he considered that they shocked a bopper audience with their 'bizarre, over-suggestive and at times degrading act'. Orrel was particularly taken by the 'extraordinary' Zal. The critic thought that Cleminson would have been working in horror films if he wasn't such a capable guitarist. Also at the Leeds gig was Charles Shaar Murray who wondered at Alex – the demonic circus ringmaster: 'His lips peel back over his teeth in such a way that you are never quite sure whether he's going to laugh at your joke or pass a knife through your ribs.'

On 26 May, the band checked into the Glasgow Apollo and was given a rapturous reception by the 3,500-capacity crowd. The next day, Alex, obviously still buzzing from the crowd reaction, told the *Scottish Daily Record*:

We called it sensational because we believe we are the best band in the world. We are into showbusiness, we are not so much a stage act but a movie. Every take is different ... that way we keep our music fresh. We've never had a hit but when we go to America this year we will insist on the red carpet at the airport.

The SAHB fan club was expanding fast and next to sing their praises was Mott the Hoople's Ian Hunter. Writing in *Sounds* in July, he said the SAHB's new single 'Sgt Fury' was incredible.

One sure way of achieving maximum exposure was to get on the bill of one of the massive open-air festivals, which were so much in vogue during the 1970s. In 1974, the SAHB struck lucky when they appeared at the first ever Knebworth Festival in Hertfordshire. Promoter Freddie Bannister had pulled together some of the hippest bands of the time for what was dubbed 'The Bucolic Frolic' on 20 July. A £2.75 ticket bought fans the privilege of listening to Tim Buckley, John McLaughlin and his Mahavishnu Orchestra, The Doobie Brothers, Van Morrison and The Allman Brothers through a 25,000-watt sound system. As a sign of their growing reputation, the SAHB were the only British-based band, aside from Van Morrison, on the star-studded bill. Interestingly, Alex and the rest of the group were especially delighted to share the bill with the avant-garde jazz guitarist McLaughlin whom they thought was the latest breakthrough in contemporary rock.

The SAHB were second-bottom of the bill and followed Tim Buckley on stage, but they still managed to eventually get a delirious response from the 60,000 crowd. The hour-long set started with 'Faith Healer', 'Midnight Moses' and 'Can't Get Enough' before the band played their new single 'Sgt Fury', which was released on the same day as the festival. Alex playfully told the crowd that the event was actually being staged to tie in with the single's launch! With the audience now on his side and confidence coursing through his veins, Alex strutted about the stage in a black frock coat, jeans and jock strap, flexing a teacher's cane while wearing a stocking mask over his face.

Next up was another song from the new album, 'The Return of Vambo', followed by 'The Man in the Jar', 'Money Honey', 'The Impossible Dream' and 'Dance to the Music'. During parts of the show, the crowd seemed to be relaxing too much in the summer sun for Alex's liking and he yelled at them: 'Will you get your asses off the ground? You gotta make some sort of movement, you're getting stagnant, don't be stagnant. C'mon, even if you slide your ass across the grass. C'mon, we want to tell if you're alive – make some movement!' Other stand-out songs were 'Framed' and 'Anthem' – during which the audience responded by waving hundreds of flags and banners in unison.

The music press loved the performance – *NME* called it a magnificent show. But the festival compere John Peel was one of the few present who was less than impressed. Later he reflected that it was:

impossible to feel indifferent to the SAHB. What little I saw of their set at Knebworth I found mildly embarrassing. That they have a real ability seemed clouded by all the theatrics. However it's those same theatrics that have some critics with A-levels writing about 'street-rock' and mentioning in passing several central European philosophers and their probable thoughts on the matter. I remain uncommitted.[3]

The general good vibe of the dope-soaked event was tested to the limit by an incident backstage when the Doobie Brothers apparently demanded the right to change in the Alex Harvey caravan. Alex allegedly told the organisers to 'tell the Doobies that if they want to get their hands on this caravan then they may come and fight us wi' knives'. Not surprisingly, the offer wasn't taken up by the Americans.

Although he generally felt a bit frustrated by the laid-back nature of these outdoor events, Alex was back at the Reading Festival for the second year running in August 1974. The only difference this time was that the SAHB were topping the bill on Friday night. Again, the crowd, who had paid £2 to get onto the site – and who had been warmed up by bands like Hustler, 10cc and Camel – loved the SAHB set which ended with pipers in kilts playing 'Anthem'. Critics said that the Scots seemed to be in their element playing in the miserable wet weather.

In *NME*, Pete Erskine thought the show was pretty amazing and added that Alex was 'teetering on the razor edge between real emotion and jive, the show gets more manic by the week ... Alex Harvey has this whole pack of dramatis personae all based around the same character.' *Sounds* critic Steve Peacock was more restrained and commented that he felt like a spectator at some curious ritual.

Gigs in Germany followed during the autumn – but one concert in the town of Heidelberg was marred by audience violence. Alex met the problem head-on and started aping the crowd by smashing up the stage. But the stunt backfired when his hand was sliced open by a bit of wood. There was blood everywhere and Alex required stitches before the tour could continue.

A 13-date tour of the UK in October – supported by a band named Slack Alice – included the prestige gig headlining on Sunday night at the London Palladium. Having spent years supporting the likes of veteran Scots comedian Jimmy Logan at similar venues, Alex must have enjoyed the feeling of finally being the top of the bill. At York University on 12 October the nervous MC told fans that they were banned from standing up or leaving their seats during the show! He backed up the statement by threatening that if anyone disobeyed, the gig was off! The result was perhaps the most restrained SAHB gig ever.

Confirmation that Alex Harvey had finally made the big time came when the new album charted on its release. After almost 20 years in the business, he had finally got himself a hit record in the UK. Recorded at the legendary Abbey Road studios, *The Impossible Dream* eventually peaked at number 16 in the Top 30 album charts, but only stuck around for four weeks.

The title of the record was telling – the songs on the album represented many of Alex's fantasies and dreams. Reviews were almost all positive and Charles Shaar Murray said the album was the first rock 'n' roll comic book, adding that it was:

populated with thumbnail sketch characterisations, splashy musical primary colours and peculiar verbal shorthand. *The Impossible Dream* validates the trash aesthetic with triumphant ease ... one mo-fo of a rock 'n' roll album ... make no mistake about it they are a first division band even though not enough people have sussed it ... [it] should bring a lot of innocent pleasure into your dull and tedious lives.[4]

Pete Makowski in *Sounds* was slightly more cautious, but he too recognised that the album caught the full dynamics and insanity of the group. Indeed, the album, which had a cartoon Sgt Rock (aka Alex) on the cover, still sounds mighty impressive today.

The standout track was – and still is – 'Sgt Fury', an engaging, amusing mix of 1930s dance band and vaudevillian jump rhythm, which was arranged by Alex's old pal from the *Hair* days, Derek Wadsworth. The number didn't have any deep significance or meaning – it was just an exuberant homage to the song and dance era. It should have been a number one but when it was released as a single, it somehow managed to miss the charts completely. Despite Alex imploring 'I wanna be rich and famous' in the chorus, the single-buying public refused to help him along the way.

The other instant classic was 'Man in the Jar', part of the introductory 'Hot City Symphony'. This was a bizarre parody of the Mickey Spillane pulp fiction crime novels with Alex adopting a weird mid-Atlantic accent as he narrates the tale of a man who feels he is a failure and wants to smash his way out of the glass cage that surrounds him. It ends with an epic brass finale. The other part of the 'symphony' is 'Vambo' – full of weird Pidgin English phrases and phonetic spellings, it was a reflection of the way kids in Glasgow spraypainted the walls.

Another excellent song, 'The Tomahawk Kid' was apparently recorded in an hour and emerged after a lengthy jam session. It soon became a concert favourite with its perverse retelling of Robert Louis Stevenson's *Treasure Island* myth. Throughout the album, the band provides mature back-up to Alex. Zal in particular plays some incendiary riffs, most notably on 'Long Hair Music', which had originally been titled 'Can't Get Enough'. The haunting, moody 'Anthem' closes the album and some of the Mountain team thought that its strongly nationalistic feel would appeal to the Anglo-Scot Rod Stewart – who at the time was looking for a follow-up to his number one hit 'Sailing'. Sadly the idea never got off the ground, but for Alex this was just a minor setback. Everything else seemed to be going nicely to plan.

12

TOO MUCH AMERICAN PIE

'He's bizarre and crazy, one great rock 'n'
roller. When America gets a taste of him they
will flip. He's paid his dues and is ready to
break out.'[1]
Elton John on Alex Harvey

1974 also saw the band make their first trip to the
USA. In the 1970s, cracking the American market was
a dream for every British band. Those that succeeded –
like Led Zeppelin and The Who – were guaranteed to live
the dollar-laden fantasies of sell-out tours, glamorous
groupies and platinum albums. But it meant gruelling
treks from coast to coast, which were time-consuming
and held no guaranteed assurance of success. American
audiences then – as now – were fickle in selecting which
British bands to take to their heart. Some groups who
couldn't put a foot wrong in Britain and Europe – like
Slade or Status Quo – were struggling to conquer the
Americas. The SAHB's fellow Scots rockers Nazareth had

already found out how tricky it was to make money in the States – on one US tour they reportedly lost £27,000 and all record royalties were used up paying the bills.

Nazareth's lead vocalist Dan McCafferty says they, like most other bands of the time, fell into the trap of believing that the luxury hotels and stretch limousines were laid on for free. On the radio documentary *Old Wild Men*, Dan explained: 'Then you'd get the bill at the end of the tour and you go "Oh, we were paying for that!" We could have got a taxi pal!'

The SAHB were fired with optimism that they could buck the trend, and over the next few years they threw a lot of energy into the American dream. Ultimately, although they toured the States four times, they were to fail and that setback was to contribute greatly to their demise. But back in 1974, the USA seemed to be theirs for the taking.

To prepare the people of America for what they could expect, Alex recorded a promotional interview, *Alex Harvey Talks – About Everything*, which was dished out to radio stations in cities where the band was due to play. Aside from the usual healthy plugs for the new album and explanation of the rationale behind the songs and the character of Vambo, Alex also provided some helpful guidance to the listeners. After explaining away his unusual accent by telling them that he was from Glasgow, he made doubly sure they understood by informing them that Glasgow is in Scotland. The rest of the interview is well worth hearing, just to get a handle on Harvey's lateral thinking and his scattergun philosophy on life. Harvey could have won international caps talking for Scotland and if you want to know about growing up in the Gorbals, the strengths and weaknesses of Alice Cooper's stage-show, or even about George Bernard

Shaw's views on phonetic spellings, then this is the album for you.

In one section of the interview, Alex gave an interesting insight into what drove him on to be a success and how he wanted to use his fame positively:

When I was a kid, I never ever thought that I would ever have anything like this – a successful band drawing in thousands of people into different venues ... I always thought though that I would be involved in something that would be ... big. I always think that I can give something back to humanity, especially to those kids I see in the streets. Because the same energy that a kid going wrong and going wild and being abandoned [sic] – if that energy goes in a different direction you could have a very useful member of the community.[2]

The first SAHB tour of the United States began on 8 November 1974. For Alex, who had been brought up watching Hollywood films and listening to Gene Autrey, the visit to America was the ultimate trip, however, he told friends that he found the modern American music scene jaded – the only band that caught his eye were The Tubes, an anarchic mob that had much in common with the SAHB and who soon became regulars at Alex's shows. Soon, the SAHB press machine was feeding stories that headline acts were wary of following the Scottish band on stage. Fleetwood Mac apparently cancelled a gig in California rather than be shown up by the SAHB. That may be true, but American audiences were to remain largely indifferent to Alex and his extreme act. Only small pockets of the vital US market such as Cleveland were to succumb to the groups' charms.

But even though seeing the States was a dream fulfilled, the ever philosophical Harvey had mixed feelings on visiting a country in the throes of the post-Watergate crisis:

I always wanted to see Hollywood, I guess that comes of being one of the cinema-going generation. But I found it was a false-fronted, disposable sort of place. I love America for itself, however. It may have shown itself up as a corrupt society, but that's only part of it. It's a less cynical society than ours. Americans think they have the answer to the world's problems, and I'm not sure they are not right – because although people here may laugh gently or even sneer at the day-to-day diet of God, country and flag, at least they do have definite principles. Maybe it's a naïve place, but that's perhaps not a bad thing, even though when it comes to sex, you'd think they had invented it![3]

Alex also had an interesting insight into life on the road and in particular to the persistent attention of female groupies. In America, he said young women had no qualms about approaching him on tours and making direct sexual propositions to him and the band. That approach apparently didn't appeal to Alex's moralistic side:

I'm old fashioned – or maybe just old – but this 'Here I am, help yourself' attitude does not turn me on at all. As a contrast, what I find back here at home is that I'm getting letters from girls like the kind they send to newspapers, y'know: 'Dear Mr H, I'm in love with this boy and he doesn't seem to know I'm alive, what should I do?' That's a different kind of naïvety and maybe I find it more acceptable because I have two kids of my own. What seems to happen in the States is that lacking in cynicism as they are, there youngsters having discovered both sex and freedom are developing an attitude: it's new, let's try it. It won't work out in the end.[4]

But overall, Harvey was undoubtedly a bit disillusioned with the reality he found in America. He seemed to be under the impression before travelling there that it really was the Promised Land, where everyone had swimming pools in the backyard and success was almost guaranteed. Instead he found that cities like Cleveland had just as much, if not more, poverty than in his native Glasgow, and that breaking the US market was going to take a massive amount of work.

The trip to the States rounded off 1974 neatly and included the band's New York debut. By way of preparation, a road manager had been sent on ahead to secure the services of two bagpipe players. On that trip, Alex fulfilled one of his lifelong ambitions when he met Marvel Comics boss Stan Lee during a special luncheon given in honour of the band at the swanky Plaza Hotel. A breathless Alex told the *NME*: 'Can you imagine ... Any man like that who would just come to my party, well, it's fantastic ... Charles Shaar Murray met him in London and told him how much I idolised him ... I've got so many of those comics.'

The US tour, which covered 22 cities in 29 days, had gone very well. Alex later told the *Daily Record* that from the reaction of the fans one would have thought they were already a major act in the USA. Iggy Pop was among the new converts to the cause, going to see them at the Whisky a Go Go club in LA where the audience were so engrossed that bar receipts fell spectacularly while they played.

One particularly impressed member of the audience that night was Barbara Birdfeather, a journalist who wrote a glowing review of the gig for a local newspaper. Barbara, who now lives and works in Los Angeles, recalls:

I had been in the business for a number of years but I had never seen anything quite like them – they just knocked me out. Around that time, David Bowie and a few other people would get dressed up on stage but none of the working-class bands got dressed up. None of them had stage props like the SAHB and no one – but no one – had bagpipes on tour with them! In so many ways they were ahead of their time.

The Whisky was a real working-class kind of club and there would probably have been a couple of hundred people there to see Alex. They gave the band a great reception and Bill Fehilly was pleased beyond compare. I told him I was really impressed and that I was going to write a great review, and he asked if I could help them in the States by becoming their PR. I told him I had never done publicity before – but I ended up being with them on all their American tours.[5]

Life on the road with the group was one long party and Barbara still sheds (happy) tears when she recalls the madness that was the SAHB on the road:

They were the original party animals – it was continual! At the time I was still drinking quite heavily and doing other stuff, so memories of that era are a bit fuzzy, shall we say.

Zal was always very quiet, but the rest of them loved to party. That included the pipers and the roadies that we always used – they were very quiet, straight young men who liked a beer but who never in their wildest dreams thought they would be on the road with a rock 'n' roll band.

So at the start of the first tour they were very quiet and gentlemanly. Then Alex started to influence them and they started drinking more and more, and flirting with the girls. In the end we ended up having to search for the roadies – as well as the band – in the mornings after a show!

A typical day on the road would start in the morning with Alex and the rest of the gang meeting up in the hotel lobby while Derek Nicol settled the bills. While he was doing this we would all go to the bar and have one or two Bloody Marys or Screwdrivers. Then while Derek and the roadies were getting the suitcases and instruments together at the airport we would go to the airport bar and have another couple of drinks while we waited to get on the plane.

On the tour when they supported Jethro Tull we visited secondary cities in the American South and that meant we went through Atlanta airport a lot – it's like the hub airport for the South. After a while the bartenders at the airport would just look up and see us coming in and say, 'your usual?'

We would get on the plane to, say, Charlotte, North Carolina and the first thing the stewardess would ask is would we like a drink! Once we arrived in the city, while Derek organised the suitcases again, we would go to the airport bar. It was the same routine while Derek checked us into the new hotel. Then

I would set up some interviews with local press, which Alex did, in the bar. Once we got to the gig, we made sure that the rider in the contract always ensured there was more vodka and Scotch whisky.

But the band were never drunk enough not to perform, their tolerance of booze was amazing. No one would have guessed by looking at them play just how much they had drank. They were always very professional. And then after the show, that's when the real carry-on started! Derek would tell them to be back in their rooms by one o'clock, but sometimes they would just go to a local club and end up out all night long.

Alex might have smoked marijuana with me once or twice, but it wasn't his cup of tea and I never ever saw a hint of needles lying around or anything like that. And they weren't destructive, they didn't trash their hotels or throw things out of windows, they respected other people's property.

But Alex was always very mischievous – he came over to my apartment once and I was in the kitchen doing something and when I came out he had spray-painted one of my walls with the Vambo slogan!

He was extremely cheeky – he always tried pushing people to the limits to see how far he could go and how much he could get away with. He would promise to do things but the minute our backs were turned he would just do whatever he wanted to do. He was like a little boy that knew when people loved him – he was quite irresistible. He knew that we all loved him so much so he could get away with murder.

The SAHB in America were like little kids who were away from home for the first time with no supervision they tended to go a little overboard, they were inevitably just going to get into mischief. They had a certain Scottish innocence about them. When their wives or girlfriends came across to be with them it was completely different – it was like the teacher had just come back into the classroom. They didn't even swear. Being with the SAHB was more than good fun – it was magic, a sort of magic that has never been duplicated.[6]

Eddie Tobin gives an insight into the way that the band enjoyed the traditional rock 'n' roll diversions while they were touring:

At the beginning everybody was drinking seriously. Let's be honest. Everyone was taking a sample of everything. Smoking dope was a way of life for most people. They didn't do a lot of cocaine, I have to say, it was mostly soft drugs. Alex wasn't a big acidhead. But cocaine was not unknown. But it's very difficult when a band is having to tour, go to receptions, stay awake – it's very hard. Sometimes you just need something to keep you awake. Cocaine was a drug that kept them awake and – from time to time – it might be appropriate.[7]

Whatever the distractions, the SAHB were winning Stateside admirers. On a visit to Cleveland in 1974 they played at the local Agora Theatre in front of an enthusiastic sell-out crowd which included Janet Macoska. Janet would eventually become one of the leading rock 'n' roll photographers through her shots of artistes like The Rolling Stones and The Who, but back in 1974 she covered the SAHB gig for a local college newspaper. She was so impressed that she immediately penned an article that asked if Alex was destined to become the next rock superstar. When Alex and Bill Fehilly saw the piece they immediately took Janet into their 'family', and she remains close to the Harveys today.

Janet remembers that Alex was always brimming full of ideas, though some of them were frankly a bit unrealistic, not to mention a tad dangerous:

They played once at a club in a suburb of Cleveland that had a really low ceiling. Alex pushed through a panel and decided to crawl up into the ceiling, which was made of fibreglass or something. But he soon came crashing back through and fell ten or twelve feet onto the stage and must have knocked himself out. He just lay there – Zal came over and looked at him, then Chris did the same, but they just kept on playing, thinking he will come around eventually. Finally he came to, picked himself up and grabbed the microphone and just started singing again![8]

Macoska once travelled to Louisville, Kentucky, to do a photo shoot with the group and witnessed another example of the endearingly naïve side of Harvey's character.

Alex had this idea that he wanted to go onstage with his face blacked up like Al Jolson. For some reason he thought it was not racial and that instead it would bring the races together. All the Americans around him told him he couldn't do it and that it wouldn't be viewed in that way – we told him that black people would see it as an insult and that he might get killed. He said, 'No, I'm sure this will work' – and he vowed that he was going to ask the first black Americans he would meet and prove us wrong. As we were walking out of this big arena he met these two black State Troopers. Everyone had gone out to the car and I went back to see where Alex had vanished to – you could see from the look in the eyes of the Troopers that he was getting into serious trouble with his line of questioning. So I clicked the picture, grabbed his arm and said we have got to go now. Luckily I doubt that these two black policemen even understood a word of what he was saying![9]

As another single, 'Anthem', bombed at home, Alex and the boys consoled themselves with champagne press receptions in New York, Boston and Philadelphia. The American media had been invited to a show in Trenton, New Jersey, and saw the SAHB on top form – encoring with versions of 'School's Out' and 'Jumpin' Jack Flash'. The band also recorded a show for New York radio stations at Electric Ladyland studios and then played the week of concerts at the Whisky in LA. The audience at one of the shows included Elton John who was at the time the biggest star in the business. Elton told the music press that Alex had paid his dues and now his time had come.

However, fans of Blue Oyster Cult – who topped the bill at many of the shows – were less charitable and like the UK's Slade fans, they gave the SAHB a roasting. The trouble invariably began with the tango introduction to 'Next'. Alex admitted to Pete Erskine of the *NME*:

Aye, they gave us some stick in Chicago, the guy from the record company was nearly in tears – but we got some unbelievable press off it. It's the sixth time it's happened to this band ... that particular point in the set is very much touch-and-go for people who have never seen us. I think a lot of them get really disturbed by 'Next' – they think it's a piss take. But the thing is that nobody's eyes left the stage ... ultimately these people turn out to be the best fans we can get because they remember us.[10]

Harvey also denied Erskine's assertion that the act had a latent air of sadism about it, and argued that by illustrating violent acts on stage he was helping to ensure it did not happen in the crowd. He viewed it as a kind of exorcism.

Another all-conquering Scots group, the Average White Band, caught up with the SAHB at the Boston Orpheum and later told reporters that the gig had a real tense atmosphere with a large percentage of the crowd hurling abuse at the pipers dressed in full regalia. Alex just blew the crowd kisses. When that didn't work he swore at the rowdy fans and told them to listen and learn as the songs were all about their ancestors. The audience didn't like that either and the atmosphere got even more hostile.

Mountain Management was also finding that Alex's unpredictable stage manner was bringing problems. Derek Nicol recollects:

On the first US tour we played a concert at the Philadelphia Spectrum with The Edgar Winter Group headlining. As you know he is an albino and as a result, everything they had on stage – like the big PA speakers – was painted white. The SAHB were only given eight feet of space in front of their kit and I could see Alex thinking this isn't right. So during the Vambo

Rools part of the show he spray-painted that slogan from one side of the stage to the other! Of course, we were kicked off the tour straight after that!

Another time we got a bill for $2,000 from the Roxy in LA after he had spray-painted Vambo Rools across the big velvet drapes they had as the backdrop of the stage. [11]

Back home, Alex reflected on the tour and concluded that they had got the most positive reactions in working-class cities like Cleveland and Detroit and among black fans:

One fella – a huge boy he was – came into the Cleveland dressing room, picked me up in his arms and swore allegiance. I told him that I'd been warned not to go to the black clubs and he said nobody'd mess me about if I went with him.

Alex also took time to mouth off about British bands that behaved like animals on tour, wrecking hotels and driving expensive cars into swimming pools:

They think they are big boys because there's always someone to clean up the mess and pay for their damage. I've spoken to the people who work there (the waiters and the maids and the janitors and so forth) and they just have contempt for those people. Someone has to clean up when they've smashed up a room, and paying for it does not make it right. If I'm ever staying there and there's someone like that riding motorcycles around the ninth floor or doing anything to disturb my sleep I may have to go up there and exchange a few words wi' them and make sure that they stop. I'll ask them very nicely indeed. They have got to be alone sometime and they won't see me coming. I do not care who they are. Anybody who does that is an asshole and I want you to print that.[12]

13

LIKE ALL YOUR HOGMANAYS ROLLED INTO ONE

'I don't want to be on the road forever, so a
hit single wouldn't be too bad, I mean it's all
down to showbusiness really.'[1]
Alex Harvey

1975 began with the SAHB and the Scottish music scene
in general in the ascendancy. In March, *Melody Maker*
even went so far as to devote a cover story to the Scottish 'phenomenon'. The paper wondered somewhat optimistically if Scotland was the 'new rock 'n' roll capital
of the world'. Along with Maggie Bell, the Average White
Band and the Bay City Rollers, Alex was seen as part of
a distinct music scene that – according to the editorial
– was apparently generating as much excitement as the
Merseybeat did in the 1960s. *NME* was also keen to praise
Alex, and in January it ironically presented him with a
'life begins at forty award for getting himself together at
an age when most of his contemporaries are out tilling the
allotment'!

Eager to capitalise on the hype, the SAHB released their fourth album *Tomorrow Belongs To Me* in April – just six months after *The Impossible Dream* had charted. Like a lot of the SAHB catalogue, it was mostly written on the road, on planes and in dressing rooms during the American tour of December 1974. The new album boasted a bizarre cover that parodied the trippy-Roger Dean style artwork that Yes used to decorate their album covers during the 1970s. Charles Shaar Murray was as enthusiastic as ever in his *NME* review of the new record, calling the set of songs a collage of fantasies and 'a gorgeous mess'. The wide range of styles on offer led him to compare Alex to Frank Zappa and Murray argued that one song, 'Give My Compliments To The Chef', was the best thing Harvey had ever done. (Hugh McKenna still thinks that this track is second only to 'Faith Healer' in the list of best ever SAHB songs.) Pete Makowski in *Sounds* thought that overall the album was the SAHB's finest yet.

The general public seemed to agree that the album was another winner and despite the lack of a hit single, the record became the band's only Top 10 album in the UK, eventually reaching number nine and staying in the charts for ten weeks. But although Hugh McKenna and Zal Cleminson are outstanding, for some the album somehow fails to hit the spot. 'The Tale Of The Giant Stoneater' is best viewed as an interesting experiment. In bedtime-story style, Alex narrates a tale replete with images of a desolate past and future where stone is in short supply. The track has Hammer horror-style guitar plus a country hoedown section thrown in for good measure. It was Harvey's favourite track on the record, and had its roots in a holiday he had taken in the West of Scotland, where he was angered to see an enormous bulldozer paving the way for a new motorway through previously unspoilt land. Another track, 'Action Strasse', with its recollections of glory days and painted ladies in Hamburg, is also a strong song.

But perhaps the best song on the album though was the title track, a wistful version of 'Tomorrow Belongs To Me' which had featured in John Kander and Fred Ebb's 1972 hit musical *Cabaret*. The inclusion of a song that had become a favourite of neo-Nazi sympathisers raised some eyebrows back in the mid 1970s when the Neo-Fascist movement was beginning to rear its ugly head in some British cities. Overall, however, the public seemed to like the album – but in retrospect it has just too much filler on show to be regarded as a classic. The album closes with a chant promising the return soon of the alter ego Vambo and hints at a future project called Vibrania.

After rehearsing at Shepperton Studios, on the set next to where director Ken Russell was shooting his latest movie *Lisztomania*, the band embarked on a massive UK tour in May, 1975. It kicked off at Newcastle City Hall on the first and ended 25 days later at the Southend Kursaal, after 19 concerts. The most unusual date was an open-air gig on 17 May at the Stoke City football ground, supporting Yes. All the dates were sell-outs, and the enthusiastic crowds found a band on top form. Charles Shaar Murray caught up with them at the Edinburgh Usher Hall and raved about how slick and tough the band sounded and how Alex was still the most 'outrageously cheapo showman around'. As at many gigs around that era, Harvey had to calm the frenzied crowd, telling them that if they rioted it would put future gigs at risk.

On 24 May, the group played at the Hammersmith

Odeon in London with the entire band proudly donning Scottish football strips – even though the international team had just been whipped 5–1 by England at Wembley. The group booted footballs into the crowd and told the English fans that their team had been lucky that afternoon! Keen SAHB fan, Steve Toal, who was in the audience that night, recalls that Alex's intensity was at times unsettling – especially when he repeatedly asked the audience whether they preferred the group to him.

Interviewed that month, Alex gave an early hint of his increasing disillusionment with the business and made it plain that his long overdue success wasn't delivering the satisfaction that he had hoped for:

I'm not all that interested in success, whatever that is. There's more to life than being big. What use is popular success, if it's not acclaim for what you wanted to do in the first place? I can't understand it, people keep asking me if it feels good to be a success. I just ask, what does that mean? In my own terms, I've been a success for years.[2]

Next up was the SAHB's second appearance on the BBC2 rock show *The Old Grey Whistle Test*. The show had long had a soporific hippie image problem. The SAHB changed all that with epic performances of 'Give My Compliments' and 'Delilah'. For the latter, Zal and Glen camped it up wildly, while Alex playfully decapitated a doll.

Written by Les Reed and Barry Mason, 'Delilah' had been a hit for Tom Jones in 1968. Jones performed it in dramatic, macho, humour-free fashion. By way of contrast, Alex – who had first done the song in London's 800 Club in the same year – latched onto it and made the song his own. He made sure everyone knew that the killing depicted in the song was brutal and sleazy, but he did so in his own witty way. It was typical of Alex

– entertaining and educating at the same time. Alex effortlessly parodied the original, turning the 'hero' into a menacing psychopath.

The decision to record 'Delilah' came at a rehearsal and originated from Bill Fehilly, who thought something offbeat or comical was needed to break the SAHB into the charts. Initially the band considered covering Frankie Lane's 'Jezebel'. But then Hugh McKenna, continuing the biblical theme, suggested 'Delilah'. Twenty minutes later the band were running through their new version. Though the group had originally played it as a joke, the song became the surprise showstopper on their spring tour of the UK and the decision was soon taken to release it as a single. A bemused John Peel only gave the single a three-star review, concluding rather unfairly that Alex would try any old trick in the quest for a hit. Whatever the motive, the song had 'hit' written all over it and entered the UK charts on 26 July 1975. It stayed there for seven weeks and peaked at number seven before beginning a slow, stately decline.

At long, long last, after 20 years in the business and at the tender age of 40, Alex Harvey had a hit single in the charts. Chris Glen recalls that 'Delilah' had just been a song they threw into the live act – during which he and Zal did a bizarre, mincing dance across the stage. Phonogram's decision to release it as a single and the subsequent chart success came as a surprise to the band. They had to fly back hastily from America to do promo work in the UK, after being told of the success in a transatlantic phone call from Donald Zec at *The Daily Mirror*. They even appeared on *Top of the Pops*, in front of an audience of kids who seemed mystified by their antics. Back in Scotland Harvey told the *Daily Record* that he was loving every minute of his success: 'It's the greatest news I've ever had. Having a Top 10 single is something you dream about. I never thought it would happen because I've tried so hard for so long'.

Backstage at the Reading Festival in August, Alex was to come across John Miller (aka John McKillop) – a colourful Scot who had served in the Brigade of Guards before becoming a soldier of fortune. Miller would eventually become the singer's part-time bodyguard/tour manager, and his full-time best friend. At Reading, he and Harvey immediately hit it off especially when John – who was working for security at the music festival – barred Bill Fehilly from the stage area because he didn't have the right pass! At six foot three inches in height, John Miller was always an imposing character. But he would latterly gain international fame as the man who carried out a couple of ingenious but ultimately unsuccessful bids to kidnap the Great Train Robber Ronnie Biggs from Brazil and bring him back to justice in Britain! (Alex was one of the few people who was aware that Miller was planning to snatch Biggs.)

In August, with 'Delilah' still high in the charts, and the surprise hit adding markedly to the sales of their album back catalogue, the SAHB signed for the legendary Atlantic Records label in America. The following month they set out on another US tour supporting Jethro Tull – their third visit in nine months.

Barbara Birdfeather says that although Alex was getting used to life Stateside, he still had a lot to learn when it came to the weather:

The first date on that tour was Salt Lake City and we were staying in a fancy hotel. Well, organisation was never Alex's strong suit – which was quite the opposite of Ian Anderson of Jethro Tull, who is organised to the max.

Anyhow, we all warned Alex not to stay out in the sun as he

would get burned, because his skin was so fair. But of course he met some young ladies and hung out with them at the hotel swimming pool and ended up really red as the proverbial beetroot. He was really sunstroked but he had to do a show that night and he ended up having to take a bath in cold water mixed with baking soda!

By that point he was also a little bit drunk and didn't want to get into the tub so we had to force him into the water. But he went on that night and did a fabulous show. We were all so annoyed because we had all warned him – but that was typical of Alex, he always came through for the audience. I believe to this day that he truly loved the kids in the audience. He had a kind of patriarchal feel for them and for us – like he felt responsible for us all.[3]

NME despatched star writer Charles Shaar Murray to Miami's Jai Alai stadium where the SAHB were supporting Jethro Tull. The influential music paper even went so far as to put Alex on the front cover, resplendent in an iron diving mask in a memorable photo by Joe Stevens. On the same week, back home in the UK, the *Live* album of the Hammersmith Odeon show was entering the charts at number 25.

Murray found an audience zonked 'on some pretty vicious local smoke' struggling to come to terms with two pipers – Mark and Kyle – skirling their way down the aisle in full Highland dress. This was not what the wasted Tull fans had come to see and they got even more confused when Alex emerged dressed in a pirate coat, with hooped T-shirt, Levi's and red, white and blue cowboy boots to introduce the 40-minute set – which had no encores. Not to be outdone in the fashion stakes, Hugh had donned a white silk bathrobe.

The day after the show, the whole SAHB entourage visited the Miami Seaquarium. Alex had always been fascinated by sharks and with the movie *Jaws* popular at the time, he was in his element. Trudy Harvey had quietly to dissuade him when he – somewhat optimistically – threatened to climb into a shark's tank for a swim with the eight-foot long predator. Alex kept shouting, 'It's OK, they only attack when they're hungry!' 'Maybe they are hungry!' came the nervous reply from everyone in the immediate vicinity.

But the band's good humour was tested to the limit in Miami when the truck with all their gear was stolen. Alex just shrugged off the mishap, even though some of his precious *Sgt Fury* comics were among the missing items. In fact, the band lost all their instruments, including some with great sentimental value. A snare drum which had been in Ted's family for 30 years was nicked, as was Alex's old Telecaster guitar which he had owned since 1960. Also stolen was Harvey's favourite leather jacket and his pirate coat. Jethro Tull helped out by lending the band their instruments and Ian Anderson even lent Alex his own leather jacket.

Minor mishaps continued to plague the tour and in November the band lost out on a gig supporting Little Feat at the Beacon Theatre, New York. The American band's lead singer Lowell George had seen the SAHB in Los Angeles and apparently asked for their removal from the bill, telling an *NME* reporter that the Scots band were not his type of music. Then a prestigious support slot opening for Peter Frampton at Madison Square Gardens also fell through.

Audience reaction in the States was also still problematic. On 3 November the band supported Frank Zappa at the Spectrum in Philadelphia. The SAHB may have been big fans of Zappa but Frank's fans gave the Scots a rough ride. Zappa aficionado Aaron Childress recalled how after 20 minutes of yelling and screaming abuse, the crowd finally got their way and Alex walked off stage:

Alex Harvey was booed off during his set. It was a shame, I thought his show was pretty good, although I was a fan of his and had a couple of his albums. I was surprised that Zappa didn't say anything to the crowd when he came out. I thought for sure that he would chastise the crowd for its poor showing. In the States, Philadelphia fans – whether it's sports or music – have a bad reputation for acting like jerks.[4]

Alex left the stage with a priceless parting shot to the ungrateful audience: 'Your country is 200 years old and you act like a bunch of babies!'

Despite such setbacks, 1975 was developing into a spectacular success for the SAHB. As the band were completing the US tour in September, the live album recorded at the Hammersmith Odeon in front of an adoring rowdy crowd continued to claw its way up the UK charts, no doubt spurred on by Charles Shaar Murray's enthusiastic endorsements. Many of the audience were expatriate Scots who apparently drank local bars dry in nervous expectation before the show.

The *NME* review by Kate Phillips noted sarcastically that this was chapter 599 of the longest breakthrough in the history of rock 'n' roll: 'Every year, inch by inch Alex advances more in the public esteem ... Inspiring new devotees with the kind of personal affection that survives all vicissitudes.'

The live album concept was all the rage at the time but most of the attempts – like Bob Dylan's *Before the Flood* or *Mott the Hoople Live* – failed dismally to capture the atmosphere of the concerts. The SAHB's effort is much more fun than most. It starts with a mock-heroic fanfare composed by Alex's old mate Derek Wadsworth that leads nicely into the magical gothic chording of 'Faith Healer'. 'The Tomahawk Kid' – dedicated to Robert Louis Stevenson – is also excellent. In common with all the SAHB studio albums, a lot of the magic of the live versions of songs is lost on vinyl without the visual dynamics to back them up. By the end of 'Framed,' Alex's exchanges with the audience get a tad tiresome, but overall this is a good album and a fine reminder of just how powerful the band could be live. It reached number 14 in Britain and became the only Harvey album to chart in the USA, entering at number 100 before fading away into obscurity.

In Britain, by contrast, the band seemingly could do no wrong and 'Gambling Bar Room Blues' gave them their second hit single in the UK when it reached number 38 late in the year. In October they announced plans for a string of festive concerts – two at the Glasgow Apollo on 18 and 19 December and another couple the following week at London's New Victoria Theatre. Harvey told the press that they would play without any support and that the top ticket price would be £1.75. He promised that the shows would be full of seasonal spirit and added: 'I want these concerts to say something about our band ... we really care about the people who come to our gigs and I'd like these ones to be a Xmas gift to them.'

Rumours that the shows – to be designed by a team of experts who had worked on Vegas and London West End productions – were to be spectacular one-offs meant that all four gigs sold out instantly. Another concert in Glasgow and an extra two in London had to be added. The additional shows meant that the band's equipment had to be rushed to London after the Scottish events. The extra expense incurred ensured that the Christmas spectaculars would see the group actually lose cash rather than make a profit.

Early rehearsals for the shows took place in a basement room under an antique store in a side street in London's Victoria. Geoff Barton of *Sounds* told readers that the walls of the room were lined with coarse hessian and the roof was covered with black egg boxes to help keep in the thunderous noise. Alex was suffering from the effects of painkillers after a visit to the local dentist, but was still fired with enthusiasm for the upcoming concerts. Later the rehearsals moved to the disused film studios at Shepperton.

The shows, especially those in Glasgow, were remarkable events. Zal Cleminson is not alone in believing that the SAHB never got any better than on those December nights in their hometown. The guitarist told *Radio Scotland*: 'Alex was in his element, strutting about the place, directing it … He was at his peak, his health was good and the presentation was spot on … we rolled everything into these shows.'

The blistering set had the decrepit old theatre rocking to its foundations. The band had emerged after Alex – dressed in a smoking jacket – had pulled the ribbon from a huge Christmas present. They played in front of a massive 'Vambo' stage set, which looked like a cross between castle ramparts and a dilapidated Glasgow tenement. The songs played each night were a greatest hits package, running from the early days right through to newer stuff like 'Delilah'. At some of the shows, Zal was given a solo showcase and played an acoustic love song.

During 'Cheek to Cheek', two six-foot models in sparkly backless evening dresses danced on either side of Alex. The women made sure they faced the audience for most of the song so they wouldn't realise the dresses were backless. At a strategic moment they turned around and the crowd went crazy. Alex then raised the biggest cheer of the night by kissing the dancers' bare buttocks – where roses had been strategically placed.

The seedy old building on Glasgow's Renfield Street

had become almost a second home to the band over the years. In an excellent book on the theatre by Russell Leadbetter, *You Don't Have To Be In Harlem*, one contributor wrote that the Christmas shows were like 'all your Hogmanays rolled into one' with balloons and streamers filling the air at the finale. In the same book, Ted MacKenna recalls how his only bad memory of those nights was the theft of his prized tuxedo, which he had bought on Sunset Strip. Despite this, he loved the place, adding:

There are very few places anywhere that could compare with it as far as atmosphere was concerned. It really was a rock 'n' roll gig. The audience could really see the band – you had these balconies all the way up and a high stage, plenty of room for a great performance though the people in the first two or three rows could not see the drummer. Even walking into it when it was empty was an experience. They do not build cinemas like that any more.[5]

Eddie Tobin, who was booking acts for the Apollo at the time of the shows, believes that the Christmas concerts saw band and audience united almost as one:

To paint the picture … You've got a Glasgow band who have a following from the streets. These were not just interested album buyers – this was an audience of people who adored the band. So the crowd was – to a man – totally partisan.

Some people go to concerts out of curiosity, y'know they might say, 'Well, I've heard their hits, let's see what they are like,' kind of thing. But nobody came to these Alex Harvey shows as a casual visitor. If they were there they were 100 per cent loyal. That's why Alex controlled them so well. If he asked for silence, he got total silence. That was awesome. I've seen hundreds and hundreds of acts, but it was unusual to have a crowd 100 per cent behind you. The only other bands I can think of who didn't get casual viewers were Status Quo and, maybe, Genesis.

On the night of the shows, you had this great sense of anticipation. It was almost religious. I would almost guarantee that

for anyone who was at these shows it was like a religious experience. And Alex played the part of The Man, or The Guru or The
Faith Healer 100 per cent. They came out and did 'Faith Healer'
and the crowd – from the very cheapest seat in the house – was
100 per cent with them. They finished with 'Anthem' and dry ice
drifting off the stage and the pipers. The band played out of their
skin. Bands know when they were great and the SAHB were
great on those nights.

Unfortunately, the shows were never recorded. I suppose we
thought they were going to go on forever and that 20 years on
they would still be doing the Apollo Christmas shows. That was
the mentality of the day. Everything is going to go on forever
– you believe that when you are young.[6]

At the New Victoria shows in London, Charles Shaar
Murray's own group Blast Furnace and the Heatwaves
supported the SAHB. The London gigs were just as much
fun as the Glasgow ones with Alex dancing with young
girls invited up from the audience as the band played
'Gang Bang'. Zal did his tap dance routine while reciting 'To be or not to be', and during 'Gambling Bar Room
Blues' the group mimed like cardboard cut-out figures in
front of a glamorous blonde model. It was a festive party
which put all the rest to shame.

Following the Xmas shows, Alex was awarded a trophy
given to all the bands that sold out the Apollo. In a typically self-effacing gesture he donated it to help raise cash
for handicapped kids. It was a fitting end to a magical
run of shows and a successful year. On the eve of 1976,
it seemed like Alex Harvey could do no wrong.

14

HE WAS MY BLOOD BROTHER

'The business does tend to devour people that
don't understand it.'[1]
Alex Harvey

As 1976 began, the SAHB looked to be on top of the music
world, but already rumours were starting to spread that
all was not well in the camp. One recurring difficulty was
that Alex – who had always had a robust physique and
the health of a younger man – now had health problems
and was rumoured to be drinking too much. He was
increasingly plagued by an agonising back condition,
which was made even worse when some scaffolding fell
on him while he was on stage in Germany. Unfortunately
there was little time to rest and recuperate, and the New
Year soon saw the band back in the recording, promoting
and performing loop.

In a sign of the group's pulling power, they were voted
the fourth best British live act in the annual *NME* poll,
which was published in February. It's worth noting that
they beat bands of the stature of Yes, Genesis, Pink Floyd

and Roxy Music in the vote, all acts who were arguably at the peak of their popularity at this point. Yet in the same poll, the SAHB weren't mentioned when it came to best band overall. It was becoming apparent that even if they could sell out concert halls, that didn't mean they would automatically sell lots of albums.

Despite this worry and his health problems, Alex seemed as manic as ever. In January he was pictured in *NME* taking a dip naked in a Norwegian lake immediately before going on stage to perform at a concert in Oslo! He then calmly walked through the audience, hauled himself up on stage, pulled on a T-shirt and jeans, which were handed to him by Swedish singer Monica Tornell, and introduced the band.

Derek Nicol recalls:

There was this lake in front of the stage. The band went on and started playing 'Framed', and everyone was looking around for Alex. The opening riff kept going on and on and then suddenly we saw this head bobbing up and down along the lake, wearing a plastic bag over his hair! He was completely naked when he got out and dragged himself up on stage. Someone gave him his jeans and T-shirt – and he started singing as he stepped into his jeans.[2]

Back in Britain in March, Alex showed his compassionate side again when he helped two penniless 15-year-old girls who had hitchhiked from Manchester to London to see their idol and turned up at the Mountain offices. According to the *Sunday Mail*, Alex immediately telephoned the girls' parents to reassure them that the youngsters were safe and well before taking the starstruck girls to Euston Station and buying them rail tickets for the journey home.

Later that month though the band got less favourable publicity when they held a 'Nazi party' at Alex's Finchley home. Third Reich regalia adorned the walls as the band and their wives sauntered about in Nazi uniforms wearing 'Hitler rules OK?' badges. Alex wore a Kaiser Wilhelm helmet, khaki shorts and platform boots. Chris Glen looked fetching dressed as a stormtrooper. Zal dressed in drag as a dowager and wore a monocle. The entire group took part in entertaining skits where they would act out interrogation scenes from World War II B-movies. But the party happened at an unsettled time when the National Front was on the rise in the UK, and some writers found Alex's shindig to be in dubious taste. Taken in conjunction with his military fixation, one might start to wonder if Alex had right-wing tendencies.

In reality, nothing could be further from the truth. Indeed Alex often took time out to warn his audiences about the dangers of a resurgence of the far right, telling them that Hitler should have been strangled at birth. Just to make things as plain as possible he once told *NME* that appearing on stage dressed as Hitler was only meant to be a bit of fun. He told fans at Newcastle Town Hall: 'Do not think for one minute that we think that bastard was a good man.'[3] Still, doing the Hitler impersonation at a concert in Hamburg was a bit close to the bone – German record company bosses who attended the show were left speechless by the performance.

Trudy Harvey confirms that the Nazi-themed party was just meant to be a bit of harmless fun:

From time to time – like at New Year – we would hold parties in the house. One day some of the band were here and Alex just said, 'Let's have a party – but you all have to come dressed as Germans!' It was meant to be an absolute joke, and the band entered into the flavour of it – but naturally enough there was only one person who dressed as Hitler, and that was Alex. I think it was around the time of the film *Cabaret* – and the party was very much based on that. In fact it was very humorous but

I think in retrospect the way it was portrayed ... 25 years on it doesn't look good. But Alex was a great believer that humour defuses all the horror associated with things like that. He loved the humour of *Monty Python* and of Spike Milligan.[4]

Certainly Harvey did have a leaning towards that type of comedy. Sometimes on tour, while the band were waiting to board their next flight, he would approach total strangers in the airport bar and ask them to smell some exotic Continental cheeses that he carried around with him!

Alex further enhanced his reputation for taking things to the extreme when the music press carried full-page adverts for the new album *The Penthouse Tapes* which showed a naked model answering the phone while writhing on satin sheets. It was the first topless advert ever to appear in *Melody Maker* and carried the headline 'Alex has done it again!' Critics however weren't so sure if the veteran performer could still cut it. The new single, a cover of Del Shannon's 'Runaway', paled in comparison to the original. Reviewing *The Penthouse Tapes* in *NME*, Kate Phillips condescendingly described our hero as a 'kindly, optimistic delinquent'. It's undeniable that by 1976 the SAHB were beginning to show signs of fatigue, and the album was a mixed affair, with some songs like the opener, 'I Wanna Have You Back', being little more than a pretty average hard rock workout. The country-influenced 'Say You're Mine' – written by Harvey over 20 years previously – also sits awkwardly on the record.

Elsewhere the album is crammed full of over-the-top cover versions of songs like Jethro Tull's 'Love Story' and The Osmonds' 'Crazy Horses'. Another cover was Alice Cooper's 'School's Out' – but as Kate Phillips remarked there was something slightly daft about a 40-year-old man bellowing about 'No more teachers'.

The song 'Jungle Jenny' had also been kicking around for years and had been a flop single for the band early in 1973. The song's eponymous heroine Jenny was originally a Glasgow pensioner who – at the age of 90 – still carried out a healthy trade as a prostitute! Alex always liked the hooker's nickname and when he wrote the song he used it to tell the story of a young woman who survives a plane crash in the jungle and is reared by apes.

Early on in the project, the album had been given the working titles of *The Attic Tapes* or *Alex Harvey's Greatest Hits*. The feeling back then – which still persists today – was that what eventually surfaced as *The Penthouse Tapes* was just a fulfilment of obligations to record company bosses who wanted to cash in on the success of 'Delilah'. But the album did well commercially, reaching number 14 in the UK and staying in the charts for seven weeks.

Spring 1976 also saw another massive UK tour, followed by concerts at the home grounds of three football clubs – Charlton Athletic, Swansea City and Celtic. The British tour spanned three months, starting at the end of April and ending up early in June. By now, the SAHB were bringing a whole new meaning to the phrase 'hard-working band'. Because of the Christmas shows, Glasgow and London were left off the concert hall itinerary. But just about every other major UK city was included and the band also took on two nights at Newcastle, Manchester, Birmingham and Sheffield. It was an awesome demonstration of the group's pulling power. Tickets sold for £1.25 or £2.50.

The tour had its share of problems, though. Alex's back pains meant that a couple of the 28 dates had to be called off. In May, the battle-scarred old trouper told *NME* that he would quit tomorrow if it weren't for the fans, saying they 'are just wee babies and I love them'. *NME*'s Angie Errigo was won over by a mighty concert the band played in Newcastle – she even went so far as to recommend that if Harvey really wanted to quit, he should run for Prime Minister – against David Bowie! Angie also liked the attitude of the fans, adding: 'the great thing about Alex Harvey fans is that they are there to bang their heads against walls ... but they dinna wreck the joint or each other while they are doing it!' The crowd were like kids at a pantomine, singing along at choruses and being thoroughly entertained by Alex and Zal play-wrestling to win control of the guitar. The man himself did his Hitler routine and complained about being bombed in his bunker.

Hugh McKenna was also feeling the strain again and he collapsed before a gig in Southampton. He had to pull out of the tour and was replaced on keyboards by Tommy Eyre. Doctors ordered Hugh to rest fully for two weeks saying he was completely exhausted because of overwork. A show at the Usher Hall in Edinburgh ended with the group being banned from the venue for allegedly urinating onto the crowd – a claim that they strenuously denied.

The star-studded bill for the three football ground gigs included The Who, Little Feat and The Outlaws. The tickets for the Glasgow gig on 5 June cost only £4. At the Charlton show, Alex sauntered on stage after the set by southern boogie band The Outlaws. The SAHB's set took place at dusk, during a torrential thunderstorm and with sporadic fights breaking out among the restless crowd. Alex proceeded to eat the petals of a rose while the band cranked up 'Love Story' as an opener. *NME's* Phil McNeil thought the show was 'very fierce', with tough, muscular drumming and Tommy Eyre deputising well for Hugh. At one point, Alex, who was carrying a teacher's cane in

The programme for the UK tour gives an interesting insight into how Alex was starting to see things in a 'them and us' light. It contains a cartoon story in which the SAHB battle against the forces of evil in the guise of Doctor Killjoy, who rules the country in an oppressive way through the Ministry of Boredom. Maybe the Doctor was the boss at the BBC, maybe he represented the music industry moguls who controlled Alex's output, but in Alex's fantasy, the people are led in rebellion by his band when the evil Doctor tries to ban noise! Alex dubbed himself the teacher and righter of wrongs. The band members are also given telling nicknames – Ted is 'The Buffer', Hugh is 'The Professor' and backroom boffin. Guitarist Zal is called 'The Actor', completely dedicated to pleasure, and Chris is 'The Punk', a general do-gooder.

Despite all the hassles, Alex was boosted by the fact that their albums were now to be released on Mountain Records, which had just been opened by his old mate Bill Fehilly. In July, adverts in the music press promised that the first album on that label, *SAHB Stories*, would 'Take your breath away!' Recorded at London's Basing Street Studios, the new album was produced again by David Batchelor, who also co-wrote two of the songs. It was the SAHB's sixth studio album in less than four years. Compared to the output of contemporary bands like Led Zeppelin or Pink Floyd it was a phenomenal work-rate. But inevitably it meant that previous high standards were difficult to sustain and – if truth were told – by 1976 the creative well was starting to run dry. *SAHB Stories* is an album full of songs like 'Jungle Rub Out', which had been lying around for ages, and 'Sultan's Choice'. They all have inventive hooks or killer guitar riffs but they all ultimately run out of ideas and end up relying on repetitive choruses. 'Dance To Your Daddy' can best be attributed to Alex's fondness for pretty young girls dancing. 'Dogs of War' is a less than subtle attack on mercenary soldiers.

Still, the album was by no means a complete letdown. The hit single 'Boston Tea Party', with its insistent beat and historical narrative, is a standout, and allowed Alex to indulge his twin interests of history and all things American. The song still sounds original and beguiling today. It was Harvey's typically offbeat contribution to the American bicentennial celebrations and told the story of how the imposition of English taxes on tea had inadvertently led to America's obsession with coffee!

Tellingly, the only other really A-grade track on the album is a cover version. 'Amos Moses' had been an American hit single in 1971 for Jerry Reed Hubbard, the swamp-rocker from Atlanta, Georgia. The SAHB's version was based on a typically nagging and incessant Zal Cleminson riff over which Alex recounts the tale of the cajun Amos Moses who lived in a swamp and hunted 'gators for a living. Mountain Records thought the song had potential to be a successful follow-up to 'Boston Tea Party', but when the single was released in the UK in August – with 'Satchel and the Scalp Hunter' as a B-side – it failed to chart. The latter song was a weird tale of a girl called Satchel who exacts revenge on her tormentors 'Dutch Druid and the Elders'. It was Alex's original choice for the A-side.

SAHB Stories – which remains a particular favourite of Hugh McKenna's – marked a significant shift in direction for the group, with Alex taking more of a back seat when it came to writing and recording. A song like 'Sirocco' was pretty much Hugh's project. Perhaps sensing that time was catching up on him, Harvey wanted to push the band further into the limelight. Yet he was still looking to the future and forming plans for an outlandish concept album to be called *Hail Vibrania*, which he thought had the potential to end up as a West End show. The plan was for it to feature Alex's old alter ego Vambo as ambassador for the mythical land of Vibrania. Sadly the project never saw the light of day.

During some rare time off in July, Alex, his extended family and pets took a trip to Loch Ness in Scotland to search for the fabled monster. Alex's father, Leslie senior, arrived ten days before the main party and set about arranging interviews with locals who claimed to have seen 'Nessie'. Once Alex and Trudy had reached Invermoriston – a short stroll from the Loch – they soon began the task of compiling six hours of taped interviews with locals, including a water bailiff, policeman, minister and the local laird.

When they visited the Benedictine Abbey at Fort Augustus they spoke to the staff and pupils – one of whom turned out to be a cousin of the boxer Muhammad Ali! The resultant album based on the interviews would eventually be released in 1977. Though he never once laid eyes on the monster during the week long holiday, Alex left the area fully convinced that the monster existed and that those witnesses he had spoken to were sincere.

Writing in the album sleeve notes, he commented:

If soldiers, scientists, trained observers, poachers, policemen, priests and Protestants give the evidence of their own eyes, then I believe in the existence of a family of creatures as yet not accepted by modern science.

For Alex, the trip up north was a great success and he left Scotland on Saturday 17 July in high spirits. Sadly, tragedy was just around the corner.

The wheels really started to come off the SAHB band-wagon that same month with the death of manager Bill Fehilly. The plane he was travelling in crashed into the side of a mountain in Dumfriesshire in southern Scotland. Also killed in the tragedy were Fehilly's 11-year-old son, Liam, two directors from his Top Flight Leisure Company, and a lawyer who was travelling with them, and the pilot. The party had been on a scheduled 55-minute trip from Blackpool to Fehilly's hometown of Perth when the twin-engine Piper Aztec got into difficulties. To add to the sense of disbelief, the *Glasgow Herald* of 28 July revealed that the ill-fated plane had been a late replacement for another aircraft that was unserviceable.

Trudy Harvey knew that the tragedy was a body blow for her husband:

If there was anyone who could influence Alex in his entire career it was Bill. He had a certain wisdom and stature about him and he had achieved quite a lot in his life. He was a big man in every sense of the word – the seventh child of a seventh child of a seventh child. There was an uncanny link between the names of his companies – Top Flight and Mountain – and the way that he actually died.[6]

By a weird twist of fate the news of the tragedy was broken to Alex at his London home by David Gibson, the reporter who had organised the Tommy Steele competition back in 1957. By 1976, Gibson was working for the now defunct *Sunday Standard* and when the story came over on the news wires he had to ring Alex for a comment. David recalls: 'Alex took the news very badly, I think it knocked him off his feet. Alex worshipped Bill in many ways.'[7]

The *Daily Record* reported that the SAHB and three members of Nazareth attended the funeral in Perth on 4 August. A picture of Harvey showed the star looking drawn and distraught. It was one of the lowest points in his life – some would say that it was on a par with the death of his brother. On another less emotional level, the tragedy marked a turning point in the business affairs of the SAHB. Without Fehilly's paternal guidance, the record company seemed to take less interest in the financial wellbeing of the band. In the book *All That Ever Mattered*, a history of Scottish rock, Ted McKenna commented: 'We lost a lot of money playing in America. No one was taking care of business.'

On Thursday 5 August the band members reconvened for an important meeting at Mountain Records' office in London. Phil McNeill of *NME* was also there to do an interview with Alex, and found him lethargic and in a downbeat mood after flying back from the funeral in Scotland. Asked where the band went from here, Alex growled and gave the reporter a brief history lesson:

We're carrying on. Straightforward. I've known Bill twenny years – I used ta post bills up for him. I posted bills for Count Basie, Howlin' Wolf, Muddy Waters and Big Bill Broonzy for his promotions at St Andrews Hall in Glasgow. I posted bills to subsidise the band I had at the time. I got fined a couple of times and he [Fehilly] paid the bill.

Alex explained to McNeill how Fehilly had introduced him to the blues masters of that era and how he had taken Alex and SAHB under his wing in 1972:

He was the only man I could call captain, Phil, he was my blood brother. He was a beauty ... I feel a great loss because I don't know anybody else that could say the things he said. But we're going on and Mountain's going on. It's a strong band. Mountain's a pretty tough outfit.[8]

As if to prove the point that it was business as usual, the band left the interview and headed home to pack for a trip to Finland. They were due to play their first ever concert in that country, on the same bill as Chuck Berry at the Turku Festival. If there was any doubt as to the significance of his manager's death, Alex Harvey dispelled it in the lyrics of a later song called 'No Complaints Department'. Never released on a SAHB album, it contains a lyric which states that Alex had lost his brother on the stage and his best friend in a plane crash. It couldn't be more explicit – the tragedy was a crushing blow for Alex to come to terms with.

Though the general consensus was that Fehilly's death was the catalyst for Harvey's subsequent decline, some of those close to the singer say the writing had been on the wall before then. Eddie Tobin sensed that Alex was being assailed by twin problems – his ingrained distrust of the music industry and the simple fact that the band were losing their imaginative edge:

I started to sense it was going wrong just before Fehilly's death, I think Alex was losing it. Everyone says it was Bill's death – but I think he was gone before that, I really do. Creatively he had reached a point where he was levelling off. You could see it in the records. As the albums progressed, I think the creativity was drying up. He had gone flat. The difficulty was that they had become a live band. And the wants and needs of the live public are different from those of a record-buying public.

Tomorrow Belongs To Me – what was that all about? Even I didn't understand it. When I heard the album, I thought, where is this going, where are these guys going? These songs are too heavy, they are bound to dig a hole for themselves. There was nobody in that band that was heavy enough to go down that road and I think subsequent events proved that. They were lost when they made that album.

I think the frustration over the lack of creativity fed the excesses and the anger. It's not that the band didn't have the ability. But remember he was the leader. The band was so accustomed to him conducting. And when the conductor stops conducting, the band just looks at him. This wasn't a team game, where he could say, 'I'm not going to play this week, you're going to play.' So you cannot really blame the band, because the format was Harvey the creative genius and you guys fill in along the way.

The difficulty was that Alex had lost it. His brain was going off in so many directions. Remember, he suffered the death of Leslie, I think that hurt him very badly. The business arrangements surrounding Les's death – especially the fact that the management just frankly wiped their hands of the whole thing. As soon as he was dead it was over.

That disturbed Alex and made him nervous. He never did have much time for the business anyway. Eventually, Alex didn't believe anything anybody said. He thought the business was full of sharks whose sole purpose in life was to rip guys off. That cynicism reached frightening proportions. He simply did not believe anybody – except Bill Fehilly.[9]

Griefstricken and in constant pain because of his recurring back problem, Alex could at least console himself with the fact that *SAHB Stories* had sold well in the UK, peaking at number 11 in the charts during the summer of 1976. Few would have guessed that it would be the last time Alex was to have a hit record in his home country. Everyone who knew him agreed that he was in need of a long rest but the lure of the business drew him back.

In the autumn of 1976 the band set out on an ill-fated tour of Europe. For a while it was fun, with Alex enjoying sightseeing in Paris and climbing the Eiffel Tower. But the years of hard living and hard drinking were starting to catch up on him. He had been touched by tragedy once too often – and drinking a bottle of vodka a day wasn't going to help matters. Those closest to him began to notice that Alex was starting to lose his grip and couldn't keep up with the rest of the band. Zal even recalls having to boot him up the backside to wake him while they were performing at a gig in Malmo. The omens were clear from the start of the European tour. In Hamburg, he suffered a minor collapse, but decided to soldier on with the shows.

But halfway through the sell-out tour, the inevitable happened. In Lund, Sweden, Alex fell ill early in the show but after a short break he completed the set. Backstage after the show, he collapsed. He had to be carried back to the hotel, where the decision to fly him home the following day was taken.

NME reported that the 'seriously ill' star was being flown home suffering from exhaustion, and added that the remaining dates on the tour had been cancelled. A Mountain Records spokesman said:

Alex was seriously ill at the weekend and he has been ordered to take a complete rest ... he is now confined to bed ... We assume that the pressures of the past year have caught up with him and that he is totally exhausted.

The wise money was on Alex not being back on stage till the following spring. In fact, it was July 1977 before he would work again.

15

1977

'Rock 'n' roll has got to grow up in a hurry –
it's getting effete and out of date. What I want
to hear now is something that will blow me
down like "Heartbreak Hotel" or Little Richard
doing "Lucille".'[1]
Alex Harvey

Alex rested up at home during most of the winter, including an eight-week spell when he apparently slept on
a wooden board at night in a forlorn bid to try and cure
his back pain, thought to be caused by a pinched nerve
in his vertebrae that had damaged part of the spinal nervous system. Doctors seemed unable to cure it.

Some people close to him believed that the back
problem was at best an excuse to cover up a much more
serious health problem. Eddie Tobin for one had serious
doubts and still holds them today:

He was in hospital in London. We were trying to get him back
on stage and someone suggested that Alex hadn't chipped his

spine and that in fact he had a serious drink problem. People were still slipping him drink while he was in hospital.'

Tobin says that Alex was taken to see a doctor, who confirmed that alcohol was the real problem:

All this money had been spent on a chipped spine, which was simply not true. I don't believe there was anything wrong with his back.'[2]

True or untrue, Alex had to wear a back brace, but despite the pain, he still had a healthy appetite. He told a *Daily Record* reporter that he was regularly dining on a traditional Scottish breakfast of square sausage, fruit pudding, black pudding and potato scones – which he bought at Fortnum & Mason's in London. He also apparently feasted on raw steak as part of a carefully controlled diet!

Around this time, Mountain Management was concerned that Alex's behaviour was becoming more erratic, as the prescribed drugs he was taking mixed badly with alcohol. The company decided to employ a bodyguard to keep an eye on him. Derek Nicol recalls:

Towards the end we had to get John Miller to act as a minder for Alex. He was there just to make sure that Alex would get up and go to the show on time. He also got Alex into training and running to try and get him fit again.[3]

Alex took to the new regime well and proudly told friends that he could now run a half-mile and then swim another half-mile soon afterwards.

Miller was to remain very close to Alex right up until the end of his life and the two came through innumerable close scrapes together. John believes that their rapport was definitely a case of opposites attracting. Miller was six foot three and an ex-soldier, while Harvey was five foot three and a pacifist/conscientious objector. One man had once hurt people for a living while the other wouldn't hurt a fly. Whatever the differences, the two had shared interests – both were Scots and both had a total respect for military matters and alcohol. Miller says the two men confronted a lot of demons together:

Regarding his health, Alex was in whatever condition he wanted to be in. Alex was the greatest actor I've ever met. We used to go into seedy Belgian and German clubs, and he used to roll towels up and put them under his shoulder and he would threaten to beat people up who were seven foot tall. I know he was drinking a lot, but Alex was always like that – I never saw him any other way. Alex never had any pretensions to grandeur – he never spent money, never had a car and he dressed like a bagman. I never saw any of the trappings of success. He never overindulged with fancy houses or fancy holidays – in fact one of the few holidays he took was down in Cornwall. We wanted to get him off the drink and so went down there for two weeks just fishing and going out to visit places. I was the one who sat with him in the room for a week and said to him, 'Alex, if you are going to be putting whisky into Coca-Cola cans at least let us know you are doing it!' He was the biggest influence I had in my life. He was just so creative, it was that creativity that messed his head up as much as anything else.[4]

Miller says that unusual behaviour became more and more common with the star seeming to revel in doing the unpredictable. Miller recalls that once, at a big festival in Belgium, Harvey found out that Richard Attenborough had just completed filming on the movie *A Bridge Too Far* nearby. Alex sent Miller to go to the film set and commandeer a Bren Gun carrier. The SAHB then piled into the vehicle and tried to drive up on to the stage to begin their set.

John Miller also says that Harvey was by now playing mind games with just about everyone he came into contact with:

Alex was one of the calmest people I ever met. I never saw him angry or saw him play the part of the big rock star. But he was an incredible head games player. He confiscated all the band's pornography one day and put tape over all the dirty bits! Sometimes I would meet him in a pub in London and he would tell me that I should pretend I didn't know him and that I should pick an argument or a fight with him! He also used to play these wee games during interviews with the press where Alex would turn to me and say, 'No, you shut up about that,' and I would say, 'No, I'm going to tell him that story.' And the reporter would be going, 'What story, what story?' On one tour he said to me, 'I'll see how good you are – the minute I get the chance I'm off for a drink.' So I handcuffed him to a flight case to stop him getting out – but I still ended up having to go down to the pub to get him and the flight case. We had these mad schemes like SAS – stalk a stalker, where we would go after stalkers just to show them what it felt like to be stalked. We used to go out at dead of night in weird garb and actually stalk people. I never saw him raise his hand or his voice to anybody. I can honestly say that. Sure, he got emotional towards the end but I've never seen him not do a gig or pull a stroke on a promoter. Anything that was emotional was out of artistic frustration. There were things he wanted to do and things he knew were going to happen and he just needed five years. He knew he didn't have time to finish what he wanted to do.[5]

In November 1976 Alex had bullishly told the *Daily Record* that he was planning a major UK tour for spring 1977, but only for selected venues where the band would play up to a week at a time. When asked about his state of health, he added:

I was certainly exhausted and overworked ... But it was all blown out of proportion. Anyone who thought I was finished with the business had better think again. I have never felt fitter.

Alex was also cheered and flattered by the large number of fans who had written to wish him well while he was ill. While he recuperated he grew a Che Guevara-style beard and worked on his pet project – the much anticipated *Vibrania* album which he hoped to have ready by the middle of 1978.

The long lay-off left the other band members at a loose end. The solution was for them to head for Air Studios and Basing Street Studios in London to start work on their own album. The plan was not a direct result of Alex's illness – the group had been contemplating such a project since the completion of the last SAHB tour of the UK in the summer of 1976. No one doubted that the guys had the ability to make a decent record, and now of course they had a large fan base eager to hear if they could cut it without Alex. The last troubled tour of Europe had given them an early chance. With Alex needing to rest during sections of the show, the band had played on their own, with the McKenna cousins sharing vocals on new songs like 'Smouldering' and 'Outer Boogie'. Recording the 'solo' album was actually a release for the band, as they often found it tricky in the past to write with the extrovert Harvey in mind. The new songs were smoother and more relaxed – many of them just wouldn't have suited Harvey's manic style.

Alex was supportive of the new venture and helped to choose and produce some of the new songs for what was to become the *Fourplay* album, released in January 1977. The promotional photos featured Alex, bound and being abducted by the rest of the band on the back of a lorry on Hammersmith Broadway in London. To add a bit of excitement to the photo shoot, Alex started yelling 'Help! They're CIA agents! Rescue me!' His cries for help were apparently extremely convincing and the local police reported that 15 passersby tried to intervene and free Alex.

When the record was issued, fans first had to work

out who the guy on the left-hand side of the album cover photo was. Closer scrutiny revealed that it was Zal without his make-up! The photo hinted at the fact that the band wanted to make a break from the past and explore new musical directions. Listening to the record – dedicated to 'Big Bill' Fehilly – backs up the notion. Without Alex, the band seemed to have one eye on the lucrative American AOR market which was just emerging on the back of FM radio. A song like Hugh McKenna's 'Love You For A Lifetime' is lyrically honest and smoothly produced. It wouldn't be out of place on a Michael Bolton album.

Critical reaction to *Fourplay* was generally favourable, with even *NME*'s new star writer – darling of the new wave, Tony Parsons – remarking that the album 'rocked like a laidback bitch on heat'! When Parsons asked the band how they differed from the old Tear Gas outfit, Zal told him with some degree of sincerity that they were probably now a lot poorer.

But despite a 29-date tour of the UK in January and February, and an appearance on *The Old Grey Whistle Test*, the concept of the SAHB without Alex was difficult for the fans to embrace. The live shows featured a sterling cover version of 'Stay' from David Bowie's *Station to Station* album, together with some SAHB songs like 'Delilah' and stuff from *Fourplay*, but sadly, both the album and excellent single 'Pick It Up and Kick It' failed to chart.

The SAHB weren't the only established band suddenly finding that things were changing in British music. Ever since late 1976, the old guard 'progressive' bands had been getting a long overdue wake-up call from the wave of punk bands and their supporters in the music press. So, while Alex recuperated, bands like the Sex Pistols and The Damned were stealing away his fan base with their new raw sound.

It may sound cruel but by 1977 Alex was seen as yesterday's man in the pop business. Of course he wasn't
alone – many of the SAHB's contemporaries like Wish-
bone Ash, Yes and Deep Purple had also been badly damaged by the punk rock revolution. One day they were hip
and making lots of money, the next day they were past
their sell-by date.

Many of those bands had become so pompous and out
of touch that they deserved all they got. The same could
not be said of Alex. When most rock stars drove around
in flashy classic cars, Alex didn't even have a driving
licence. By way of explanation, he jokingly told people that
when he was young there were no cars, just coaches and
horses! While most stars lived in Hollywood mansions,
Alex seemed quite happy with his wife and kids living in
East Finchley. Also, despite the fact that he was one of
the oldest stars in the business, Alex always had a real
interest in whatever youth culture was in vogue. When
young aspiring musicians visited the Harvey home, they
were usually spirited away by Alex to the room where he
kept his record collection. There they were given the Alex
Harvey version of the history of rock 'n' roll, listening to
the type of music that had influenced him as a youth.
The youngsters would eventually leave the house with
dawn breaking – bleary-eyed but wiser.

Unlike many of his contemporaries, Alex had a punk
sensibility, and he liked to champion the underdog. In
many ways he was the original British punk rocker. And
although the hippie days in London during the Swinging Sixties had infused in him a desire for a peaceful life
under any conventional political or religious system, he
also shared a sneaking admiration for the punks' devotion to anarchy and rule breaking.

As early as 1973, he astutely pointed out in a *Sounds*

interview that the music industry was stale and desperately in need of a wake-up call:

Somebody's got to come along that won't be in the format, and I haven't got a clue what it's going to be. Something that will be the equivalent of rock 'n' roll, which came along and said 'Fuck you' to all this about being in tune ... and we'll all ask, 'What's going on?' I would like to see something that broke the rules.[6]

(Interestingly, *NME*, which fast became the bible of the punk rock movement, paid an oblique tribute to Alex. In the autumn of 1976 they had introduced one of the first ever articles on the Sex Pistols – a review of their gig at London's Screen on the Green – by using the above quote from Alex.)

Alex could see that rock 'n' roll was becoming ridiculously pretentious. He knew that in reality it was a pretty disposable art form and that it shouldn't take itself so seriously. What was needed was the same type of radical shake-up which he had been part of back in the mid 1950s, when the old guard were the crooners and the dance bands. Now, in 1977, he was part of the old guard that was under threat.

Feeling a natural affinity towards punk, he decided to try and embrace it head-on. He spoke out in its defence, telling reporters how much he loved Adam Ant's music and how he wanted to manage the Sex Pistols. Later, in 1978, Alex played at the Vortex, the legendary punk club in London, with a back-up band that included two Highland pipers; he traded insults with any punks in the audience who had the nerve to gob at him.

The Vortex was at the time owned by Harvey's friend John Miller, who recalls the crazy nights when Alex showed up:

He used to go to the *Melody Maker* and say 'I've got a great gig – Miller's giving me £200 a night not to play!' They published these stories – he would go down there with a piper and play 'Anthem' for an hour. The punks just stood there – they were spellbound.

He was a permanent item on the guest list – but every night he used to come to the club, the bouncer would phone me up and say 'Alex Harvey is at the door and wants to get in'. I would tell them to just let him in. And the bouncer would ring back and say that Harvey wants me to search him, because he's carrying a blade. I'd go every night and strip him until I found this fucking blade. And he used to joke about it, saying 'one day I'll get in here with a blade and do someone badly!'[7]

Music journalist Billy Sloan has since revealed how John Lydon once told him that Alex was the only old rocker for whom he had any respect. The Sex Pistols lead singer thought Harvey was a visionary whose punk attitude greatly influenced the Pistols. Alex would have loved to have heard that compliment, though sadly that type of recognition only came to light in the years after his death. He adored the Pistols and always hankered after managing them. He thought 'Anarchy in the UK' had the same quality as classic rock songs from a previous generation like 'Be-Bop-A-Lula', 'Heartbreak Hotel', and 'Tutti Frutti'.

Tom Robinson was one of the new wave of musicians who found a ready friend and ally in Harvey. Robinson told me how he first met the star after watching Alex and his post-SAHB New Band perform at Newcastle Polytechnic:

I'd enjoyed the show and risked going backstage for an autograph. Not only had Alex's macho onstage persona featured prominently in the music press throughout the 1970s, but more recently so had mine as a gay activist. My plan was to nip in anonymously amid the well-wishers, grab an autograph and beat a rapid retreat, but Alex clocked me instantly.

'You!' he yelled. 'You're Tom Robinson, aren't you?' I mumbled a terrified 'Yes' as the room fell silent. 'You're the one that did THAT SONG.'

'Erm, "2-4-6-8 Motorway"?' I mumbled, clutching at straws.

'No – the other one. GLAD to be GAY.' He stressed the words, fixing me with a penetrating stare. 'That's fuckin' TERRIFIC!'

He invited me back for a drink at the hotel – where he told me the tale of his first night at sea as a teenager. Apparently a stoker known on board as The Phantom Gobbler turned up in his cabin armed with a shovel in one hand and his dick in the other. 'As a matter of fact Ah quite enjoyed it,' said Harvey with a laugh. 'But these days Ah'm intae bein' married an takin' the dog fae a walk!'[8]

The two men became close pals, and Robinson recalls a night at Alex and Trudy's East Finchley home, when he was treated to highlights from Harvey's vintage rock and blues collection, blasted from the living-room speakers.

The small reproving figure of Alex's youngest son Tyro suddenly appeared in the doorway. 'Dad,' he demanded, 'can you turn down the rock 'n' roll, please? I'm trying to sleep.' Robinson was struck by this complete reversal of the traditional parent–child conflict over loud music!

When the Tom Robinson Band played a Rock Against Racism gig at the nearby Alexandra Palace shortly afterwards, Alex joined them on stage. His performance left an indelible impression on everyone in the hall – especially Robinson:

The punk era was big on sound, fury and thrashing around with guitars, but watching Alex work was an object lesson in stagecraft. He didn't even bother rehearsing – just showed us the chords to Bob Marley's 'Big Tree, Small Axe' in the dressing room beforehand and told us to watch and follow his cues.

At showtime he walked calmly out to the front of the stage, pointed at the left side of the crowd and sang 'Big Tree ...' He then pointed at the other side and sang '... Small Axe'. Within ten seconds he had the whole crowd singing their parts on cue, while we played loud or quiet as he raised or lowered the neck of his guitar. Mostly it was quiet, and the audience was spell-bound. I learnt so much about economy and dynamics from those four minutes on stage with Alex – it was a masterful performance.[8]

Back in 1977, he may have been staring extinction in the face, but Harvey was not taking the hint and would not be going quietly. His immediate response to punk was typically offbeat. In April he finally released the album based on the legend of the Loch Ness Monster. Work on this project dated back to the holiday the previous autumn when, just prior to Bill Fehilly's death, the Harvey clan had decamped to Loch Ness. Derek Nicol recalls that Mountain funded the project – mainly because they felt that Alex needed to have some time off, to get out of London and clear his head. The family stayed in caravans and Alex spent his days interviewing locals, including a monk, who had allegedly seen the monster.

The weird and wonderful result was an album with highly effective narration by Richard O'Brien, Alex's old mate from *Hair*, that detailed the menace of the 'dark, cold and deep stretch of water'. Alex added some fanciful songs, and the package contained a map of all the reputed sightings of Nessie. Promoting such an offbeat project was always going to be a nightmare – indeed some people told me that Harvey opted for such an un-usual and esoteric project just to 'mess with the heads' of the record company executives who were beginning to get on his nerves. When the record company K-Tel got into financial difficulties the entire project seemed jinx-ed. The album flopped and tens of thousands of copies of the disc still remain unsold. For the first time since the formation of the SAHB, Alex seemed to be out of synch with what audiences wanted to hear. He was simply going out of fashion.

Undeterred, the SAHB regrouped and in the summer of 1977 they started work on what was to be their final album *Rock Drill*. But the previously rock-solid band showed its first signs of disunity with the departure of Hugh McKenna in a dispute over time-keeping. The band that Alex used to liken to a family or clan was starting to show signs of wear and tear. Hugh recalls how, underneath the genial exterior, Alex could be a tough taskmaster, and says he felt that the group was not moving on as it should. After a request by Hugh to see a copy of his contract seemed to be ignored by management, the keyboard player decided to deliberately miss a rehearsal.

When Alex told his song-writing partner that he was now 'on probation', Hugh, perhaps understandably, told him in no uncertain terms what he could do with his job. He walked out on the band and was once again replaced by the prolific Sheffield-born keyboard-player Tommy Eyre. Hugh says: 'I told Alex to shove the band. My departure from the group could have been more graceful – but my inclination was that I wanted to do something different.'[9]

Hugh's replacement, Tommy Eyre, had gained an impressive reputation playing with bands like Juicy Lucy, Aynsley Dunbar's Retaliation and Joe Cocker's Grease Band. When he was just 19 years old, Eyre earned his place in the rock 'n' roll roll of honour when he arranged and played the seminal Hammond organ introduction to Cocker's single 'With A Little Help From My Friends'. Despite Tommy's best efforts, Hugh's departure was a body blow to the group. He and Alex were the strong songwriting partnership of the band, and that was always going to be difficult to replicate. The general consensus was that much of the SAHB's special chemistry was lost when Hugh departed – some critics doubted if the group itself would survive much longer.

In August 1977 the SAHB released their final single, 'Mrs Blackhouse', a less than subtle attack on Mary Whitehouse, the elderly puritan who prided herself in being the nation's moral guardian. Alex was no fan of censorship and was particularly annoyed when Mrs Whitehouse attacked the *Gay News* newspaper. Alex told *The Sun* of 27 August that Mrs Whitehouse was 'a poor misguided woman who is trying to make civilisation go backwards'. Mrs Whitehouse responded by saying that she had no interest in Alex Harvey or his views on life. Maybe if she had listened to the lyrics of 'Next' she might have formed an opinion. Tom Robinson remembers:

Alex was incandescent that Whitehouse should have sued *Gay News* for blasphemy and won. To him it was inconceivable that someone being gay should even be an issue, bless him.[10]

'Mrs Blackhouse' and another *Rock Drill* track, 'King Kong' both got an airing on 28 August 1977 at the Reading Festival. The group had warmed up for the crucial gig by appearing at the Blitzen Festival in Belgium on 21 August. Alex was at last in good health again having gained weight, and friends hoped that he was mellowing out after taking his break from the wild touring schedule. Others felt that he was rushing back to work too quickly and was still drinking too heavily.

Topping the bill at Reading should have been a springboard for a SAHB comeback – instead it turned out to be the band's last stand. Booze and illness may have ravaged him, but Alex still managed to be a showstopper. In a move surely aimed at further upsetting Mary Whitehouse, he even played the role of Jesus during the song 'Framed'. As he dragged a massive polystyrene crucifix across the stage to a perspex mound, Alex told the audience he was a carpenter whose mother was a virgin! Other crew members who were dressed as Romans helpfully nailed him to the cross. Chris Glen then added to the mayhem by coming on stage on a skateboard coinciding with Alex being 'stabbed' by his minder. The stage floor was by now covered with blackcurrant juice 'blood'. Everyone on or near the stage was in hysterics by the time Zal slipped on the juice and fell into the pit.

Derek Nicol sensed that the crucifixion act was ill-judged and over the top:

The Reading audience didn't like his Jesus impersonation at all. It was all a bit too much for them – his minder John Miller was dressed as a centurion and was whipping Alex who was wearing a crown made out of barbed wire. His forehead was actually bleeding, that's how honest a performer he really was.[11]

Ten of the songs played at Reading resurfaced in 1998 on the double live CD *The Gospel According to Harvey*. The messy recording sounds as if it was made from the audience, but it's still worth a listen. Photographer Janet Macoska was at the Reading Festival and recalls an incident after the show that highlighted just how uncomfortable Alex was becoming with the strains of being a star:

We were all in the car, ready to leave and there were fans outside the car looking for autographs or trying to talk to Alex. There was one guy in a wheelchair with his leg in a cast, and he wanted Alex to touch him, like he could heal him. That really freaked Alex out. He kept saying, 'How can they think I can do something like that?' He was not comfortable with the idea that he had such power. He really had a problem with it. I don't think Alex could have handled huge success like cracking America. It's strange but true to say that he was not really comfortable with that type of adulation. He didn't know what his responsibility was with that kind of power.[12]

Janet also thinks that the passing of Elvis Presley in August 1977 marked a turning point for Harvey. Elvis was born in the same year as Alex and he died aged just 42:

Elvis's death floored him. He couldn't believe it. Elvis was one of his first heroes in rock 'n' roll. The realisation that Elvis was mortal took a lot of steam out of Alex – I think that he started to think about his own mortality.

Later on, Alex was a man who was in some pain – whether it was physical or emotional. One time I met him, he was about 20 or 30 pounds heavier than I had ever seen him. He was depressed and just seemed kind of lost – he didn't have his enthusiasm for music or the fire that I originally saw in him any more.[13]

16

THINGS FALL APART

'I have eleven silver and gold discs, but
suddenly I was told I still owed money. I don't
understand being asked to do a tour under
financial pressure.'
Alex Harvey[1]

Soon after the Reading Festival show, details of a tour of
Scandinavia, Holland, Germany, Belgium and Switzer-
land were unveiled with the promise of a major UK tour
in December. Sadly, it would never happen and the final
curtain was about to fall on the SAHB era.

In late October, the *Daily Record*'s Gordon Blair reported
that Alex had walked out on the band during rehearsals
for a prestigious BBC2 *Sight and Sound* show at Shepperton Studios. The dramatic exit came just four days
before the start of the European jaunt. A candid Alex
revealed: 'I was halfway through the second song when
I realised it just didn't make any sense any more.' One
version of the walkout is that Alex got angry when union
technicians turned down his request to use a ten-foot

ladder as a prop during the show. They said it would be too dangerous and refused to listen to Harvey's argument that he had used the ladder at the Parkhead show without any mishaps.

Eddie Tobin has a different and much more bizarre take on the *Sight and Sound* debacle:

The BBC people were there checking the lighting and all that stuff. It was all ready to record, Alex was in the studios but then he walked past me and went out. I didn't think much of it – it was a big place and everyone was walking about. Then I went looking for him and couldn't find him. I was told that he had got in a taxi. Again, that was nothing unusual, because something could have just pissed him off. So I drove to his house in East Finchley, where he told me that he had seen a purple light and that he couldn't cross water!

Remember, we were just about to begin a European tour which was starting in Scandinavia. The company had given guarantees that he would appear. The promoters were so uncertain that we had actually flown around Europe assuring them he was coming.

So the impact of his non-appearance was going to be enormous. Because these were personal assurances which we had given. But he decided that he couldn't cross water. He couldn't be convinced to change his mind. I phoned Derek Nicol who was on holiday and we offered Alex a thousand pounds a day. He turned it down. Nothing could convince him. We would say to him, 'Do you realise you could be killed for not going on this tour?' and he just said, 'Fuck it.' It was over, and I said that to Derek.

There was nothing we could do. It was finished. He had drawn the line, physically and mentally. But he had picked a real inopportune moment to do it.[2]

In the book *All That Ever Mattered*, Ted McKenna explained how the final split came on a day that he had arrived late for a rehearsal:

Alex tore a strip off me, then turned around and said, 'That's it, I'm finished.' I left my riser and sat down beside him. We'd both lost belief in the situation, and when I mentioned the cab that brought me there was still around, he went out and got into it. I shook his hand and said, 'It's been fucking great, Alex,' and he left.[3]

A Mountain Records spokesman confirmed that all the continental gigs were off and also revealed that the rest of the band was far from happy with the situation. The spokesman dramatically added that Alex would never appear live again. The following month, *NME* seemed to confirm this, announcing that the star had 'retired'. Furious Mountain Record management soon began a lengthy legal battle against Alex, claiming he had broken a contract with them.

All those years after the break-up, Eddie Tobin still sounds upset about the way it ended:

I felt that the manner of his departure was quite insulting to the other guys in the band. I can understand him insulting Derek Nicol or insulting me, but not the band – those are people he had lived with. He woke up and he went to sleep with them. They were on buses together touring America, Germany... bad times, good times. I just thought it was dreadful. It was a 100 per cent mess near the end. I don't blame him, it's just that it wasn't right. The band stopped dead that day.

I hadn't offended him. No one had said anything or done anything to my knowledge to offend him. His lack of faith in the industry had just reached such a level that he just drew a line and said, 'That's it, I'm gone'.[4]

Tobin recalls how he later broke the news to Alex that the company was taking out an injunction against him:

I handed him with the writ from Mountain when he was walking his dogs in East Finchley. I had said to the lawyer that I wanted to do it because I didn't want it to seem impersonal and also because I liked the band. He opened the letter and he was delighted with it – because it was signed by a baron! He had never received anything that was signed by a baron before! He really found this quite exciting and he said he would frame it and put it on show in his house. So that's how much he was worried about the writ. He had reached the point where he didn't give a shit!

I think the injunction was very reasonable – especially as the company was sitting on a large debt. There was an injunction on him disposing of the equipment that belonged to the company and disposing of his talents when at that time they still belonged to the company. Let's be honest, business is business. I don't think Alex was selected for unfair treatment.[4]

Although he was undoubtedly in physical pain, Alex told the *Daily Record* that illness was not the major factor behind his decision to split the band. For the first time he hinted that all was not well financially, telling the reporter that he resented being told to tour to pay off debts. It was difficult for him to grasp that he owed money despite selling lots of records.

Almost unbelievably after five years of sell-out gigs and chart success, the band members found that their management were taking out court injunctions to recover money owed to them. Alex's widow Trudy recalls that near the end of the SAHB era, the band discovered that they were in debt to the tune of £250,000. The financial problems were to drag on even after Alex died.

Derek Nicol states that, despite the veneer of success, the SAHB never even made it close to being in the financial big league:

To be quite honest with you, The Sensational Alex Harvey Band never made any money. The reasons for that were that they were never a huge-selling album band and also that they never made it in America. They were one of the biggest live draws in the UK, they were on a par with Rod Stewart and Elton John. The SAHB were fantastic live. But if you listen to the albums, they were always very culty. They were never great songwriters. Mountain hired the Carnegie Hall in New York and played the

SAHB there – again that was a huge hype, it was a PR venture.[5]

Nicol believes that Alex's uncompromising attitude to his roots and his music worked against the SAHB in the long run – especially in the crucial American market:

If you listen to an original Soul Band record, he sounds American. Most Scottish singers around that era sounded like that. But with the SAHB, it was Alex Harvey, no compromises. His intonation was a real Glasgow accent and that in itself limits how far you can go. Americans would say, 'What's he talking about?'

There was certainly disappointment when he walked out. I was on a four-day cruise to Miami, and I got a marine telephone call from the office saying Alex Harvey's walked out and that he had decided to retire. It was one of the biggest shows that they could do and I'm stuck in the middle of the Caribbean – nothing could be done. Maybe he was just tired of being on the road – the band worked very, very hard trying to break new markets.

Alex was a lovely guy – for me he was a genius. I gave him his freedom on most things creatively. He would come up with some great ideas. But sometimes you had to try and pull the reins in a bit. With people like that there's always a line that has to be drawn.

The idea of *Vibrania* sounded fantastic – it could have been a movie or concept album. But it was one of those projects that would have needed a million pounds even in those days to do properly. And at the same time he needed to keep the band going because there was this huge debt, they were always out gigging trying to recoup money. Nazareth sold lots of records, had a long, long career and made money – the SAHB never got beyond that point.

We were all working hard trying to make it successful, but it never ever got there. They were successful in terms of credibility, probably as a cult artist, as a performer, there was no one bigger.[5]

Barbara Birdfeather's work as the group's American PR gave her first-hand insight into the dire straits they were in financially and also of the reasons for their failure to crack America:

They never had much money and they were always bitching about how little they were paid. Often they would end up asking me for five dollars just to buy cigarettes! I would give them the money and then send the bill to Fehilly!

In America, the fans that actually got to see them loved them. But I think that band were too far ahead of their time. The combination of hard rock and costumes was just too much for some fans to take. If more people had got to see them or if they had got more airplay it might have been different. The lack of airplay really killed them. It was really difficult to get radio people along to the shows, they would only want to see the main act and were very condescending to the SAHB. Alex didn't suffer fools gladly, so he couldn't really get along with some of the pretentious assholes in the business. That's why they went down so well in blue-collar towns like Cleveland.

But Alex always gave his heart wherever he played. He never held anything back – that's why the fans loved him. If they were not responding he would work so hard to get them to react. Like the crowds who came to see Jethro Tull – they were a bit more austere and would often walk into the concert late – he would work so hard on them and by the end of the concert, he would have won them over.[6]

Nearly 30 years on from the demise of the band, there is little ill-feeling among the people I talked to about the financial problems. Those closest to Harvey seem to dismiss any notion of a rip-off. There's a general realisation that, with a few honourable exceptions like Led Zeppelin or The Rolling Stones, being a rock star in the 1970s did not mean instant riches. This was an era long before the days of 'artistes' being awarded million-pound contracts for miming rather than singing.

Hugh McKenna cites a couple of facts that sum up the difference between then and now. At the peak of his career with the SAHB he was on a retainer of about £400 a week, which roughly works out at about £2,000 a week in modern-day terms. And despite being one half of the songwriting team, Hugh never got any royalties, aside from PRS, from a record company until around 1992. When he and Alex wrote the Top 30 hit 'Boston Tea Party', Hugh was told six months later by an accountant that it had only wiped off £6,000 of his debt to the company. Hugh says that an accountant who looked through the books after Mountain folded found that Hugh was owed £60,000 in unpaid advance royalties. In the end the keyboard player was awarded £3,000 by the liquidator.

Looking back on the messy demise of the band, Hugh takes a typically easygoing viewpoint:

Why didn't it make money? You are asking the wrong guy, because I have no real grasp of how people do business and I have absolutely no first-hand knowledge of what happened to any monies. Anyway, what's the point in me wasting my life away worrying when I'm enjoying my life now making music?

We had always been led to believe that, on the one hand, management had invested so much money into things like buying a PA it was always my sort of understanding that we had to be paying this back. But on the other hand there were stories flying around about journalists getting taxis from London to Birmingham and the charge being added to the band's debt.

For me personally it's all sorted out now and I don't have any wish to open up any can of worms or point fingers at anybody. All I know is that Universal Songs have got my part of the back catalogue now and since they took it over I've been getting regular royalties twice a year – not big amounts but certainly enough to help pay the phone bills.[7]

Eddie Tobin is dismissive of the idea that the SAHB were in some way ripped off.

There was no money to divide. You cannot be in private hospitals and enjoy a very high quality of life when you don't play. They weren't a band that sold 20 million albums – they were a live band. And in the last two or three years of his life he didn't gig much. Hiring a place like Shepperton Studios for rehearsal and all the lights for the European tour is really expensive. He pulled out of the SAHB two or three days before the start of a European tour and that meant that we had all the costs. It was ludicrous to think that they should have had any money – it wasn't as if all the songs were number one in the charts.

Fehilly lost money. Fehilly would say that he wanted to recoup, but he was always happy, win or lose. Fehilly understood it was a gamble. He won the gamble with Nazareth. What would have happened had Bill lived – who knows? Would he have made earth-shattering decisions that would have changed the world and Alex would still be with us? I don't know.[8]

John Miller noted the depth of Alex's growing distaste of the business that he had devoted his life to.

I think he got pissed off that Mountain had this big four-storied office with marble floors in Mayfair, with about 32 people walking about doing next to nothing while the band is out grafting. We finished a tour once and Alex said to me, 'I want you to go and take some money off some cunt for me.' I said, 'Who?' and he said, 'This guy miscellaneous.' We looked at the tour accounts and the only thing that had made money was this 'miscellaneous'![9]

Trudy Harvey is sure that the financial hassles were just one of many factors affecting her husband. He was also exhausted from touring and had lost his creative edge. She knows that the pressures of fame were telling on him and that he felt uneasy about being recognised in the streets. Alex may have initially yearned for success, but when it came his way, it brought all sorts of unwelcome factors into his everyday life.

As Trudy Harvey describes it:

Alex's ambition was to make an impression. He was an extremely political person and he believed that the world was quite a controlled place and that the powers that be were corrupt. He wanted fame in the sense that it would allow him to try and change things – to make the world a fairer place. He wanted to bring injustices to light and he was full of an impotent rage when he found out that in fact he couldn't change things. So it wasn't as if he had a great personal ambition to be the famous Alex Harvey – he just wanted to use that fame as a vehicle to help others. In many ways he actually hated fame. I remember times when we would be shopping in Muswell Hill and we would see three or four young women walking down the road towards us. He could see that they were recognising him and he just didn't like it at all. Another time, we were in a newsagent in Glasgow and Alex took a girlie mag off the top shelf and was looking through it. He looked out the window and there were all these little boys peering in at him! He really wasn't someone who was at ease with being recognised away from the stage.[10]

*

In 1977 with the SAHB dissolving in a sea of litigation, Alex was depressed and drinking heavily. There's certainly no shortage of stories about Alex Harvey's excessive habits. But some of those closest to Harvey question how – if he was drinking a bottle of vodka a day – he managed to keep up such a busy work schedule during his final years. They also disclosed to me that the doctor who carried out the autopsy after Alex died said some of his organs were like those of a young man. There was no evidence of cirrhosis of the liver or of cocaine or other drug abuse. Some would argue that stories of his alcoholism should be left out of this book – and indeed some stories have been omitted. But Harvey's whole persona was built around his drinking and he was often drunk on stage later in his career. His boozing wasn't exactly a secret, and to leave it out of this book would be a cop-out.

Trudy Harvey explains her husband's decline and heavy drinking by saying:

You have to realise that Alex was very frustrated towards the end of his life. Things hadn't gone right for him. He had lost his brother and he'd lost his manager. Also when his manager died, the SAHB were in debt to the tune of £250,000, which was an awful lot of money back then. The band had done strenuous, gruelling tours of the USA where they toured for maybe six weeks with only, say, three days off when they didn't have a gig. And they would sometimes be getting on two planes a day. I think Alex was very frustrated that when he had been working so hard all he had to show for it was this debt. I don't think Mountain Management were to blame – it costs a lot of money to do things like go on tour with Jethro Tull.

The big idea was to break in America and the method was just touring, touring and more touring. But in the event they only broke in pockets of the States, like in Cleveland where they were massive. Whereas over here once they put an ad in the music press the shows just sold out. Alex never did things by half. Every night on tour he would put 100 per cent into the gig. I don't think he was very good at pacing himself. He would come back home from tours really zapped. He would just go to his bed for two or three days. And you have to remember that he was 12 to 15 years older than most of the guys in the band.[11]

Like many other observers, Trudy believes that Alex was ahead of his time and would have been much more of a success in the modern age:

He and the band had such fantastic ideas that would have been brilliant in the age of video. It would have been a whole different ball game for that band if it had all just happened for them a little bit later. I know he was frustrated by the attitude of some people in the business towards the ideas he had. For instance we went to Morocco for a couple of weeks holiday and we made friends with a lot of the local musicians. They tried to teach Alex some Arabic music and he in turn would teach them stuff like songs by The Beatles. Alex came back to Britain very, very fired up and said, 'I've got my support band – I want to bring these guys over here.' But whoever was in charge at Mountain Management said, 'You cannot do that!' It was as if he was being told, 'Don't do anything other than what you are doing 'cos what you are doing is on the way to making it'. Nobody did that type of thing back then, whereas nowadays every band seems to use musicians from Asia or Africa. Alex was incredibly creative and ahead of his time. Part of the frustration he undoubtedly had was that he couldn't sell those ideas – which seemed quite zany back then – to the people who controlled the pounds, shillings and pence.[12]

Alex was beginning to resemble the punch-drunk ex-boxing champ still aiming for a tilt at old glories. In March 1978, *Rock Drill*, which had been influenced by Alex's liking for a statue by Sir Jacob Epstein at the Tate Gallery, was released, but it flopped. Reviews were mixed, with even the arch-Alex fan Charles Shaar Murray finding little to enthuse over. Murray was less than complimentary about the influence of the band's new keyboard man Tommy Eyre, and he concluded that, although it had good moments, when the album was bad it was 'tedious in the extreme'. Reviews like that led many old fans to give the album a wide berth, but listening to *Rock Drill* now one can't help feeling that the critics judged it too harshly.

The tracks sound every bit as good – if not better – as some of the songs which filled the SAHB albums in the mid 1970s. True, it doesn't have any classic songs which would rank alongside 'Next' or 'Midnight Moses', but considering *Rock Drill* was recorded after a long lay-off for the band, they sound as tough and ballsy as they ever did. It's all the more credible when one considers that they cut the record just as all the health and financial worries were surfacing. If anything they sound re-invigorated, and they had lost none of their capacity to experiment – witness the offbeat homage to the Loch Ness Monster, 'Water Beastie', and the use of Austrian composer Max Steiner's stirring instrumental soundtrack to the 1933 Fay Wray movie *King Kong*.

Lyrically, Alex also showed that he was still not afraid to take a risk and the excellent introductory line to the album, which wonders why zebra crossings abound where antelope used to roam, shows his green credentials. In a song like 'Rock 'n' Roll' he even throws in references to Nietzsche and Engels, which perhaps reinforces the notion that the band were a cut above the competition in the hard rock stakes.

According to Trudy Harvey, the track 'Booids' with its thunderous Burundi-style drumming came about after she and Alex watched a TV programme on Persian history in which huge bands tried to recreate the music of that era. Alex, ever eager to adapt something different into rock 'n' roll, tried to get the SAHB to play in that style. Interestingly the final track on the album should have been 'No Complaints Department', a reworking of a song from Alex's 1964 album *The Blues*. Harvey fanatics swear that the song was one of the best things the SAHB ever did, but for whatever reason it was jettisoned at the last minute. In its place is the worthy singalong 'Mrs Blackhouse', which never really hit the spot back in 1978 and sounds even less convincing today.

John Miller recalls that the making of *Rock Drill* had seen a continuation in Harvey's hostile attitude to his bosses:

After we had done the album, Alex said to me, 'I need some money for drugs for the boys.' I told him he wouldn't get any more money until the management heard a couple of tracks, because at that time nobody has heard anything. But Alex insisted that I go to London and tell them I need £400 to get Jazz Clarke to play in a session. I asked him who Jazz Clarke was and he said, 'He's no cunt, but they won't know that – they'll say, "Wow, how did Alex get Jazz Clarke to play?" So I went to London and told them all this and it went all around the office,

'Hey, Alex has got Jazz Clarke to play on the record.' And of course they ended up giving him the money.

Towards the end of SAHB, I used to tell him that he had to try and conform a bit – give the record company what they wanted. But by then he had lost momentum and he had lost the band – it's like Plant without Page, Rotten without the Sex Pistols, or Laurel without Hardy, the whole thing was very much him and the band. He knew he had so much to offer but he didn't have the vehicle to offer it in. It's like being an athlete – if the Olympics are in June, it's no good peaking in January. The Sensational Alex Harvey Band just peaked too early.[13]

17

THE NEW BAND

'No one knows yet how long you can go in pop music. If I use my head I do not see any reason why I should give it up. After all, Louis Armstrong was 70 when he finished playing.'[1]
Alex Harvey

For the first time in six years, Alex faced the prospect of life without his trusted band to back him up. Given his health problems, it certainly would have been advisable for him to slow down, or even take the big step of moving away from performing to try something different. Perhaps he could have joined the ranks of rock stars who dabbled in acting. (His eldest son Alex is today a respected actor on the Scottish scene.) Instead, the old trouper chose the gruelling option of forming a new band together with Tommy Eyre and an 18-year-old English guitar prodigy called Matthew Cang. They drafted in a second guitarist Suzy Tinline, drummer Phil Mount and bassist John Peerless.

The newly formed group only played one gig – a spectacular Sunday night show at the London Palladium. Harvey was obviously up for the gig and told the expectant audience 'This is costin' me a lorra fucking money, so youse berra shurrup an listen!' Aided by pipers, drummers, the cast of the show *Camelot* and a troupe of dancing girls, the concert was a one-off spectacular. Some of the crowd called out for Zal, but they had to make do with storming renditions of old favourites like 'Midnight Moses' and 'Vambo' alongside a waltz version of the Sex Pistols 'Anarchy in the UK'!

But plans to premiere *Vibrania* – the concept album Alex had been working on for ages – were scuppered by record company bosses who issued an injunction forbidding Alex to perform it. One of the audience that night was Alex's old colleague from Giant Moth, the drummer George Butler, who recalls being less than impressed with what was on offer:

The band were like a bunch of narcoleptic session musicians … Alex came on with this big marine guy who was his bodyguard shuffling him up to the mike. I was thinking, is this an act like James Brown used to do? He was slurring his words shouting, 'I'm back with the best band in the world!' It sounded more like a plea than a statement.[2]

Despite such reservations, the show was deemed to have been a success overall and when someone in the crowd yelled, 'Welcome back!', Alex replied, 'Ah ain't everr bin awae, bebby,' to rousing cheers.

But Alex soon decided to shuffle the pack again and start afresh with yet another new band, which with an unerring degree of logic he called The New Band. Keyboard maestro Hugh McKenna returned to the fold, though later that year he was again replaced by Tommy

Eyre. After jamming sessions the new line-up was settled upon – Harvey, Tommy Eyre along with Gordon Sellar on bass, Simon Charterton on drums, sax player Don Weller and guitarist Matthew Cang. In October, details were released to the music press of the band's first major gigs at the Venue in London the following month.

Harvey's choice of Matthew Cang showed that he still had a keen interest in nurturing young talent and was not averse to taking risks. Matthew was fresh out of school when, in the autumn of 1977, he learned from a friend that Alex was on the look-out for a new band. Matthew remembers that it took a number of telephone calls to the Harvey household before he struck lucky and got to speak to the man himself:

One day, Alex picked up the phone and I told him I wanted to play in his band. I think he was a bit taken aback by it. But a month or so later I got a call to come down for an audition. It was just after New Year 1978. I met him at the old Vortex club in London, we had a jam and that was it! I don't remember ever being told, 'You've got the job' – I just started getting calls saying 'Rehearsals start on Monday at such and such a place – see you then.' The first band was put together mainly for the gig at the London Palladium in March 1978. But that was the only gig that band did. Shortly after that, they split, and I got a call from Alex saying he wanted to try something new – to write some new material and form a new band with me included.[3]

The New Band toured around England and Europe during the latter half of 1978 but most of the following year was spent off the road, rehearsing and recording at Morgan Studios in North London. Alex did however make an unusual appearance at the Glastonbury Festival in June 1979. Peter Gabriel had included him in an eclectic mix of performers including Tom Robinson, Phil Collins, Steve Hillage and Nona Hendryx. Harvey appeared on stage dressed in a kaftan and proceeded to trade insults with some members of the audience.

His friend Tom Robinson was seriously alarmed by his behaviour.

Alex was clearly drunk and out of control. This was a chance for him to shine on stage alongside a bunch of big names in front of a massive audience, and he blew it. It was such a shock after his charismatic performance at Ally Pally with the TRB only a few months earlier – I'd never seen that self-destructive side of him before. But that's what alcohol does to people.

Robinson's own star was waning by this point and the two men never appeared together on stage again. As to why Alex might have been turning to the bottle, Robinson offers some intriguing parallels to his own career:

Even from my own 15 minutes of fame, I remember how crushing it felt when that sudden celebrity was taken away from me, having longed for it all my life. And any former teen idol's self-esteem takes a hit when he nears the age of 50. You lose your looks, energy levels subside, and the slog of touring small venues again starts to feel like seriously hard work.

The bass player with The New Band, Gordon Sellar, had joined the group following a suggestion from Brian Adams, a Scot who was briefly fulfilling the role of Alex's manager and who had also previously bossed Sellar's own early 1970s band, Beggar's Opera:

The SAHB had split and Alex had done the Palladium show. Not long after that he got hold of Simon Charterton who was a friend of Matthew Cang, and then Brian suggested they get hold of me. Alex obviously remembered Beggar's Opera, and we were soon rehearsing with him at a wee place in Euston. That's where we worked on the album. We rehearsed all the stuff there and then took it on the road.

During the recording of the album Alex was fine. We put the

basic tracks down fairly quickly, we had been on the road, done Europe and Scandinavia and all the rest of it. So we knew the stuff back to front – the only difference was that Tommy Eyre had come back by that time. Hugh McKenna wasn't that well again.[4]

November 1979 saw the release of The New Band's one and only album, *The Mafia Stole My Guitar* – the obscure title referred to the incident in Miami back in 1975, when the band's gear was stolen. Apparently they learned subsequently that the equipment was stolen to order by the Mob and had been smuggled to Cuba within hours of the theft.

The new single, a cover of Johnny Kidd's signature tune 'Shakin' All Over' got an encouraging *NME* review from Alex's old friend Charles Shaar Murray. Murray warned readers that the single was not for the squeamish and Alex's voice was 'Glasgow's answer to nuclear attack'. *Melody Maker* also gave the album guarded praise saying: 'It's a deceptive achievement ... His writing still has bravado but he seems wiser and more reflective now.' The reviewer John Orme went so far as to say that if it wasn't for a couple of oddball tracks the record would be nearly faultless.

The Mafia Stole My Guitar confounded many of the snipers who thought Alex was all washed up creatively. Indeed, in many ways Alex seems to have got a new lease of life during the recording of the album. Much of the credit goes to The New Band who play superbly throughout. In a way Alex seems to revel in the freedom of playing with new musicians and the choice of the jazz veteran Don Weller was an inspired one. It's a confident, energetic record which remains a favourite with many fans and with Alex's immediate family. It also contains an overlooked classic in the closing track – a cover of

Louis Prima's 'Just a Gigolo/I Ain't Got Nobody'. The song would become a hit a few years later when Van Halen's frontman David Lee Roth sang it, but Harvey's version is infinitely superior – when he sings about how sad and lonely he is, it would bring a tear to a glass eye.

Before the important shows at the Venue in November, The New Band headed north for a warm-up concert at York University. It was meant to be the start of a brave new chapter for Alex. Instead it turned into a drunken shambles which sadly was to become quite common in the next couple of years. Gordon Sellar says the problems started halfway up the motorway:

We travelled up on a luxury bus with all the wives and girl-friends, and lots of food and drink. Anyway the bus broke down and we had to jettison some of the company. Then we all squashed into a 12-seater transit. And Alex just sat there, and put his coat over his head and started saying 'It never changes.' He must have said it about 40 times before we got to York.

We were a bit late in arriving, and things were already a bit traumatic. A certain amount of alcohol was in the dressing room before the gig, and Alex fortified himself rather too much. He did have a chip on his shoulder about students anyway – he was always saying that they sponged off the state. So he ended up shouting at the students. He spent most of the night berating the audience. The audience was for lynching him – all hell was breaking loose and we went off the stage – but he stayed on and carried on insulting the audience while they shouted back at him. We had to go back on, play an encore and haul him off.

I said to Hugh McKenna, 'Is he always like this'? And Hugh just replied, 'Aye'! Anyway, we finally got the luxury bus back, and on the way back home, Alex had got himself together, and he smiles and he says, 'I was a wee bit nervous tonight'! And that was all he said – it was never mentioned again. That was our very first gig and it was the worst night of the time I spent with him.[5]

The Venue shows – the band played two shows a night for three nights – went much better, with Alex's old friends Billy Connolly and Richard O'Brien showing up and introducing the new group to the audience. Gordon Sellar says crowd response was generally favourable, though some fans seemed a bit annoyed that 'Delilah' and 'Framed' were the only SAHB songs they played.

However, sales of the new album were sluggish and four showcase gigs in Glasgow, Newcastle, Birmingham and Sheffield in January 1980 did little to dissuade anyone from the belief that Alex was increasingly irrelevant to the music scene of the new decade. The *Daily Record* even poked fun at Alex for planning yet another comeback calling him the 'Rocky of Rock'. Alex hit back and told the paper that he was fighting fit but still angry about the legal problems. Asked why he still bothered, he told the reporter that rock 'n' roll was the only life he knew. He seemed to take pride in the fact that he was the only one of his contemporaries who had started out with him back in the 1950s who was still singing.

Alex was especially looking forward to the Glasgow Apollo concert on 10 January – the only problem was that hardly anyone else was, and ticket sales were poor. Six days prior to the gig, Alex told Andy Collier of the *Glasgow Herald* that he was one of rock 'n' roll's great survivors and also tried to convince readers that *Mafia* was one of his strongest ever recordings. He said he felt invigorated by the young musicians who now backed him, paying fulsome tribute to them and to the punk bands, especially the Sex Pistols, whom he adored.

Collier gained rare access to Harvey's domestic life with his wife Trudy, his two sons and two pet dogs. The family lived in a comfortable terraced home in Finchley, North London, where Trudy worked as a potter in her small studio. Alex talked passionately to the *Herald* reporter about the need to preserve wildlife. He then proudly displayed his incredible collection of Victorian and Edwardian toy soldiers and admitted to having a fascination for the 'dreadful days of the British Empire'.

In what was to be one of his last major interviews, Alex argued that he saw no reason to quit, saying age hadn't stopped some of his old jazz heroes from playing on, concluding:

I've lasted in music because I have done everything you can name in the business. But nothing counts as much as a few close confidantes.[6]

Unfortunately the interview did little to boost interest in the concert. Only 300 tickets were sold for what was meant to be a triumphant return to the scene of the SAHB's greatest conquests. In a bid to boost numbers, tickets were given away to people passing by the Glasgow Apollo. The fiasco apparently cost the band's recording company, RCA, £1,400. The *Glasgow Herald* reported that it was 'a shamefully attended welcome home party' and reporter Andy Collier concluded that Glasgow's most famous ever rock star was no longer popular in his home city. Collier added that those who had bothered to show up were noisily enthusiastic and were royally entertained by the jazzy New Band which featured two saxophone players. The reporter thought Alex had 'reached new heights of maturity – quite simply he's better than ever now, it was an honour to see him'.

Despite such plaudits, Alex was unhappy. According to friends, the poor turnout hit him hard. He had to face the fact that for the first time in years he could no longer command the automatic respect and admiration of his public even in his native Glasgow. Gordon Sellar says word was getting about that Harvey just wasn't cutting it any more:

I played the Apollo twice with him. The first time was in 1978, but by 1980 I think folk had kind of sussed that it wasn't the same level of show that he had been putting on before. He may have been hurt – though he didn't let it show really. But all of it was going on inside really.

After the Apollo gig there was a reception for the group at the Lorne Hotel, where his family were present. I didn't think there was anything of Alex in his dad – he was quite a mild-mannered wee fellow.[7]

Unsure of what to do next, The New Band gradually drifted apart. However Matthew Cang still has fond memories of the group and his time with Alex, especially when they played together on stage:

All the gigs I did with him were usually memorable! There was a small tour we did in 1980 (just after the Iranian Embassy siege in London) with the whole band dressed as the SAS in black with ski-masks, and Alex came on dressed as the Ayatollah!

We also did a gig at Leyhill prison, which was ... different. Songs like 'Framed' and 'Delilah' have a different intensity in front of an audience like that – you did feel that some members of the audience had a certain empathy with the subject matter! In the studio Alex was always willing to try new things, so I remember it as being a pretty creative time. He was always into trying new effects on his voice, as well as trying to get the right take on tape. I found him very generous to work with – he gave me a lot of room to work. If I wanted to experiment, he would always back me up and let me try things.[8]

He also adds to the theory that, contrary to the way he has been portrayed by other writers, Alex was not a complete shambling wreck in the years after the SAHB split.

I don't know how much he drank before I knew him, but he wasn't overly excessive at that time, as I recall. We'd often go out and have a few pints, but I rarely saw him drink more than that. He never seemed to be overly depressed about his business affairs, although I know they played on his mind – I remember him saying, 'How can I have worked for a record

company for so long and still owe them this much money?'
Maybe it was my youthful enthusiasm, but I was more interested in us doing something new and fresh, so I didn't pay too
much attention to the legal stuff.[8]

Eddie Tobin has a different take on Alex's drinking habits and what caused them.

He was never incoherent through drink, but I believe he was
drinking very heavily. Vodka was his drink of choice. He could
hold it but it was impairing his judgement. Was it depression?
Was it frustration? Was it anger? I don't actually know what it
was. He was someone who wanted to create something but who
wasn't achieving it. I think he was angry with everybody when
he really should have been angry with himself.[9]

18

THE FINAL YEARS

'The best gigs I ever did in my life were with
him – but the worst ones were
as well.'[1]
Gordon Sellar on his time with Alex Harvey

Alex Harvey's final years weren't the best ones of his
life. Not many people were buying his records, and fans
weren't going to see him perform in large numbers. By all
accounts he felt frustrated, even angry about the way his
life had turned out. He was in debt and had lost all faith
in the men in suits who were meant to be pushing his
career in the right direction. And of course he wasn't in
the best of health. He was drinking heavily and also taking prescription pills from a Harley Street doctor, which
weren't mixing well with alcohol.

One man who spent a good deal of time with Alex in
his last few years was Ray Conn, a fellow Scot who first
met the singer in the 1960s. Then they were both young
men hoping for a career in the music business and hanging out together at the Giaconda Café and other haunts

in London's Tin Pan Alley. The pair remained friends and Ray travelled extensively with Alex on one of his last tours of the UK. He also worked on the *Soldier on the Wall* album, penning 'The Poet and I' and providing backing vocals on other songs. His memories of the star are tinged with sadness and he remembers that at times he was in every sense a shoulder for the troubled star to cry on:

Alex sometimes would literally just cry in my arms like a baby. He would come up to me and throw his arms around me and just start crying. It was like there was something wrong but he couldn't tell me what it was. It was a really disturbing thing to see. I think in a way that he probably knew he was pretty ill late on in his life. But he was also frustrated because he wanted to do more, he told me he wanted to go into production or into films. I wanted to help him because I had connections in the film industry. Alex always used to say 'I don't want to end up like another Tony Monopoly – the guy who won *Opportunity Knocks*'. He was also very disappointed with his record company RCA. He didn't feel that they were 100 per cent behind him, and I think he had heard backroom talk that they were saying he was finished and all that. If you listen to the song 'Poet and I' when he sings about Highland Mary, he is crying his eyes out.[2]

Public appearances were becoming increasingly problematic – before a gig at Nottingham Rock City club, Alex did an interview for a local radio station, which had to be cut short when he turned up drunk and started swearing during the recording. However, even though there were obviously serious problems in Alex's life, Ray is adamant that he was still performing brilliantly. Sometimes, though, it was touch and go:

For two days before the last Newcastle gig he was more or less unconscious. We carried him onto the bus to go to Newcastle. We were literally ten seconds away from cancelling the concert. The first band had already been on and you could hear the crowd screaming and Alex was still unconscious. But we managed to stir him and – amazingly – he got up and did a handstand. He stood on his head for about five seconds! And then he went on to do the best gig I've ever seen him do. After the gig the band headed off in the coach, and Alex and I got a taxi to Birmingham and charged it to RCA!

I organised the concert at Leyhill Open prison. We came inside the prison gates in a van and the governor came out and said 'where is this famous pop star?' So we opened the van door and again, Alex was actually drunk and unconscious in the back of the van when we came inside the prison gates. We said, 'Oh, he's just asleep,' – but in fact he was totally out of it.

I also organised a concert down in Brighton for Greenpeace where Alex ended up having a fight on stage with Gary Holton, who used to sing with The Heavy Metal Kids. Holton came into the hall dressed in all his leather gear and shouted out, 'Alex Harvey is a wanker,' and Alex stopped the concert. All these Greenpeace tweedy types were looking on amazed and Alex says, 'Who are you calling a wanker, you bastard? Come up here on stage and say it.' I ended up throwing a Russian flag over the pair of them. Alex ended up not getting his fee for that concert. We were at the Venue one night and Bill Wyman of The Rolling Stones was there. Alex was on and he died a death – he was crap that night. I asked Wyman why he was there and he replied, 'I've come to see the master – Alex Harvey.'

The day Alex left for his final tour of Europe, I met him at the Warwick Arms pub in Maida Vale and bought him a case of beer. I was on my way to Nice the next day, so the last thing I said to him was, 'I'll yodel over the mountains for you'. And we gave each other a hug. That was the last time I ever saw him.[3]

Bass guitarist Gordon Sellar played on and off with Alex for almost four years, eventually leaving him just six months before Harvey's death. Gordon has mixed views of his time spent with Alex and gives an honest reply when asked if he enjoyed those days:

Overall, I have to be genuine and say it's 50/50 – which is sad, because the best gigs I ever did in my life were with him – but the worst ones were as well. He wasn't constantly drunk – it came and went. Sometimes he would start off a set of gigs brand new but gradually he would go downhill. He was drinking by himself, shutting himself away in his room. It wasn't like he would always be drinking openly and falling over in pubs all over the place – although that did happen as well.

His mood drifted one way and then another. Even latterly you could have fairly positive conversations with him. But the gigs were getting worse and he was letting people down. One time we went all the way to Luxembourg and never did the gig. We just did the sound check and then had to come home.

It did become quite a worry. We did a whole tour once where he had forgotten his passport. We went all over Europe and every time we went over a border, he had to be hidden under a pile of clothes in the back of a van.

We did the Marquee club once, and he wandered on stage in his normal clothes and stripped to his Y-fronts before getting into his stage clothes – all in front of the punters. He had this wee tuppence halfpenny cassette player and he put it up to the mike and told the crowd, 'Listen to this' – it was a tape of the old jazz guy Bix Beiderbecke – and he just stood there listening to this tape for three and a half minutes. And then he says, 'Isn't that fantastic?' Then we did a song.

By that time he was spending all day speaking to people on the phone and messing around, then come three o'clock in the morning he would get creative, but by that time we were knackered. He was an insomniac. In the hotel, you had to lock your door at night, you'd hear a knock on the door at five in the morning and you'd just lie there pretending to be asleep.

But he was a very, very genuine guy. He went with his heart all the time. He was very well-read and very intelligent. He was a gentleman when he was OK. There was no malice about him.[4]

Zal Cleminson was also finding life after the SAHB somewhat difficult. In the immediate aftermath of the split he formed the Zal Band, along with Ted and Chris and two new recruits, Le Roi Jones on vocals and Billy Rankin on guitar. Le Roi had previously been with the outrageous American band The Tubes and had met the SAHB gang on tour. When Alex quit the band, Chris Glen contacted Le Roi and asked him to take over the vocal chores. Zal rehearsed in a cramped garage at the rear of Glen's London home before embarking on UK and Swedish tour dates. But, soon after, Zal called a halt to the group.

After that short-lived project, Zal teamed up with fellow Mountain Records veterans Nazareth in October 1978. But by the early 1980s, the man who had thrilled tens of thousands of fans only a few years earlier was working as a London cabbie. In James McNair's *Mojo* article, Zal recalls how by sheer coincidence he picked up Alex and Matthew Cang as a fare one day! Soon afterwards, Alex invited Zal to listen to some new songs he was working on and sound him out about reforming the SAHB. Zal turned him down:

I remember thinking, these songs don't sound very good to me and I told him I was happier with what I was writing myself. Looking back it was a cruel thing to say considering what I felt about Alex in the long term, but I was trying to be honest.[5]

Zal also told *Mojo* how he met Alex for the final time at a Mountain Records drinks reception for Nazareth in London:

Alex turns up, and the doors are all locked. He's banging at the windows shouting, 'Let me in' – and I'm in the foyer looking at him. Behind me all the band and the hangers-on are giving it laldy. I'm saying, 'Can we not let him in?' But I'm hearing, 'No, don't. Don't let him in!' Alex was in front of me and my new life was behind me. I turned away from the window and Alex must have gone home. It was an odd moment, a terrible moment, if I'm honest.[5]

The Mountain organisation went into liquidation in 1980. Derek Nicol explains:

We tried to create a career out of the SAHB without Alex and also with Zal, but it never worked. The whole thing was like a big family pushing in the same direction – not like a normal record company, which is a completely cold unit with no relationships. When things don't happen, I suppose there are bound to be grudges at the end. The trouble is that musicians never understand the economics of funding a band. You want a limousine, yeah, you can have one, but that's another lot of records you have to sell to recoup the cost. Mountain was a very successful record company with a great reputation at one stage, but of all the acts we had, only Nazareth made money.[6]

Despite his health problems, Alex began 1981 still seeking out the old buzz of the music business. After almost a year away from the UK stage he played some gigs in February, concentrating on the club circuit and with the same four-piece band – which was now to be known as The Alex Harvey Band. *NME* of 14 February reported that, after the concerts, Harvey was heading to Germany to do nine shows there, then it was back to Britain in March for five more. This time though, the personnel of the band changed – with Ian Taylor on lead guitar and Alex's old friend Bill Patrick on sax as two new recruits.

In August, Alex was billed to play at the Reading Festival. Where he had once been the headline act, now he was fifth on the Saturday line-up behind groups like Samson and Trust. Ian Gillan topped the bill. In the final few months of his life, Alex was still out on the road and in the recording studio, but in August 1981 he did agree to take a break and go with his family on a walking holiday around the west coast of Scotland, calling at places like Campbeltown and Ardrossan and meeting old friends along the way. By a bizarre coincidence, he bumped into one of the guys in his old group, Giant Moth, as they strolled along Brodick beach. In October he did some of his last gigs in the UK on the club circuit.

By December 1981, work continued on his final album *Soldier on the Wall* with a new band called The Electric

Cowboys that hailed from the Rhonda Valley in Wales, featuring Jack Dawe on bass and Ian Taylor on guitar. Alex and Kevin Nixon of Power Station Records produced the record. But fate was to intervene before the finishing touches could be put to the record. The album was released posthumously in November 1983, after being remixed by Roy Neave of Fairport Studios in Hull. Roy remembers being told that the original recording had been difficult:

The tapes were unfinished and there was quite a lot of tarting about to be done on them. Kevin told me that the vocals on one track apparently had originally been recorded with Alex lying drunk on the floor singing into the bass drum mike while the drums were being played! But these were just guide vocals, apparently when he died he was just on the way back to England to redo the vocals, so the whole thing was a bit cobbled together.[7]

Live gigs around this time were pretty shambolic affairs – frequently Alex had to be helped on stage at the start of the show. On other occasions he looked uninterested, swigging beer and often missing his cue. One young man who travelled with Alex's last band on a tour of clubs in the north of England was Daniel Bennett who was then a 14-year-old schoolboy. Daniel – who is now a conservation biologist – played truant from school to tour and hang out with Harvey and the group. He says that the old trouper was still capable of great things on stage, but adds:

That was the only time in the 24 hours that he seemed to be alive, there was absolutely nothing out of him during the day. He just slept all day and at night he was drinking heavily. When he woke up he looked as rough as anything. He would wake up half an hour before he would start performing and then he would be really lively.

One time we were in Hull and discovered that the manager of

the hotel we stayed at had been a policeman in Glasgow in the 1950s who had arrested Alex over some whisky that had gone missing! They recognised each other and stayed up all night drinking. We were woken at five in the morning by the sound of Alex wrestling this huge Alsatian dog! He was crazy during the nights. Sometimes when he woke up he would get this wee Casio keyboard out and start banging about on it and singing this song 'The Tombstone Trail'.

He used to talk about all his friends that had died and I got the impression then that he knew he did not have long left. He looked as rough as anything till about ten o'clock at night when he got on that stage and he was incredible, electrifying. He was probably pissed on stage but he was 100 per cent professional.[8]

So when the moment was right he could still summon up some of the old magic. A bootleg video of the Electric Cowboys playing in Vienna can still be bought at record fairs, and although it's a very poor recording from the crowd, it's a snapshot of Alex playing live near the end of his life.

Throughout the 95-minute tape, Alex looks seriously under the weather. At times he seems to be in a trance, smiling sweetly out into the small audience. On other occasions he grabs his guitarist or bass player in an emotional hug. Then he has extreme difficulty getting his own guitar plugged in. When he finally manages to do so, he drops his plectrum. With anyone else the whole debacle would be an embarrassment but somehow the affection of the audience and the band members towards Alex pulls him through. The band open with a blistering 'Faith Healer' before playing lengthy jams on a couple of new songs – 'Snowshoes Thompson' and 'Flowers Mr Florist'- to cover up for the fact that Alex had missed his cue and is wandering around aimlessly backstage.

A slovenly 'Delilah' sees Alex entertaining the roadies by taking advantage of an inflatable doll at the side of the stage. He introduces a new song 'The Ballad of Billy Bolero' by saying he wrote it for his friend Clint Eastwood. When some of the crowd laugh, Alex tells them 'I'm no fuckin' jokin'!' The old showstopper 'Framed' is also peppered with expletives before Alex at last gets his act together and does a passable impersonation of Marlon Brando in *The Godfather*. Things get a bit silly during 'Gang Bang' when Alex tries to get the docile audience involved, inviting around 15 of them up on stage – where they stand around looking bemused and wasted. The drunken ringmaster eventually remembers he has company and they all go into a huddle to sing the chorus. The concert ends with Alex making painfully naïve – if well meant – comments to his Austrian fans about the Nazi occupation of their country during World War II. By now Alex has given up any pretence of singing in tune, and the whole affair is a glorious mess, even though the audience seems to enjoy the spectacle.

Even if live concerts were increasingly hit-or-miss affairs, Alex still was hooked on touring and performing. Janet Macoska recalls speaking to him prior to his final tour of Europe. Alex told her that he was off the booze and he sounded in good spirits and genuinely enthused about his latest band, asking the photographer if she thought they would do well in the USA.

The Christmas before he died, he travelled to Scotland to visit his parents and his older son. Alex junior was by now starting to play a bigger role in helping his father and he worked alongside management to set up tentative plans for an Australian tour that would have gone ahead in the spring or summer of 1982. Sadly it was never to happen – within a matter of weeks Alex Harvey would be dead.

19

TIME FOR TRIBUTES

'I couldn't care what they do to me when I'm dead. They can cut me up in quarters... or distribute me to the poor.'[1]
Alex Harvey

On the morning of 3 February 1982, the phone rang in Councillor Jimmy Wray's Glasgow office. A secretary took a message and passed it on to Wray when he arrived at work the following day. The simple message read, 'Alex Harvey needs your help.' Whatever was behind the plea was to remain a mystery – for on the same day, 4 February, Alex Harvey died. Wray had kept in contact with his old friend from the Gorbals, the two occasionally exchanged long phone calls and talked about the old times. Just before his death, Alex had expressed an interest in doing a fundraising concert in Glasgow to help a drug rehabilitation project that Wray was involved with. Twenty years on, Wray – now a Member of Parliament – recalls:

I was really shocked when I heard Alex had died. I didn't hear from him that often. Once he went away on the road and gained success, very few people saw him up here in Glasgow. I think he changed a lot. I've heard stories I wouldn't repeat.[2]

*

On 5 February the people of Scotland woke to discover that one of their favourite sons had passed away. A three-paragraph news digest item hidden away on page five of the *Glasgow Herald* detailed the facts in a perfunctory way:

Rock star, Alex Harvey, 46, veteran of the sixties R&B boom died from a heart attack yesterday as he was about to return to Britain from a European tour. He had reached Belgium and was with tour manager Gordon Rowley when he collapsed. He died later in hospital.' His agent in London, Shirley Stone, told the newspaper: 'Alex Harvey leaves a wife, two children and a lot of fans.[3]

Even on a quiet news day, the country's other leading broadsheet *The Scotsman* could only manage a four-paragraph tribute, though it did recognise Alex's great theatrical flair, and his 'raw gritty tone and expressive phrasing'.

There was something terribly apt about Alex dying while he was on the road. After over 30 years in the business he was still entertaining his fans right up to the end. He had arrived in Belgium at the end of a four-week European tour with The Electric Cowboys. Harvey was waiting to board a ferry in Zeebruggen. One account was that Harvey stopped walking and clutched at his chest, saying, 'This is it, boys,' before collapsing. The ferry was held up to see if Alex would revive, but when it became clear that his condition was serious he was rushed to hospital. He had suffered a massive heart attack from which he could never recover. While in a coma in hospital, he had a second heart attack and died – one day shy of his 47th birthday. Harvey had lived a hard, strenuous life and in the end his body just gave in. His heartbroken band members were given the news halfway across the English Channel.

Alex's funeral took place at Golders Green Crematorium. Hugh McKenna played a poignant rendition of 'Anthem' on the piano. Alex's elderly father was dressed in a black velvet jacket and made a point of shaking hands personally with everyone who attended. Leslie Senior, who had survived both his sons, did an Indian chant at the coffin in a tribute to his son's love of cowboys and Indians. He urged people not to cry at the service, but when a lone Highland piper started to play the emotions were uncontrollable. Derek Wadsworth recalls: 'At the funeral, Alex's father stood up and raised his hands to the sky and said, "God, I give you my last son".' Afterwards most of the congregation adjourned to a nearby pub for a party that went on well into the night. But despite the booze and smokes, the atmosphere was by all accounts pretty despairing.

Exactly one year after Alex's death, his father passed away.

*

On the day Alex Harvey died, three guys who had played with him at different times in his career got together in London. Matthew Cang remembers:

The day he died, Hugh and Ted McKenna came over for a jam with my brother and me, and although I think we all felt shocked, it seemed fitting to play together for the evening. The last time I saw Alex was about six months before he died. He called me one day and asked me if I'd come and play a one-off gig in Nuremberg as someone in his band had gone AWOL. So I did, and we had a right laugh. On the journey home, Alex and I sat talking for hours and that's my last memory of him. Alex was one of those people who left a big shadow, even for a short-arse! I still miss him – he was an important person in my life ... and he was older than my Dad![4]

Even though his career had been nose-diving in latter years, there was an air of genuine sadness when news of Alex's death broke. After a few days, heartfelt tributes began to appear. Jimmy Wray penned an affectionate article in the *Glasgow Herald* of 11 February, reminding readers that there was more to Alex than the star in the spotlight. He reminisced about the old days in the 1950s and described Alex as a man of the people who

put the smiles on thousands of OAPs' faces at the many performances he gave them free of charge. [He] helped to take them on bus tours, decorate their homes and ran Christmas parties. This was the Alex Harvey we all loved and respected – the boy from Thistle Street ... Many of the residents could see Alex in the early hours of the morning walking through the Gorbals with his guitar slung over his shoulder returning from a gig in Glasgow. He was a dedicated musician endeavouring to make the big time and success could have come to no better – because this man was a giver in so many ways.

So we, the people of the Gorbals, would like to pay our last respects to a man who gave us many happy hours in times of strife and to a real nice guy.[5]

Another old friend, David Gibson – who had organised the Tommy Steele of Scotland competition all those years ago – also paid his respects writing in the *Sunday Standard* of 7 February 1982. Gibson estimated that Alex had generated an income of £15 million in his career, but said Alex saw little of that sum. The writer also noted that Harvey was way ahead of the musical trends.

He was a punk before youngsters even thought of it ... he was heavy metal when the rest of rock was in the Stone Age and was perhaps always just a little bit too far ahead of the trends.[6]

But it was left to Alex's most eloquent supporter, Charles Shaar Murray, to pay the most affectionate tribute in *NME* on 13 February. First of all Murray gave praise to the SAHB – calling them one of the 'craziest, most honest, most creative and most courageous bands of their time'. He then went on to wish that everyone could have known the real Alex, a warm, humorous and generous guy:

> who had a grin that hit his face like an earthquake. He had the kind of voice that most English people would consider to be archetypically Scottish and he embodied warmth, compassion and an all-consuming interest in and concern for other people. He was also one of the least bitter people I have ever met ... He commanded the same kind of love, trust and respect that Ian Dury does, the kind that comes from a relationship with the audience that is based on honesty ... Alex Harvey was my sergeant, I never met anyone quite like him and I never will again.[7]

The BBC paid tribute to Alex just a week after his death by showing a 15-minute interview he gave to the Scottish singer B.A. Robertson for the *Jock 'n' Roll* TV series. Alex talked in eloquent and amusing fashion about his career, from the early days when he toured the Outer Hebrides with his band impersonating Johnny and the Hurricanes right through until the Hamburg years. He told anecdotes about gigs at the Bonnybridge Miners' Welfare Club and at the Star Club. Not surprisingly, Alex came across in the interview as a genuinely decent guy.

On the radio show *Vambo Rools OK* in 2000, some other well-known singers also took time to pay their respects to Alex. Lulu said Alex was a great singer and a sweet guy – news of his death had left her with a great sense of loss. Noddy Holder of Slade recalled him as a fantastic frontman whose records were now ingrained on the memory of his fans. Billy Connolly hoped Alex had

left a simple legacy – that there is nothing that you cannot achieve in life: 'He never forgot who he was or where
he came from, though he didn't wear it around his neck
like a big millstone.' Meantime Zal Cleminson spoke for
many when he said simply that it had been a real pleasure to have known Alex.

Hugh McKenna reflects honestly on the complicated
relationship he had with his fellow songwriter:

If Alex was still alive, and if I met him now I think we would
get on an awful lot better. I had two nervous breakdowns when
I was with the band. I can look at them in retrospect ... and
see that my relationship with Alex had something to do with
the breakdowns. I'm a recovering alcoholic – I've had two-and-
a-half years without drugs or alcohol. I stopped for 11 years
before that – I didn't drink for 11 years, but I thought I could
dabble in a couple of lines of Charlie.

I have a different perspective on it all now – I've been in
therapy and worked through a lot of stuff. I realised that a lot
of the problems between Alex and me were to do with me feeling
threatened by him ... when he talked enigmatically and his persona – it kinda spooked me. Back then, I was so raddled with
alcohol, I didn't know at the time that I was an alcoholic and I
didn't know that Alex was drinking too much at the time too.[8]

Ray Conn was one of a number of people I spoke to who
said that Alex's death had left a gaping hole in his life. It
was like losing a brother or father figure: 'I had just got
back from France and my mother phoned me up to say
that my friend was dead. I lost a very good friend in Alex
and it hurt me for years.'[9]

When I interviewed him in Glasgow recently, Eddie
Tobin gave a characteristically blunt appraisal of the
Alex Harvey he knew.

I'll tell you my honest feeling – God knows, in my life I've met
a lot of bands touring the world, but there are certain people
who have an aura and I believe Alex was one of them. But he

was never going to be a world success because he wouldn't allow that.

The reason for Alex Harvey's 'failure' was that he would never compromise. Was he afraid of that level of success? I think he may have been. Essentially he was a Glasgow guy, and he had reached where he was going. To go beyond that stage and become as big an act as, say, Queen – I don't think that's what he wanted to do.

After the SAHB split, I think what he did forming a new band was right. I just think that he needed very, very strong management to stop his excesses – and I don't just mean the drink, I mean musically, performance-wise. Trim the rough edges off because his New Band was a very good group – I liked the *Mafia* album.

But maybe his time had just come and gone. Everyone had 15 minutes and his 15 minutes was up. If it was destined to have gone on it would have. Sometimes people just have difficulty admitting that. But he had no money. And that's what he did ... he couldn't move into acting – he didn't have that amount of talent. He had reached the ceiling of his talents. If you go further you are exposed. He didn't go beyond because he literally couldn't go beyond. But in performance terms, he could perform like no one I have ever seen in my life.

It was very difficult to know him and not to get attached to him. He's like many characters that attract people. No matter what level you were at, if you met Alex Harvey you remembered him. Because not many people have that aura.[10]

Harvey's eldest son, Alex junior, reflected on how things could have worked out so differently if his dad had made different choices when the SAHB split. He believes his father was far from finished on his journey and still had much to offer the world:

I miss him an awful lot, but I also feel sorry for other people who have also lost something because he's gone. My old man was a teacher – a natural teacher. When the SAHB broke up, instead of trying to reform three bands, which he did, I think he should have used that energy for a change of direction. That could have meant him doing something like acting or even taking some young musicians under his wing.

But it must have been dead hard for him to let go of performing – it was maybe like a boxer trying to get back in the ring again, not knowing when to let go.[11]

No one was going to find it easy after Alex died. The other members of the band were all extremely competent musicians and were never going to be out of work for long. Tommy Eyre went on to play for numerous bands including Greg Lake's and Ian Gillan's. He also somehow ended up playing with Wham! but perhaps his most impressive post-SAHB work was on John Martyn's classic 1980 album *Grace and Danger*. Tommy settled eventually in California where he married Scarlet Rivera who had played violin on Bob Dylan's *Rolling Thunder Revue* tour. After moving to the States, Tommy continued to be feted as a top session musician and arranger.

Tommy Eyre died in May 2001 aged 51 after a long battle with oesophageal cancer. A mark of the respect in which he was held came when, as his condition deteriorated, friends organised benefit concerts in Hollywood and at the Café de Paris in London to help finance the treatment.

As mentioned previously, Zal had formed his own band after the SAHB split and then played lead alongside the likes of Midge Ure and Nazareth. Latterly he gave up music and worked in the computer software business. He now lives in the West End of Glasgow.

Drummer Ted McKenna sat behind a variety of bands, including the late, great Rory Gallagher, Womack and Womack, The Greg Lake Band and Michael Schenker Group. He also passed on his expertise to young drummers through a musician's tuition centre. In 1996, the *Glasgow Evening Times* reported that he was teaching unemployed kids in his native Coatbridge about the pitfalls in the music industry and how to deal with record companies and contracts. The drummer told the newspaper that he had been ripped off himself. Ted also taught music at a Glasgow college and toured the UK with American bluesman Amos Garrett. Bassist Chris Glen also played with the Schenker Group and now lives in London. Hugh McKenna is still involved in the music business and enjoys passing on his expertise to younger bands.

Occasionally the guys have got back together again – Nazareth's Dan MacAfferty and Maggie Bell were two of the singers who accepted the unenviable task of filling Alex's shoes. In the early 1990s the SAHB briefly reformed, playing as The Party Boys with Stevie Doherty on vocals. When they did some gigs in 1993, it was the first time that Zal had played seriously for years. Doherty deflected some catcalls from Harvey diehards in the audience by claiming he was Alex's son!

A CD, *Live in Glasgow 1993*, with Doherty on vocals was released on Meantime Records, and though it sold poorly, it sounded remarkably good. Despite the long layoff, the band was as tight as ever – Zal in particular still plays beautifully. Stevie Doherty must have known that trying to replace Alex was always going to be a thankless task but, aside from a tendency to lapse occasionally into a heavy-metal shriek, he did an admirable job.

Record-wise, the SAHB catalogue has been picked over and a number of greatest hits albums have surfaced – most notably *The Best of The Sensational Alex Harvey Band* in August 1982 and *The Collection* in September 1986. The 1990s also saw the release on CD of the SAHB's seminal recordings for BBC Radio One and *The Old Grey Whistle Test*.

The only release of new material after Alex's death came in November 1983 when *The Soldier on the Wall* was issued to lukewarm reviews and lacklustre sales. The album was released by a small Yorkshire independent label Power Station Records with the full backing of the Harvey family, who rightly felt that the songs were too good to be left lying around gathering dust.

But although there are a few classy moments, overall the record is marred by some poor production and sloppy, repetitive songs. Many critics thought that it was an ill-judged posthumous release. In a vain attempt to cash in on early 1980s fashion, the album, which had been recorded in November 1981, is keyboard-heavy with excellent guitarist Ian Taylor wasted in the mix. The only song which comes close to matching the menace and power of the SAHB in their glory is 'Nervous'. Even the most charitable of fans would have to agree that, on the evidence of this album, Alex's days as a relevant and influential artist were long gone.

The first track on the second side, 'The Poet and I' was released as a single in November 1983 – a tribute to the great bard Robbie Burns, its lyrics are punctuated by references to the characters in the poet's work. With the possible exception of 'Anthem', no other song by Harvey captures so well his pride in being Scottish, and it shows clearly that his native land was in his music as well as his blood. It's also one of the most simple, sentimental and moving songs he ever recorded. While some may question the wisdom of releasing the album, it was surely better to have such songs in the hands of the fans rather than lying unheard in a vault.

The SAHB back catalogue still sells well – most notably in Scotland and in the European countries they conquered in their 1970s heyday. America remains largely unmoved and the band's CDs are now only available there as pricey imports. Predictably the one American city where sales remain high is Cleveland, where record store dealers apparently struggle to keep pace with the demands of local fans. Whenever new stock arrives in town, signs go up in the windows and queues form. It's all terribly ironic given the sweat and tears that the band shed in a vain bid to break America during the 1970s.

Over the years since his death, there have been a number of failed attempts to immortalise the Alex Harvey story. In March 1989, the lyricist Pete Brown announced plans for a film on Alex's life through the London production company Hunky Dory and he contacted the *Glasgow Evening Times* in an effort to track down people who knew Alex well. unfortunately the film never materialised.

Two years later, plans were revealed for the unveiling of a blue plaque in Glasgow to commemorate Alex's career. On occasion these plaques have been produced to mark sites which played important roles in rock music history, such as the house in London where Jimi Hendrix lived or Widnes railway station where Paul Simon supposedly wrote the classic 'Homeward Bound'. The original plan was to place the plaque on West Regent Street in Glasgow, where Alex first saw Tear Gas play at the Burns Howff pub.

Eventually, on 26 June 1991 the unveiling took place on a children's playground in a housing scheme. It was as close as the experts could get to the tenement at 49 Govan Road where Alex had been born in 1935. A scattering of fans mingled with the press and some of Alex's old musical buddies as the plaque was unveiled. It was the first of its kind in Scotland. The event only took place after some degree of confusion. Local historians were convinced that the correct site was opposite a public convenience. No doubt Alex would have preferred that the slightly pompous affair took place close to a toilet!

He would have been even more amused by the fact that the plaque has vanished. Alex junior and I looked in vain for it, and no one at the local town hall could shed any light on its whereabouts. But the blue plaque was certainly an overdue honour – it's just a shame that the impetus for it came from outside Glasgow. To this day the local council seem unwilling to pay a similar tribute or even name a street after the singer. The feeling persists that some people in powerful positions resent the fact that Alex left his native city and lived for almost 20 years in London.

However, in June 2000, the General Manager of the Pavilion Theatre, Ian Gordon, told the *Glasgow Evening Times* how he hoped to develop a stage show based on Harvey's life. Gordon told the newspaper that Alex's dad Les had been a stage doorman at the Pavilion and had also worked across the road at the now defunct Apollo Theatre. Again the proposal came to nothing.

In February 2001, on what would have been Alex's 66th birthday, BBC Scotland aired a 30-minute documentary that told Harvey's life story in an affectionate, if somewhat predictable, way. Narrated by the award-winning Scots actor David Hayman, the show featured interviews with all the original band members, Maggie Bell and Eddie Tobin. Alex's widow Trudy and his two sons, Tyro and Alex, also made contributed. Journalist Billy Sloan, Noddy Holder and Jim Kerr paid tribute to the man and his legacy.

A young, up-and-coming Glasgow band, Cosmic Rough Riders, were filmed playing a rather laboured cover version of the SAHB's 'Action Strasse' before a teenage audience at the city's King Tut's. The band's Danny Wylie said correctly that he would be a fool to even try to top Harvey's stunning stage performances.

The idea was to show that Alex's musical impact was still felt 20 years after his death. While that may be true, most Harvey fans would have preferred to see more clips of the man in action.

True, there was some footage from 1970s shows like *Supersonic, Top of the Pops* and *The Old Grey Whistle Test,* including an interview done on Alex's 40th birthday, where he grinds his teeth and looks unshaven and cool. But a rare clip of SAHB doing 'Framed' at the London Marquee in the days before Zal wore make-up was cut short to show more of the Cosmic Rough Riders. Still, it was a real treat to see Alex back on the small screen again. Jim Kerr even managed to round off the whole show with the tale of how Simple Minds' manager Bruce Findlay's record shop in Glasgow was once raided by masked robbers who stole the contents of the till. On the way out, one of the thieves turned and returned to the counter to ask for 'two copies of the new Alex Harvey album'! Kerr maintained jokingly that 'it was Harvey himself under the balaclava'.

Thirty years on from the demise of the SAHB, the group's hard-core fan base remains as loyal as ever. Followers of Alex from around the globe keep in contact with one another online, swap lyrics, check out photos and exchange views and rare records. A number of sites have been established which pay tribute specifically to Alex. The man behind one such site, Wade McDaniel, had hoped to organise a trip to some of Alex's old haunts in 2002 – the 20th anniversary of his death. The plan was for a tour to Glasgow, Loch Ness, Hamburg and London, but the ambitious project, which drew interest from as far afield as the USA, Canada and Australia, had to be shelved due to the costs involved.

*

Since the hardback edition of this book was published in 2002, there has been an upturn in SAHB-related activity. The studio albums have all been re-released and repackaged. In August 2003 *The Soldier on the Wall* was reissued by Demon Records, and a couple of excellent compilation CDs, most notably *Considering the Situation* on Mercury, chronicle Harvey's less known work.

*

As I write, The Sensational Alex Harvey Band (current line-up Hugh McKenna, Ted McKenna, Chris Glen, Max Maxwell and Julian Saxby) have announced two live shows in Edinburgh for Christmas 2008, and there are persistent rumours of a project called simply 'Alex' which will see several Harvey aficionados sing versions of classic songs. Among the names being mentioned are Nick Cave, Billy Connolly, Alice Cooper, Joe Elliot, Jim Kerr, Irvine Welsh and Donny Osmond! Now that has got to be worth waiting for.

POSTSCRIPT

Tomorrow Belongs To Me isn't just the title of one of Alex Harvey's best albums, in many ways the phrase sums up his career. This was a guy who was hitting 40 when he had his first Top 30 hit. For almost 20 years before, fame had passed him by and he took an awful lot of knocks along the way. Ironically, when he did find stardom, it only lasted a few years before he fell out of the limelight again.

Of course, Alex Harvey's legacy is much more significant than mere chart hits. He brought delight to his fans through some inspired music and truly memorable concerts. But most importantly we should remember just how special a person he was. Everybody who met Alex was touched by him and will never forget him. He inspired great loyalty and affection among those who came to know him.

When you look at old footage of Harvey performing in his prime, the guy looks almost superhuman, untouchable. As this book has shown, in reality he was just the same as the rest of us – vulnerable and at times difficult and weak-willed, but that should never outweigh the greatness he achieved.

'Just A Gigolo/I Ain't Got Nobody', the final song on his last album released before he died, is a classic Harvey performance. When you hear him sing about how sad and lonely he was, and how nobody loved him, it's hard not to feel a lump in your throat. Maybe he knew his time was almost up and he picked that song to check out on, but hopefully he didn't really mean it when he sang those words. The truth is that just about everybody who knew him or bought his records loved Alex Harvey. And 26 years on they still do.

SOURCES

1 He Was Just a Child ...

1 Alex Harvey: *Sounds,* 24 November 1973
2 Alex Harvey: *Melody Maker,* September 1975
3 Alex Harvey: *NME,* 17 August 1974
4 Alex Harvey junior: interview with the author
5 Alex Harvey: *Glasgow Herald,* 5 January 1980
6 Trudy Harvey: interview with the author
7 Eddie Tobin: interview with the author

2 ... When His Innocence Was Lost

1 Alex Harvey: *NME,* 14 April 1973
2 Alex Harvey: *NME,* 19 January 1974
3 David Gibson: interview with the author
4 *Sunday Mail,* 28 April 1975
5 David Gibson: interview with the author
6 David Gibson: interview with the author
7 Alex Harvey junior: interview with the author

3 Big Soul Band

1 Alex Harvey: *Glasgow Herald,* 5 January 1980
2 Alex Harvey: *Sounds,* 4 May 1974

3   George McGowan: interview with the author
4   Jimmy Grimes: in *Blue Suede Brogans: Scenes From the Secret Life of Scottish Rock Music* by Jim Wilkie, (Mainstream, 1992)
5   Maggie Bell: *Sounds*, 16 February 1974
6   Jimmy Grimes: *Sunday Standard* obituary of Alex Harvey

4 Hamburg and Home Again

1   Alex Harvey: radio interview, 1974
2   Ricky Barnes: in *The History of Scottish Rock and Pop: All That Ever Mattered* by Brian Hogg (Guinness Publishing, 1993)
3   Alex Harvey: *Sounds*, 24 November 1973
4   Trudy Harvey: interview with the author
5   Loudon Temple: interview with the author
6   Bob Fish: interview with the author

5 The Giant Moth Experiment

1   Alex Harvey: *NME*, 17 August 1974
2   Alex Harvey: *Glasgow Evening Times*, 10 March 1975
3   George Gallacher: interview with the author
4   George Gallacher: interview with the author
5   George Gallacher: interview with the author
6   George Butler: interview with the author
7   George Butler: interview with the author
8   Alex Harvey: *NME*, 17 August 1974

6 *Hair*

1   Manni Ferri: interview with the author
2   Derek Wadsworth: interview with the author
3   Derek Wadsworth: interview with the author
4   Marianne Price: interview with the author
5   Derek Wadsworth: interview with the author
6   Laurie Scott Baker: interview with the author
7   Laurie Scott Baker: interview with the author
8   Derek Wadsworth: interview with the author
9   Richard O'Brien: *Mojo* April 2000
10   Trudy Harvey: interview with the author

7 From Tears to Tear Gas

1   Alex Harvey: early radio interview, source unknown
2   Maggie Bell: *Mojo*, April 2000
3   Trudy Harvey: interview with the author
4   Alex Harvey junior: interview with the author
5   Eddie Tobin: interview with the author
6   Zal Cleminson: *Sounds*, 20 December 1975
7   Zal Cleminson: *NME*, 20 March 1976
8   Ted McKenna: *Mojo*, April 2000
9   Hugh McKenna: interview with the author
10   Hugh McKenna: interview with the author
11   Eddie Tobin: interview with the author
12   Alex Harvey: *NME*, 3 May 1975
13   Hugh McKenna: interview with the author
14   Eddie Tobin: interview with the author
15   Ted McKenna: interview with BBC Radio Scotland
16   Zal Cleminson: *NME*, 20 March 1976

8 So Sensational

1   Alex Harvey: *Sounds*, 24 November 1973
2   Hugh McKenna: interview with the author
3   Alex Harvey: *Sounds*, 24 November 1973
4   Alex Harvey: *Glasgow Evening Times*, 10 March 1975
5   Hugh McKenna: interview with the author
6   Alex Harvey: interview with Tony Hadland, 1974
7   Zal Cleminson: *Sounds*, 16 February 1974

9 Everything Is Coming Up Roses!

1   Alex Harvey: *Sounds*, 11 August 1973
2   Derek Wadsworth: interview with the author
3   Derek Nicol: interview with the author
4   Derek Nicol: interview with the author
5   Alex Harvey: *Sounds*, 11 August 1973
6   Alex Harvey: *Sounds*, 11 August 1973
7   John Waterson: interview with the author
8   Alex Harvey: *NME*, 17 August 1974
9   Alex Harvey: *Sounds*, August 1973
10   Derek Nicol: interview with the author

10 Next

1   Alex Harvey, *Sounds*, 24 November 1973
2   Alex Harvey: *Sounds*, 24 November 1973
3   Alex Harvey: *Sounds*, 11 August 1973
4   Noddy Holder: interview for BBC Radio
5   Steve Toal: interview with the author

6 Hugh McKenna: interview with the author
7 Alex Harvey: interview with Tony Hadland for Belgian radio
8 Tony Hadland: interview with the author
9 Steve Toal: interview with the author
10 Alex Harvey: interview with Tony Hadland for Belgian radio
11 Hugh McKenna: interview with the author

11 Living the Impossible Dream

1 Alex Harvey: interview with Tony Hadland, August 1974
2 Alex Harvey: *Sounds*, 4 May 1974
3 John Peel: *Sounds*, 4 August 1974
4 Charles Shaar Murray: *NME*, 12 October 1974

12 Too Much American Pie

1 Elton John: *NME*, 14 December 1974
2 Alex Harvey: *Alex Harvey Talks*, promotional interview
3 Alex Harvey: *Glasgow Evening Times*, 10 March 1975
4 Alex Harvey: *Glasgow Evening Times*, 10 March 1975
5 Barbara Birdfeather: interview with the author
6 Barbara Birdfeather: interview with the author
7 Eddie Tobin: interview with the author
8 Janet Macoska: interview with the author
9 Janet Macoska: interview with the author

10   Alex Harvey: *NME*, 18 January 1975
11   Derek Nicol: interview with the author
12   Alex Harvey: *NME*, 3 May 1975

13 Like All Your Hogmanays Rolled Into One

1   Alex Harvey: interview with Tony Hadland, 1974
2   Alex Harvey: *International Musician* magazine, May 1975
3   Barbara Birdfeather: interview with the author
4   Aaron Childress: interview with the author
5   Ted McKenna: *You Don't Have To Be In Harlem* by Russell Leadbetter (Mainstream, 1995)
6   Eddie Tobin: interview with the author

14 He Was My Blood Brother

1   Alex Harvey: *The Old Grey Whistle Test*, February 1975
2   Derek Nicol: interview with the author
3   Alex Harvey: *NME*, 15 May 1976
4   Trudy Harvey: interview with the author
5   Alex Harvey: *NME*, 10 July 1976
6   Trudy Harvey: interview with the author
7   David Gibson: interview with the author
8   Alex Harvey: interview with Phil McNeill, 1976
9   Eddie Tobin: interview with the author

15 1977

1   Alex Harvey: *NME*, 23 October 1976
2   Eddie Tobin: interview with the author
3   Derek Nicol: interview with the author
4   John Miller: interview with the author
5   John Miller: interview with the author
6   Alex Harvey: *Sounds*, 24 November 1973
7   John Miller: interview with the author
8   Tom Robinson: interview with the author
9   Hugh McKenna: interview with the author
10 Tom Robinson: interview with the author
11 Derek Nicol: interview with the author
12 Janet Macoska: interview with the author
13 Janet Macoska: interview with the author

16 Things Fall Apart

1   Alex Harvey: *Daily Record*, 28 October 1977
2   Eddie Tobin: interview with the author
3   Ted McKenna: *The History of Scottish Rock and Pop: All That Ever Mattered* by Brian Hogg (Guinness Publishing, 1993)
4   Eddie Tobin: interview with the author
5   Derek Nicol: interview with the author
6   Barbara Birdfeather: interview with the author
7   Hugh McKenna: interview with the author
8   Eddie Tobin: interview with the author
9   John Miller: interview with the author
10 Trudy Harvey: interview with the author
11 Trudy Harvey: interview with the author
12 Trudy Harvey: interview with the author
13 John Miller: interview with the author

17 The New Band

1   Alex Harvey: *Glasgow Herald*, January 1980
2   George Butler: interview with the author
3   Matthew Cang: interview with the author
4   Gordon Sellar: interview with the author
5   Gordon Sellar: interview with the author
6   Alex Harvey: *Glasgow Herald*, 4 January 1980
7   Gordon Sellar: interview with the author
8   Matthew Cang: interview with the author
9   Eddie Tobin: interview with the author

18 The Final Years

1   Gordon Sellar: interview with the author
2   Ray Conn: interview with the author
3   Ray Conn: interview with the author
4   Gordon Sellar: interview with the author
5   Zal Cleminson: *Mojo*, April 2000
6   Derek Nicol: interview with the author
7   Roy Neave: interview with the author
8   Daniel Bennett: interview with the author

19 Time for Tributes

1   Alex Harvey: *NME*, 19 January 1974
2   Jimmy Wray: interview with the author
3   *Glasgow Herald*, 5 February 1982
4   Matthew Cang: interview with the author
5   Jimmy Wray: *Glasgow Herald*, 11 February 1982
6   David Gibson: *Sunday Standard*, 7 February 1982

7   Charles Shaar Murray: *NME*, 13 February 1982
8   Hugh McKenna: interview with the author
9   Ray Conn: interview with the author
10 Eddie Tobin: interview with the author
11 Alex Harvey Junior: interview with the author

UK TOUR DATES

This list is taken from selected British music papers. It is far from complete and should be approached with caution. Some of the concerts may have been cancelled or the dates may have been changed.

December 1972
4 – Marquee Club, London
5 – Nightingale, Wood Green
6 – Gloucester Art College, Cheltenham
7 – Greyhound, Fulham
8 – Youth Centre, Burton on the Water
9 – The Boat Club, Nottingham
10 – Stoneground, Manchester
11 – Windsor Hotel, Dumfries
13 – Caledonian Hotel, Inverness
14 – Glasgow Art College
15 – Strathclyde University
16 – The Kinema, Dunfermline
17 – Watermill, Paisley
20 – Weymouth Grammar School
23 – YMCA, Bellshill

January 1973
12 – Thames Polytechnic
13 – Chichester Bishop Otter College
14 – Chiswick Chevalier Lodge Club
18 – Marquee
19 – Skegness Festival Pavilion
20 – Nottingham College of Education
22 – Manchester Hardrock
23 – Bournemouth Hardrock
25 – Northampton Fantasia
26 – Newcastle Polytechnic

27 – Bolton Institute of Technology

February 1973
2 – Sheffield University
3 – Preston Guildhall
8 – Northwich Memorial Hall
9 – Brixton Sundown
10 – Durham Van Milder College
15 – Cardiff College of Technology
16 – Brighton Polytechnic
17 – Bristol St. Matthias College
18 – Finchley Torrington
19 – Birmingham Town Hall
22 – Glasgow Greens Playhouse
24 – Edinburgh Empire
25 – Newcastle City Hall
28 – Exeter University

April 1973
8 – Marquee

May 1973
10 – Hull Intercon Club
12 – Kingston Polytechnic
13 – Watford Palace Theatre
16 – Marquee
24 – Norwich Memorial Hall
25 – Edinburgh Students Centre
26 – St Andrews Cosmos

249

May–June 1973
(the infamous tour supporting Slade)

May
31 – Glasgow Greens Playhouse

June
1 – Edinburgh Empire
2 – Newcastle City Hall
3 – Civic Hall, Wolverhampton
6 – Brighton Dome
8 – Birmingham Town Hall
9 – Bristol Colston Hall
10 – Cardiff Top Rank
11 – Southampton Guildhall
12 – Sheffield City Hall
13 – Blackburn King George's Hall
14 – Hanley Victoria Hall
15 – Leeds University
uncertain date – London Earls Court

June 1973
20 – Marquee
22 – Scarborough Penthouse
23 – St Albans Richmond Hall
29 – Northampton Moulton College
30 – Manchester Stoneground

September 1973
15 – Cambridge Corn Exchange
28 – Sunderland Locarno Ballroom

August 1973
5 – London Music Festival – Uriah Heep top the bill

October 1973
3 – Sheffield Polytechnic

5 – North Staffordshire Polytechnic
6 – Doncaster College of Education
7 – Gravesend Civic Hall
12 – Scarborough Penthouse
13 – St Albans City Hall
14 – London Sundown

November 1973
8 – Warwick University
9 – Manchester Stoneground
11 – Ayr Pavillion
12 – Falkirk Town Hall
13 – Perth Salvation Hotel
14 – Hamilton Town Hall
16 – Bristol Town Hall
17 – Northampton County Cricket Club
18 – Southport Floral Hall
19 – Derby Kings Hall
20 – Hull City Hall
22 – Middlesborough Town Hall
23 – Newcastle Polytechnic
24 – Hemel Hempstead Pavilion
26 – Reading Town Hall
27 – Hanley Victoria Hall
28 – Barnsley Civic Hall
29 – Liverpool St George's Hall
30 – Edinburgh University

December 1973
1 – Cromer Links Pavilion
2 – Croydon Greyhound
3 – Wolverhampton City Hall
5 – Blackburn King George Hall
8 – Dagenham Roundhouse
9 – Plymouth Guildhall
10 – Barry Memorial Hall
11 – Salisbury City Hall
12 – Sheffield City Hall
13 – Huddersfield Polytechnic

14 – Chatham Central Hall
15 – Cambridge Corn Exchange
17 – Harrowgate Royal Hall

March 1974
7 – Oxford Polytechnic
8 – Slough Community College
9 – London Imperial College

May 1974
9 – Leeds Town Hall
10 – Sheffield City Hall
11 – Liverpool Stadium
12 – Preston Guild Hall
13 – Swansea Top Rank
15 – Brighton Top Rank
16 – Hanley Victoria Hall
17 – Newcastle Mayfair
18 – Nottingham University
19 – Guildford Civic Hall
22 – Perth City Hall
25 – Dundee Caird Hall
26 – Glasgow Apollo
27 – Edinburgh Caley Cinema
28 – Manchester Free Trade Hall
29 – Birmingham Town Hall
30 – Bristol Colston Hall
31 – Hull City Hall

June 1974
1 – Leicester Polytechnic
3 – Wolverhampton Civic Hall
7 – London Rainbow
8 – Southend Kursaal
9 – Norwich Theatre Royal

October 1974
3 – Leicester de Montfort Hall
4 – Birmingham Town Hall
6 – London Palladium (Sunday night)

8 – Portsmouth Guild Hall
9 – Sheffield City Hall
10 – Bradford St George's Hall
11 – Lancaster University
12 – York University
13 – Glasgow Apollo
14 – Edinburgh Usher Hall
16 – Manchester Palace Theatre
18 – Newcastle Mayfair
19 – Southend Kursaal

May 1975
1 – Newcastle City Hall
2 – Edinburgh Usher Hall
3 – Dundee Caird Hall
4 – Glasgow Apollo
7 – Liverpool Empire
8 – Bradford St George's Hall
10 – Leeds University
11 – Preston Guildhall
12 – Manchester Free Trade Hall
13 – Sheffield City Hall
15 – Birmingham Odeon
16 – Portsmouth Guild Hall
17 – Stoke City Football Ground (supporting Yes)
20 – Leicester De Montfort Hall
21 – Watford Town Hall
22 – Cardiff Capitol
23 – Bristol Colston Hall
24 – Hammersmith Odeon
26 – Southend Kursaal

April 1976
April 30 – Ipswich Gaumont

May 1976
1 – Southend Kursaal
2 – Coventry Theatre
3 – Oxford New Theatre

5 – Hull ABC Theatre
6/7 – Newcastle City Hall
8 – Leeds University
9/10 – Manchester Free Trade
   Hall
11 – Liverpool Empire
12 – Preston Guildhall
15 – Bracknell Sports Centre
16 – Stoke Trentham Gardens
17/18 – Bristol Colston Hall
20 – Southampton Gaumont
21 – Bournemouth Winter
   Gardens
24/25 – Birmingham Odeon
26/27 – Sheffield City Hall
28/29 – Edinburgh Odeon
31 – Charlton Athletic Football
   Ground, London (The Who
   topped the bill)

June 1976
1 – Portsmouth Guildhall
2 – Eastbourne Congress
   Theatre
3 – Taunton Odeon.
5 – Glasgow Celtic Football
   Ground (Parkhead – The Who
   topped the bill)
12 – Swansea Football Ground
   (The Who topped the bill)

ALEX HARVEY BAND

November 1978
6/7/8 – The Venue, London
   (two shows per night)

February 1981
1 – Hardstuff Shoulder of
   Mutton
6 – Newcastle Mayfair

7 – Liverpool Warehouse
8 – Leeds Fforde Green Hotel
11 – Swansea Circles
12 – Nottingham Rock City
13 – Blackpool Norbreck Castle
14 – Retford Porterhouse
15 – Redcar Bowl

March 1981
4 – Edinburgh Playhouse
5 – Sheffield Limit Club
6 – Lincoln Theatre Royal
9 – London Marquee

May 1981
8 – Nottingham Rock City

August 1981
29 – Reading Festival, Gillan
   top the bill

October 1981
date uncertain – Newark Palace
   Theatre
17 – Grimsby Central Hall
18 – Doncaster Rotters
19 – Maesteg Town Hall
20 – Sheffield Polytechnic (with
   Hot Gossip)
21 – Mansfield Leisure Centre
22 – Plymouth Palace Theatre
24 – Southampton University
date uncertain – Bradford
   University
28 – Mountain Ash New
   Theatre
29 – Birkenhead Gallery Club
30 – Middlesborough Town Hall
31 – Hull Tower Cinema.

BIBLIOGRAPHY

The Gorbals: Historical Guide, Ronald Smith, Glasgow
   City Council, 1999
You Don't Have To Be In Harlem, Russell Leadbetter,
   Mainstream, 1995
*Melody Maker History of Twentieth-century Popular
   Music*, Nick Johnstone, Bloomsbury, 1999
*Blue Suede Brogans: Scenes from the Secret Life of
   Scottish Rock Music*, Jim Wilkie, Mainstream, 1992
Hamburg: The Cradle of British Rock, Alan Clayson,
   Sanctuary, 1997
Former Soldier Seeks Employment, John Miller, Pan,
   1989
The Knebworth Rock Festivals, Chrissie Lytton Cobbold,
   Omnibus Press, 1986
*The Complete Book of the British Charts – Singles and
   Albums*, Tony Brown, John Kutner and Neil Warwick,
   Omnibus Press, 2000
*The History of Scottish Rock and Pop: All That Ever
   Mattered*, Brian Hogg, Guinness Publishing, 1993
The Great Rock Discography, Martin C. Strong,
   Canongate, 2007
Simply Devine, Sydney Devine and Matt Bendoris, Black
   & White Publishing, 2005

Since the hardback edition of this book was first published
in 2002, the official biography of the band, *The SAHB
Story* by Martin Kielty, was produced by Neil Wilson
Publishing – excellent and well worth a read.

The Sensational Alex Harvey

Alex carried out many radio and TV interviews during his career, and some of the most helpful are listed below.

BBC *Rockspeak* radio programme, 1974: interview with Brian Matthews
US promotional interview, 1974: *Alex Harvey Talks – About Everything*
In August 2001, Ted McKenna and Nazareth's Dan McCafferty were among those interviewed for BBC Radio Scotland's series *Old Wild Men*.

Music papers of the 1970s like *NME*, *Sounds* and *Melody Maker* are vital sources for tour dates, record and concert reviews, together with features on Alex and other band members. Scottish daily newspapers also occasionally featured interviews with Alex. Listed below are some of the most detailed articles.

Sunday Mail, 28 April 1957: 'He is Scotland's Tommy Steele! Back Streets Kid Wins Stardom Chance' by David Gibson
NME, 14 April 1973: 'The Vandal Reforms' by Steve Clarke
Sounds, 11 August 1973: 'Rapping with Idol Alex' by Ray Telford
Sounds, 29 September 1973: 'The Rubber Man's Choice' by Pete Makowski
Sounds, 26 October 1974: 'Rock and Roll Warrior' by Pete Makowski
Sounds, 24 November 1973: 'Alex Harvey in the Talk-In' by Martin Hayman
NME, 19 January 1974: 'Ladies And Gentlemen, This Is What a Rock and Roll Band Is All About, Says A. Harvey, 38' by Charles Shaar Murray

Sounds, 16 February 1974: 'Zal, The Colourful Sidekick' by Pete Erskine

Sounds, 4 May 1974: Talk-In feature

NME, 17 August 1974: 'Pain-wracked Glasgow Octogenarian Fights Tooth Decay, Endorses Anarchy!' by Chris Salewicz

NME, 12 October 1974: 'Encomium for Trash Aesthetics' by Charles Shaar Murray

Circus Raves, December 1974: 'Alex Harvey Band – Rock Shimmies West' by John Tiven

Exit, 5 December 1974: 'How Scotland's Tommy Steele of '56 met Tear Gas and Found The Impossible Dream' by Clyde Hadlock and Fred Toedtman

NME, 18 January 1975: interview with Alex by Pete Erskine

Glasgow Evening Times, 10 March 1975: 'The Sensational Mr Harvey keeps on rocking . . . at 40!' by David Gibson

NME, 3 May 1975: 'Thou Shalt Have No Other Punk Before Me' by Charles Shaar Murray

Melody Maker, 31 May 1975: Alex talks to Allan Jones

Circus Raves, March 1975: 'Harvey Breaks Headliners' Hearts'

International Musician and Recording World, May 1975: 'Alex Harvey'

NME, 20 September 1975: 'Delivered From The Jaws Of Death' by Charles Shaar Murray

National Rock Star, 4 December 1975: 'The Sensational Mrs Harvey – a rare glimpse of Alex Harvey's world outside his music' by Martha Ellen Zenfell

Sounds, 20 December 1975: 'Still Crazy After All These Years' by Geoff Barton

Scene Magazine, 31 December 1975: 'Alex Harvey – He's Not Getting Older . . .' by Raj Bahadur

NME, 24 January 1976: 'How Will They Live With It?' by Max Bell

NME, 15 May 1976: review of Newcastle Town Hall gig by Angie Errigo

NME, 21 August 1976: 'SAHB Stories – When You're Ready, We'll Begin' by Phil McNeill

NME, 16 October 1976: 'Alex Collapses – Seriously Ill'

NME, 22 January 1977: 'The Sensational Alex Harvey Band Without Alex', story by Tony Parsons

NME, 25 June 1977: 'The Meat of the Matter' by Charles Shaar Murray

Melody Maker, unknown date in 1978: 'Alex in Wonderland – at the London Palladium' by Allan Jones

Glasgow Herald, 5 January 1980: 'Rock's Greatest Survivor' by Andy Collier

Glasgow Herald, 11 January 1980: 'A Shamefully Attended Welcome Home Party' by Andy Collier

Sunday Standard, 7 February 1982: 'The Sensational Life of a Middle-Aged Idol' by David Gibson

Glasgow Herald, 11 February 1982: letter from Councillor James Wray paying tribute to Alex

NME, 13 February 1982: 'The Faith Healer, Alex Harvey 1935–1982' by Charles Shaar Murray

Record Collector, no. 107, July 1988: 'Alex Harvey: The Early Years and Discography, 1964–70' by Brian Hogg

Glasgow Herald, 27 June 1991: 'Harp Beat for a True Rocker' by David Belcher

Uncut, December 1999: 'Alex Harvey's Glasgow' by Allan Jones

Mojo, April 2000: 'Let's All Drink to the Death of a Clown' by James McNair

The Cleveland Plain Dealer, 16 July 2000: 'Scottish Alex

Harvey Band Still Rates in Cleveland' by Laura
DeMarco

The Scotsman Magazine, 25 January 2003: 'No
Ordinary Hero', Nick Cave interview by Alastair
McKay

The Guardian, 20 May 2003: 'Timeless Tunesmith',
Robert Smith (The Cure) interview by Will
Hodgkinson.

WEBSITES

There are a number of good websites dedicated to Alex
and the SAHB. One of the best sites – which will give you
links to other sites – is run by Wade McDaniel and can
be found at *www.wunnerful.com/sahb*. The official band
website is at *www.sahb.co.uk*. Thanks to the band and
Stewart Campbell of Visual Hits for help with sourcing
images.

SELECTED DISCOGRAPHY

Early singles

I Just Wanna Make Love To You / Let The Good Times Roll (Polydor NH52264, January 1964)

Got My Mojo Working / I Ain't Worried Baby (Polydor NH52907, June 1964)

Ain't That Just Too Bad / My Kind of Love (Polydor BM56017, July 1965)

Agent 00 Soul / Go Away Baby (Fontana TF610, September 1965)

Work Song / I Can't Do Without Your Love (Fontana TF764, November 1966)

The Sunday Song / Horizons (Decca F12640, July 1967)

Maybe Someday / Curtains for My Baby (Decca F12660, September 1967)

Midnight Moses / Roman Wall Blues (Fontana TF 1063, November 1969)

Early albums

ALEX HARVEY & HIS SOUL BAND (live)
(Polydor LPHM46424, March 1964)
Framed / I Ain't Worrying Baby / Backwater Blues / Let The Good Times Roll / Going Home / I've Got My Mojo Working / Teensville USA / New Orleans / Bo

Diddley is a Gunslinger / When I Grow Too Old to Rock / Evil Hearted Man / I Just Wanna Make Love To You / The Blind Man

ALEX HARVEY'S BIG SOUL BAND
(Recorded mostly in London during August 1964 but never released until 1999)

The Liverpool Scene / Shout / What's Wrong With Me, Baby? / Reelin' And Rockin' / The Canoe Song / The Little Boy That Santa Claus Forgot / Hoochie Coochie Man / Long Long Gone / My Kind Of Lovin' / Outskirts Of Town / Parchman Farm / Penicillin Blues / Shakin' All Over / Sticks And Stones / Take Out Some Insurance on Me, Baby / Ten a Penny / Tutti Frutti / You Ain't No Good to Me / You Are My Sunshine / You've Put A Spell on Me/

THE BLUES
(Polydor LPHM 46441, November 1965)

Trouble In Mind / Honey Bee / I Learned About Woman / Danger Zone / The Riddle Song / Waltzing Matilda / TB Blues / The Big Rock Candy Mountain / The Michigan Massacre / No Peace / Nobody Knows You When You're Down And Out / St James Infirmary / Strange Fruit / Kisses Sweeter Than Wine / Good God Almighty

ROMAN WALL BLUES
(Fontana TL5534, October 1969)

Midnight Moses / Hello L.A.,Bye Bye Birmingham / Broken Hearted Fairytale / Donna / Roman Wall Blues / Jumping Jack Flash / Hammer Song / Let My Bluebird Sing / Maxine / Down At Bart's Place / Candy

HAIR RAVE-UP
(Pye, 1969, re-released on CD by Sanctuary Records,
CMRCD 258, June 2001)
Harvey plays guitar and sings lead vocal on a number
of tracks.
Hair / El Pussy Cat / Royal International Love-In /
Bond Street Baby / Hare Krishna / All Along The
Watchtower / Birthday / Keep Out / Candy / Movin' In
The Right Direction / I Know Where You Are

SAHB singles

There's No Lights On The Christmas Tree, Mother,
They're Burning Big Louie Tonight / Harp (Vertigo
6059070, December 1972)

Jungle Jenny / Buff's Bar Blues (Vertigo 6059075,
February 1973)

The Faith Healer (edit) / St Anthony (Vertigo 6059 098,
February 1974)

Swampsnake / Gang Bang (Vertigo 113, February
1974)

Sergeant Fury / Gang Bang (Vertigo 6059106, August
1974)

Sergeant Fury / Tomahawk Kid (Vertigo 200,
September 1974)

Anthem / Anthem (version) (Vertigo, 6059112,
November 1974)

Delilah (live) / Soul in Chains (live) (Vertigo Alex 001,
July 1975)

Gamblin' Bar Room Blues / Shake That Thing (Vertigo Alex 002, November 1975)

Runaway / Snakebite (Vertigo Alex 003, March 1976)

Boston Tea Party / Sultan's Choice (Mountain TOP12, May 1976)

Amos Moses / Satchel and the Scalp Hunter (Mountain TOP19, August 1976)

Pick It Up and Kick It / Smouldering (SAHB without Alex) (Mountain January 1977)

Mrs Blackhouse / Engine Room Boogie (Mountain TOP32, August 1977)

SAHB albums

FRAMED
(Vertigo 6360081, December 1972)
Framed / Hammer Song / Midnight Moses / Isobel Goudie (Part 1 My Lady of the Night, Part 2 Coitus Interruptus, Part 3 The Virgin and the Hunter / Buff's Bar Blues / I Just Want To Make Love To You / Hole In Her Stocking / There's No Lights on the Christmas Mother, They're Burning Big Louie Tonight / St Anthony

NEXT
(Vertigo 6360103, November 1973)
Swampsnake / Gang Bang / The Faith Healer / Giddy Up A Ding Dong / Next / Vambo Marble Eye / The Last of the Teenage Idols (Part 1–111)

THE IMPOSSIBLE DREAM
(Vertigo 6360112, September 1974)

The Hot City Symphony (Part 1 Vambo, Part 2 Man in yhe Jar) / River Of Love / Long Hair Music / Sergeant Fury / Weights Made Of Lead / Money Honey – The Impossible Dream / Tomahawk Kid / Anthem

TOMORROW BELONGS TO ME
(Vertigo 6360120, April 1975)

Action Strasse / Snake Bite / Soul In Chains / The Tale of the Giant Stoneater / Ribs and Balls / Give My Compliments to the Chef / Sharks Teeth / Shake That Thing / Tomorrow Belongs To Me / To Be Continued

THE SENSATIONAL ALEX HARVEY BAND 'LIVE'
(Vertigo 18184, September 1975)

Fanfare (Justly, Skilfully, Magnanimously) / The Faith Healer / Tomahawk Kid / Vambo / Give My Compliments to the Chef / Delilah / Framed

THE PENTHOUSE TAPES
(Vertigo 9102007, March 1976)

I Wanna Have You Back / Jungle Jenny / Runaway / Love Story / School's Out / Goodnight Irene / Say You're Mine / Gamblin' Bar Room Blues / Crazy Horses / Cheek To Cheek

SAHB STORIES
(Mountain TOPS112, July 1976)

Boston Tea Party / Sultan's Choice / $25 for a Massage / Dogs of War / Dance To Your Daddy / Amos Moses / Jungle Rub Out / Sirocco

FOURPLAY (SAHB without Alex)
(Mountain TOPC5006, January 1977)
Smouldering / Chase It into the Night/ Shake Your
Way To Heaven / Outer Boogie / Big Boy / Pick It Up
And Kick It / Love You for a Lifetime / Too Much
American Pie

ROCK DRILL
(MountainTOPS114, March 1978)
The Rock Drill Suite: Rock Drill – The Dolphins – Rock
and Roll – King Kong / Booids / Who Murdered Sex? /
Nightmare City / Water Beastie / Mrs Blackhouse

Post-SAHB singles

Shakin' All Over / Wake Up Davis (RCA PB5199,
October 1979)

Big Tree, Small Axe/ The Whalers(Thar She Blows)
(RCA PB5252, May 1980)

The Poet And I (Powerstation OHM3, November 1983)

Post-SAHB albums

THE MAFIA STOLE MY GUITAR
(RCA 25257 November 1979)
Don's Delight / Back in the Depot / Wait For Me, Mama
/ The Mafia Stole My Guitar / Shakin' All Over / The
Whalers (Thar She Blows) / Oh Spartacus / Just A
Gigolo – I Ain't Got Nobody

THE SOLDIER ON THE WALL
(Powerstation AMP2, November 1983)
Mitzi / Billy Bolero / Snowshoes Thompson / Roman
Wall Blues / The Poet and I / Nervous / Carry the
Water / Flowers Mr Florist / The Poet and I (Reprise)

Oddities

(HAIR) BAND ON THE WAGON
(Bell records 1967)
Sacrifice / I'm Living / The Yellow Bay Tree / Swansong
/ There's No Lights On The Christmas Tree Mother . . .
/ Band on the Wagon / Travelling Song / No Offence
Eddie / The Golden Egg / Electric Blues / How Deep Is
The Ocean

THE JOKER IS WILD
(Metronome 15429, Germany, 1972)
The Joker Is Wild / Penicillin Blues / Make Love To You
/ I'm Just A Man / He Ain't Heavy, He's My Brother /
Silhouette and Shadow / Hare Krishna / Willie the
Pimp / Flying Saucer's Delight

ALEX HARVEY PRESENTS THE LOCH NESS MONSTER
(K-Tel, April 1977)
Solo narrative LP

There have also been numerous almost identical
compilations of Harvey's work over the years.